The *Decameron* First Day in Perspective

Edited by Elissa B. Weaver

D1596453

Giovanni Boccaccio's *Decameron* is the best known and most read work in Italian literature next to Dante's *Divine Comedy*. In the tradition of *Lectura Dantis*, the practice of canto-by-canto critical readings of Dante's work, Elissa Weaver has collected essays from some of the most prominent Boccaccio scholars to provide critical readings of the *Decameron* Proem, Introduction, and the ten stories that constitute the first of the ten 'days' of storytelling.

The first of the twelve essays opens the volume with a consideration of the Proem, demonstrating the importance of Boccaccio's literary subtexts (Ovidian and Dantean) for understanding his poetics. The second essay, on the Introduction, discusses the title of the work and the framing tale. The remaining ten contributions treat in detail each story, examining the literary, ethical, and social concerns embodied in the short narratives and in the context provided by the comments and discussions of the storytellers, and exploring the intertextual relations within the *Decameron* and with sources and analogues. This inaugural book in a new series of critical essays on the *Decameron* will provide an important guide to reading the complex series of narratives that constitute the opening of the *Decameron* and will serve as a guide to reading the entire work.

(Toronto Italian Studies: Lectura Boccaccii)

ELISSA B. WEAVER is a professor of Italian in the Department of Romance Languages and Literatures at the University of Chicago.

The *Decameron* First Day in Perspective

Volume One of the *Lectura Boccaccii*

Edited by Elissa B. Weaver

UNIVERSITY OF TORONTO PRESS
Toronto Buffalo London

© University of Toronto Press Incorporated 2004
Toronto Buffalo London
Printed in Canada

ISBN 0-8020-4454-9 (cloth)
ISBN 0-8020-8589-X (paper)

Printed on acid-free paper

Toronto Italian Studies

National Library of Canada Cataloguing in Publication

The Decameron first day in perspective : volume one of the
Lectura Boccaccii / edited by Elissa B. Weaver.

(Toronto Italian studies)
Includes bibliographical references and index.
ISBN 0-8020-4454-9 (bound)   ISBN 0-8020-8589-X (pbk.)

1. Boccaccio, Giovanni, 1313–1373. Decameron.   I. Weaver,
Elissa, 1940–   II. Series.

PQ4287.D42 2003   853'.1   C2003-903209-4

University of Toronto Press acknowledges the financial assistance to its
publishing program of the Canada Council for the Arts and the Ontario
Arts Council.

University of Toronto Press acknowledges the financial support for its publishing activities of the Government of Canada through the Book Publishing
Industry Development Program (BPIDP).

Contents

Preface

The Decameron *First Day in Perspective* is the first in a series of readings of stories from Giovanni Boccaccio's *Decameron*, his famous collection of one hundred tales, set at the time of the Black Plague in Florence. The series, called the *Lectura Boccaccii*, takes its name and format from the much older project: readings of individual cantos of Dante Alighieri's *Divine Comedy*, known as the *Lectura Dantis*. It is a collection of essays, or critical readings of Boccaccio's text, sponsored by the American Boccaccio Association, and first delivered in a public forum by some of the most prominent scholars of Boccaccio.

This volume, devoted to the opening of the *Decameron* – its preface and introduction, the beginning of its framing tale, and the ten *novelle* of the 'First Day' of storytelling – is dedicated to the members of the American Boccaccio Association, who have patiently awaited its appearance in print. It is hoped that the volume will justify the work of its collaborators and will satisfy, enlighten, and please all of its readers, opening up for them in many and new ways the pleasures of Boccaccio's text.

Many thanks to the several institutions and members of the American Boccaccio Association for their financial support of this publication: the Italian Cultural Institute of Chicago, the Humanities Division of the University of Chicago, the Department of Romance Languages and Literatures of the University of Pennsylvania, the Department of French and Italian of the University of Texas, the Comparative Literature Department of the University of Illinois, Nancy L. D'Antuono, Pier Massimo Forni, Eugenio Giusti, Steven Grossvogel, Victoria Kirkham, Christopher Kleinhenz, Edoardo Lebano, Christopher Nissen, Regina Psaki, Judith P. Serafini-Sauli, Karl-Ludwig Selig, Marcel

Tetel, and Rebecca West. For granting permission to republish four of the essays that appear in this collection and a large section of another I thank the following presses: Esedra Editrice and Liviana Editrice (Padua), Franco Angeli (Milan), Federico and Ardia (Naples), Michigan University Press (Ann Arbor), McGill-Queen's University Press (Montreal), and the Casagrande Press (Bellinzona). Thanks also to Michael Sherberg, who translated two of the essays, and to Suzanne Magnanini, who compiled the bibliography. Finally, a special note of gratitude goes to Vittore Branca, for his encouragement of this project from its inception and for his continued support of Boccaccio scholarship in America.

The *Decameron* First Day in Perspective

Introduction

ELISSA B. WEAVER

Boccaccio opens the *Decameron* with a simile: the painful beginning is like a steep and rugged mountain beyond which lies hidden a beautiful and pleasurable plain; the greater the effort expended on the climb the greater will be the delight of the plain (Intro. §4). The difficult mountain is a reference to the description of the Black Plague that devastated Florence (and much of Europe) in 1348, narrated in great detail in the Introduction; in the delightful plain is figured the escape of the group of Florentines to the refuge of the countryside and the entertaining storytelling that ensues. Yet the image seems to stand for much more, and indeed the stories themselves begin on a negative note with a tale of great vice (I.1), and they end with one of great virtue (X.10). Critics have suggested that the collection itself replicates that movement from negative to positive by beginning with an entire 'Day' of stories about the vices, especially those of great men, and ending with a 'Day' that commemorates acts of extraordinary generosity. While the latter is explicitly stated, the former is not so patently clear: Is the *Decameron* First Day, a day ostensibly without theme, a study of vices? Is there an implicit theme that unites all ten tales? The *brigata* of storytellers decides only later (at the beginning of the second day of its sojourn) to impose a theme each day. Boccaccio is a tricky narrator, and we must be cautious in our reading of his words; indeed, as many of his stories demonstrate, literal-minded readers are foolish and can be easily duped.

The *Decameron* opens with a complex series of embedded narratives: the Proem, the Introduction and its continuation as framing tale, and, finally, the tales of Day One. The essays collected in this volume are studies of these narratives, which treat them individually and as part of a complex structure. They provide a close reading of the various levels of narration, introducing the different personae of the narrator and the imagined reader, as well as the intertextual connections established by Boccaccio with other authors and with other works of his own. While the essays closely scrutinize the detail of the text, they also seek to show how each part contributes to the larger context in which it is found, to the entire 'Day' of tales, and to the collection.

The first essay is a reading of the *Decameron* Proem, or preface. The Proem serves to introduce not only Day One but the entire collection of tales; and thus a discussion of it might be said not to belong properly to a collection of essays on the First Day. On the other hand, the Proem, the Introduction to the storytelling that follows it, and the First Day of storytelling all serve in different ways as beginnings of the work.

The Proem and the Introduction to the First Day taken together constitute a statement of purpose and dedication. They give the fictive occasion of the work, and they implicitly state the poetics embodied in it, providing interpretative guidelines for reading the book as a whole. The Introduction to the frame story (*cornice*) describes the terrible conditions in Florence, justifying the escape of the *brigata* (the group of young Florentines) to the hills and their decision to commemorate, through redemptive storytelling, their society as it was before the current devastation. The First Day inaugurates the storytelling practice: the activities of the narrators, their daily routines, the stories they tell, and the response they receive from the others. The tales that are told embody, sometimes openly, sometimes obliquely, the author's ethical, social, and aesthetic concerns, and they set into motion his narrative techniques. The *novelle*, as the tales are generally called, put into practice the poetics adumbrated in the Proem and Introduction. Michelangelo Picone, in his *lectura* (I.7), argues that the entire First Day is a metanarrative – that is, a narrative about the nature of the narration itself, which gives directions for how to read the text.

The Proem begins with Boccaccio's account of his recovery from the suffering he endured because of an unhappy love and an ill-regulated appetite. He attributes his survival to the 'piacevoli ragionamenti' [delightful conversation] of a friend: 'Nella qual noia tanto rifrigerio già mi porsero i piacevoli ragionamenti d'alcuno amico e le sue laudevoli consolazioni, che io porto fermissima opinione per quelle essere avenuto che io non sia morto' [The delightful conversation of a friend and the valuable consolation he offered gave me such relief from that pain that I am firmly convinced that that is what saved me from death (Proem §4)]. Robert Hollander's reading of the Proem stresses its Ovidian and Dantean subtexts, and for Hollander the 'friend' who has consoled the unhappy lover Boccaccio should probably be read as Ovid, meaning Ovid's *Remedia amoris*. This sort of literary consolation is what Boccaccio himself offers to the ladies of his dedication, who suffer too from unhappy love and who have no other remedy for their pain. The Dantean subtext, as critics have long noted, is introduced in the book's title rubric, 'Comincia il libro chiamato Decameron cognominato prencipe Galeotto ...' [Here begins the book called Decameron, also called Prince Galahalt ...], with its allusion to the Galeotto of the famous line in the episode of Paolo and Francesca, 'Galeotto fu 'l libro e chi lo scrisse' [Galahalt was the book and the one who wrote it (*Inferno*, V, l. 137)]. The title of the book is discussed in a number of the essays in the volume, and Dante's poem, especially, is seen as an essential key to understanding the *Decameron*.

The appeal to Ovid's ironic text warns the reader at the outset that things are not what they may seem, for example, the exclusively female readership to whom Boccaccio dedicates the book and whom he addresses consistently throughout the work. Several contributors to this book discuss this issue, but primarily Millicent Marcus, who, following on the earlier work of Victoria Kirkham and Janet Smarr, reads the ladies allegorically as a justification for writing in the vernacular and an argument for 'authorial freedom from educational imperatives of the academy and Church.'

Dante is everywhere in the *Decameron*, from the title forward. Dante's poem is a subtext throughout Boccaccio's corpus, and not just in the *Decameron*; he is an author with whom Boccaccio carries on a constant dialogue. In the *Decameron* Boccaccio sometimes agrees, often differs, with Dante but always measures himself against his great predecessor. Oddly enough Dante does not seem to be invoked in the metaphorically resonant names of the members of the *lieta brigata*, while Petrarca is remembered through 'Lauretta,' Virgil through 'Elissa,' and Ovid through 'Filomena.' Tom Stillinger's essay on the Introduction, which he calls a 'meditation on titles,' sees all of the narrators' names as meditations on titles and texts. If Dante is not in these names and titles, he is, as we have said, in the *Decameron* title, in the book from the very beginning, and indeed again and again in each beginning. As Vittore Branca has noted and Hollander reiterates, both the *Commedia* and the *Decameron* begin with reference to an autobiographical midlife crisis and to a recent escape from a life-threatening situation, which in both texts is referred to as 'noia' ('grave e noioso cominciamento' [serious and unpleasant beginning (Proem §2–§4)]; 'noia' [scene of suffering (*Inferno* 1, line 76]). The Introduction's 'orrido cominciamento' [horrid beginning], the plague description, is an earthly version of hell, and the 'bellissimo piano e dilettevole' [beautiful and delightful plain] of the storytelling, an allusion to the 'dilettoso' [delightful] mountain of the first canto of *Inferno*.[1] Moreover, we can see Dante's otherwordly scheme replicated in the movement from negative to positive suggested by the first and last tales of the collection through the character of the protagonists: Ciappelletto (I.1) is the worst man who ever lived, while Griselda (X.10) is a woman of incredible, incomparable virtue. And in that case we must also note the irony of Boccaccio's ambiguous treatment of the scheme when he has Dioneo introduce the Griselda story not as her story, the saintly woman's trials and reward, but as a 'matta bestialità' [mad beastly act (X.10.3)] of the marquis, her husband, using Dante's term (*Inferno* XI, lines 82–3) for a sin deserving the punishment of lower hell.

Franco Fido in his discussion of the first story examines all of the possible structural parallels to it in the *Decameron*, and their ramifications, strengthening the case of the Ciappelletto story as yet another in the series of introductions to the collection. Besides the opposition of I.1 and X.10, Fido discusses the contrast of the first story with X.9, the first and last stories narrated by Panfilo (and we should also remember that X.9 is the real one hundredth story – the Griselda story being the hundred and first, if we count the story Boccaccio tells us not to count, the 'half-tale' of Filippo Balducci in the Introduction to Day Four). In the case of this structural parallel, which Fido calls a case of reverse symmetry, the corrupt, blasphemous, homosexual Ciappelletto is juxtaposed to the happy husband and father, the courteous Crusader Torello. In both of these cases the first story of the *Decameron* serves as a 'foreshadowing' or 'early indication' not only of connecting elements within the stories, similar or contrasting, but also of what Fido calls a 'macro-trope' that frames the one hundred stories tying Ciappelletto to Griselda and Torello. The first story's structural connection with VI.10, the story of Friar Cipolla, is based on the analogous talents of the two protagonists for what Fido calls rhetorical 'overkill,' and for deceptive rhetoric: Ser Ciappelletto and Friar Cipolla can, for example, with words, make the simple and banal seem marvelous and extraordinary.

But to stay within the immediate context of the story, I.1 is connected by virtue of its religious subject, which Filostrato calls 'cose catoliche' [religious matters (II.2)], to the second and third stories of the day. The connections are examined at length by Fido, but also by Marga Cottino-Jones and Pamela Stewart in the readings they devote to those two stories: I.2, on the conversion of Abraham the Jew to Catholicism brought about paradoxically through the bad example of the Roman clergy, and I.3, the novella of wise Melchisedech, containing the embedded allegorical tale of the three rings. While the three interpretations differ, largely in emphasis, they all point out that the reading of each story is conditioned by the other stories in its immediate context. For Fido the structure uniting the 'religious matters' ('cose catoliche') continues, forming a triangle or wedge of interconnection together with the first two stories of Day Two and the first of Day Three. In the last of the series, the story of Masetto da Lamporecchio's cuckolding of Christ, we find what is perhaps an intentional lexical connection to Ciappelletto that serves to mark closure: Masetto is said to have placed 'le corna sopra 'l cappello di Cristo' [horns on the 'cappello' of Christ], where 'cappello' means a wreath, and, in the case of Christ, his crown of thorns. But even if the use of 'cappello' were coincidental, not meant to recall Ciappelletto, each story in the series of 'religious matters' adds retrospectively to the meaning of the prior story or stories, creating what Fido terms a 'discourse of moral theology.'

Several of the *lecturae* discuss the overall structure of Day One, all agreeing with Neri, Branca, Padoan, D'Andrea, Cottino-Jones, and others who have written elsewhere, that there is a unity to the day, if not a central theme like those that give coherence to Days Two through Eight and Ten. Day One differs from the rest of the collection, being the day of storytelling that precedes the decision to impose the rule of theme and Dioneo's exception to that rule. And, while the Ninth Day appears to be truly without a unifying principle, it is a broadly held opinion that the First Day stories are clearly linked with one another, unified, but through a different kind of organizing principle: for many they are tales of reversal, in which a world of corruption represented by wrong-headed secular and religious leaders, greedy aristocrats, and one silly widow and her thoughtless entourage,[2] are corrected, the situation transformed by the verbal wit of the protagonist through the reformatory power of the word.[3] It is generally a social inferior whose wit and verbal skill brings about the change, simultaneously demonstrating his or her intellectual superiority. Pier Massimo Forni argues for an autobiographical explanation of this mechanism, which recurs elsewhere in the *Decameron*. He points to the story of Ghino di Tacco (X.2), to messer Torello (X.9), to Cisti the baker (VI.2), and to similar episodes in other works of Boccaccio's corpus, the *Filocolo* primarily. The characters, in search of social legitimization, express the merchant-class author's similar preoccupation. Boccaccio, in his famous letter of 1363 to Francesco Nelli, discusses his association with aristocrats during his Neapolitan years, underlining, as Forni puts it, 'his social inferiority while asserting his worth.' The protagonists of Day One, mindful of their inferior social status, exhibit extraordinary intelligence and finesse by correcting their social superiors without any breach of decorum.

Two stories of Day One, the first two, are indeed reversals, but each in a slightly different way. Both Ciappelletto and Abraham 'save' themselves, albeit in very different, even humourously opposing senses of the word, through reversals.[4] Millicent Marcus rehearses this argument, stressing the meta-literary message of conversion by witty retort – the invitation to a figurative understanding of language. 'The plea to abandon literal-mindedness and consider hidden truths,' she writes, 'seems to correct for the obsessive attachment to things, to appearances, or to the flesh, which makes gentlemen and friars avaricious, abbots hypocritical, monarchs lustful, extortionary, or lethargic.' She calls this a 'moral journey from self-interest to magnanimity' through which 'each tale of Day One recapitulates the overall comic design of the *Decameron* itself ...' Michelangelo Picone argues at length for a formal unity of the Day, as distinct from a coherence deriving from content, however that content be characterized. His view does not contradict the 'reversal' thesis; he concludes, in fact, that 'if there is a theme that runs through this day, supposedly without theme,' it is the presence of the 'parola liberatrice e innalzatrice,' the word that liberates and exalts, that overcomes social boundaries creating an intellectual aristocracy. The formal unities Picone posits are many: geographical, chronological, literary, narratological, social. To illustrate here only the latter case, Picone finds that the heroes and heroines of Day One represent a broad cross-section of medieval society: at the top of the hierarchy, kings, nobles, knights, and powerful prelates, the *bellatores* (Saladino, the two kings, the feudal lord Cangrande, the Genoese magnate Erminio Grimaldi, the abbot of Cluny), and the parallel realm of upper class ladies (the Gascon lady and the marchioness of Monferrato). At the other end of the social ladder are the *laboratores*, to which category technically belong the merchants and bankers, whom Boccaccio, however, privileges, giving them near parity with the aristocrats (Melchisedech and Abraham, for example, or the 'buono uomo' [good man] at the mercy of the Florentine Inquisitor, and Malgherida dei Ghisolieri, the lady loved by maestro Alberto). The lower clergy are represented (Ciappelletto's confessor, the monk and abbot of the fourth tale, and the Florentine Inquisitor); and, finally, the *oratores*, a middle class that stands between and connects the upper class custodians of political and religious institutions and the lower class custodians of economic institutions: to the *oratores* belong representatives of the mechanical arts (the notary, Ciappelletto, and the doctor, maestro Alberto) and of the liberal arts (the goliardic literary figure, Primasso, and courtiers such as Bergamino and Guiglielmo Borsiere). And it is through this last group, the representatives of the liberal arts, that, according to Picone, the author figures himself in the text as the man of letters who lives by and for his intellectual work. For Picone, as Day One progresses, it 'tends toward the unconditional affirmation of the *homo loquens*, exalting an ideal of *humanitas* that can be achieved through full possession and total control of the art of rhetoric.' For Picone, as for Marcus, this day tells us how to read the *Decameron*; it is a day that contains stories within stories and presents a variety of other models of communication. It is par excellence a metanarrative, a 'racconto del racconto,' a story of the story that is the book.

While *novelle* 1, 2, 3, 7, 9, and 10 invite discussion of the meaningful structures and metanarrative functions that are useful in attempting to define Day One, stories 4, 5, 6, and 8, seem more inward-looking, more responsive to an analysis of their story, its message or messages. Martinez reads the tale, told by Dioneo, of the young monk and hypocritical abbot, in the light of two subtexts, the Rule of St Benedict and Dante's *Vita nuova*, and he puts the story in the context of the Day and of the narrator Dioneo's other tales. Here in the First Day 'Dioneo's parodic subversion of the rule,' Martinez argues, 'begins a trend in his tenure as a narrator,' and through Dioneo the author incorporates in the framing tale a theme of subversion analogous to the abbot's subversion of the Rule of St Benedict in this story. Dioneo's story is the only erotic action narrated on the First Day – the tenth story, as Marcus argues, in anticipation of the future role of tenth stories, is based on a sexual metaphor, but the action stops when maestro Alberto wins his lady rhetorically, leaving the erotic outcome ambiguous.

Dante Della Terza, too, in his reading of the fifth tale, looks at the story of the marchioness of Monferrato in the light of its narrator Fiammetta's other stories, the Fifth Day, over which she presides as queen, and her comments. He reads it in the context of its literary sources and its historical basis, and he uses the latter – what is known about the historical existence of the king and marchioness of I.5 – together with Fiammetta's remarks in IX.5, to help clarify the meaning of the *Decameron*'s version of the story, which he concludes to be about decorum and the importance of literary verisimilitude.

Victoria Kirkham looks to the possible allegorical significance of the narrator of I.8, Lauretta, and to the day of the week the narration takes place, a Wednesday – 'mercoledí,' that is, Mercury's day. However, the critic's attention is devoted mainly to defining the literary historical precedents for a discussion of courtesy and avarice, and to determining their meaning for the tale's protagonists, for whom they are the characterizing features: Guiglielmo Borsiere, defined by Dante as a courteous man despite his collocation in Hell (among the sodomites with a lot of Dante's friends); and Erminio Grimaldi, known as 'Erminio Avarizia' [Kirkham's translation: 'Stingy Herman'], whom Borsiere will reprimand and reform. Going from Aristotle to Dante via Brunetto Latini and others, Kirkham shows that Boccaccio's notions, though they may sound like Dante's, are very different and are grounded in his society and in the present, despite their ancient precedents. For Boccaccio *cortesia* seems to be the Greek virtue that makes for constancy in good behavior and permits getting along with others, which, as Aristotle has said, sometimes may require reprimanding them (*Ethics* 1126b–1127a). Avarice, which for Dante is 'a sin that obstructs Christian Charity,' is for Boccaccio 'a secular problem, materialism that threatens social order.'

Janet Smarr's reading of I.6, the tale of the 'valente uomo' [the good/worthy man], who is falsely accused by the greedy and hypocritical Florentine Inquisitor, proceeds methodologically in much the same manner as Kirkham's. Indeed the two stories they study have much in common. Both are about avarice. However, in I.6 faith is also a central issue, and these two themes are represented through images of simony and food. These are strange combinations, which Smarr meticulously sorts out using historical documentation, the Gospel of Matthew, and the *Divine Comedy*, especially *Inferno* XIX, the story's principal subtexts.

Only one *lectura*, Pamela Stewart's, follows the fortunes of the novella in question after Boccaccio; Stewart finds that the story of the three rings had a fortuitous rebirth and a felicitous reinterpretation in Gotthold Lessing's Germany. However, all of the essays discuss the sources and critical fortunes of the tales. Hollander's reading of the Proem and Stillinger's of the Introduction do so only to a very limited extent, a necessary measure given the paucity of work on the Proem and the vast amount instead on the Introduction. The critical approaches of the historicist tradition and the allegorical school predominate in this collection, reflecting the principal currents of American Boccaccio criticism today. The semiotic, structuralist, and deconstructionist methods are also well represented, although most essays would better be labelled pluralist for their willingness to let the texts themselves suggest the most appropriate method of analysis. The unity of this volume of essays derives from that of the *Decameron* texts considered. The essays are not without the differences of opinion that a collection of the work of a variety of readers necessarily implies, and it is our hope that these differences will serve to open up fruitful discussion of Day One, and of the entire *Decameron* as well.[5]

NOTES

English translations that appear in the essays, unless otherwise indicated, are the work of the individual authors.

1 Branca, *Boccaccio medievale*, 34 ff; and in his edition of the *Decameron* (Turin: Einaudi, 1984), Intro. §4, note 10.
2 Neri ('Il disegno ideale,' 53) sees the tenth story as an exception, much like the tenth of the other days; the other stories for him represent vices of lords and men of the cloth.
3 For Marga Cottino-Jones ('Saggio di lettura') each story ends by re-establishing the social harmony that had been temporarily disrupted.
4 Pamela Stewart ('Novella di madonna Oretta,' esp. pp. 33, 38) argues that the story of Abraham the Jew (I.2) is unlike the other stories of Day One and is an example of a paradoxical reversal, as is the story of Michele Scalza in the Sixth Day (VI.6), underscoring what she reads as a parallelism of Days One and Six. Stewart argues that the *Decameron* has a two-part structure (Days One through Five, and Days Six through Ten) created through various structural symmetries and through two programmatic beginnings, stories I. 1 and VI.1.
5 The article by Timothy Kircher, 'The Modality of Moral Communication in the *Decameron*'s First Day, in Contrast to the Mirror of the Exemplum,' appeared too late to be taken into consideration by the contributors to this volume. I have added a reference to it in Kirkham's note 6 and have included it in the bibliography. Kircher treats the subject of the exemplum tradition in the stories of the First Day, its ironic treatment by the narrators, and models of communication set up within the stories.

The *Decameron* Proem

ROBERT HOLLANDER

Points of departure are signs that lead to arrivals; finishing anything, we tend to look back to its inception, for only with the sense of the relation of those two events or moments do we feel we come in contact with whatever it is that constitutes wholeness, integrity. Given the fact that beginnings are of undisputed importance, we should be more than a little surprised that Boccaccio's *Proemio* is probably the most neglected part of the *Decameron*. Robbed of wide recognition of its rightful and important place as introduction to the whole by the (justly) closely studied *Introduzione*,[1] it is frequently forgotten and almost always underattended. Even those who announce their intention to study it at some length (e.g., Di Pino, Getto, Russo)[2] do not offer either close analyses or particularly insightful larger understandings. Indeed, the *Proemio* tends to suffer from the same sort of subjective and impressionistic responses that the *Decameron* as a whole tends to receive.

Perhaps because of the extraordinary complexity of its wholeness (even Dante's *Commedia* is easier to keep in mind in some orderly fashion), the pieces of the *Decameron* are allowed to serve us, in our hunger for meaning, as adequate specimens from which to draw our totalizing generalizations. Without wishing to offend, I would merely suggest that the *Decameron* is one of the worst read masterpieces that the world possesses. Unlike the vast, often contradictory, but generally useful hoard of scholarship that we have concerning the first two cantos of the *Commedia*, or even the slightly less imposing amount of interesting matter dedicated to Boccaccio's difficult and fascinating *Introduzione*, the unconcerted and fleeting attention paid to his *Proemio* is itself a primary indication that, as readers, most of us are not ready for the demands made on us by Boccaccio's text. In the group of those who do not understand it, I unhesitatingly include myself.

In her challenging essay 'An Allegorically Tempered *Decameron*,' Victoria Kirkham reminds us of how few of the *Decameron*'s riddles we have been able to solve.[3] Her opening paragraph reminds us how poorly we have responded to the following difficult and necessary objects of attention: the hidden 'real' names of the ten narrators, the significance of the pseudonyms with which Boccaccio says he has supplied them, the identities of those who are lovers among the *brigata*, the reason for the uneven distribution of servants among the ladies and gentlemen, the meaning of the evidently allusive ballads sung at the conclusion of each day. That is a short list, its own potential for elaboration not even slightly developed. And we can all add to it our own small heap of miseries – things in the text which seem to call out for the critic's solving balm, but resist our ministrations. Kirkham's inventory suffices to remind us how little we have accomplished in six hundred years in our attempts to grasp Boccaccio's intentions. And one wishes that more studies of Boccaccio had the good grace to insist that the texts which they purport to clarify are at the very least resistant to their clarifiers. We do the truth a disservice when we make Boccaccio sound 'easy.' The *ballate*, for instance, remain a closed book to the vast majority of critics who concern themselves with the *Decameron*. Can we not all see that they are obviously of importance, that they call out for interpretation? Yet how many of those who would tell us what the *Decameron* means even confront the fact of their puzzling presence? Very few. And some of those who have had concourse with them have produced results which are so unconvincing that those who remain silent may feel that, in some circumstances, silence is indeed golden. Yes, the *Decameron* is enjoyable, so comforting, so 'user-friendly' that we are allowed to believe we have understood it. We may, I would agree, have felt its spirit. Understanding the way in which it was put together and what it may signify, these are desires which, in my experience, remain nearly totally unfulfilled.

Let me offer only one example of the sort of difficulties encountered by an ideal Boccaccian reader. Such a reader – unlike most of the work's actual audience – comes to the book from Boccaccio's preceding vernacular fictions and Latin texts with certain expectations of the techniques and preoccupations that he or she will encounter in a fabulist who owes his major intellectual allegiance to Classical forebears and to Dante. He is, as he is often said to be, a 'pre-humanist.' What of the author who now confronts us? Everything is changed – or nearly everything (at least we may say that everything seems to be changed): gone is the narrator-in-love-who-by-this-book-woos-his-sweetheart; gone are the mythological figures who populate the earlier texts. While there has been a 'comico-borghese' element in some of the earlier works (at least for moments at a time), that style now gives the dominant tone to many of the one hundred tales, and surely sets the scene for our reaction to the work as a whole. The motives for the conscious choice (for surely it must have been one) which accounts for these major changes are obscure to us, and probably will always remain so. Our most usual form of response is to look upon the considerable earlier production of Boccaccio as little more than an apprenticeship, despite the fact that the author himself repeatedly looks back to the antecedents which he created for himself. We tend to deny the importance of the continuum and, as a result, the extraordinary nature of his change of course within it. Like native inhabitants of the New World we stare in wonder or alarm at this new vehicle without knowing anything about Genoa or that its captain came from there. Were we to know these things, we would still be amazed that he and it had been capable of such a voyage.

While some have argued that the *Decameron* is a work void of moral concern or purpose, almost all who deal with it argue with some zeal that it puts forward a vision of human life which urges a moral choice upon us. Without reviewing the centuries of debate (we are aware with what difficulty those who defended Boccaccio in the Renaissance did so, forced to tell his detractors – and themselves – that he really was a good Christian), we can make a simplified outline of the positions which have grown up alongside the book. I would describe the three major and competing views of the *Decameron* which have emerged since the Second World War as follows. (I would also be quick to insist that I am aware that my three schools force together some interpretive positions that reveal wide divergences of opinion.) It is variously held that the *Decameron* may be characterized as embodying one of the following central positions:

1 a traditional Christian/Humanist moral vision, one which essentially maintains the Augustinian/Dantean continuum (e.g., Branca, Bernardo, Kirkham);[4]
2 a literature of 'escape,' of pure amusement (e.g., Singleton, Olson);[5]

3 a new moral vision which is in polemical relation to the old moral
   order (e.g., Di Pino, Getto, Scaglione, Baratto).[6]

I do not now believe that any of these approaches enables us to understand what the *Decameron* is most centrally concerned with, if I believe
that each of them contributes an important element of understanding
to a better working hypothesis. The first view is undoubtedly correct in
understanding that whatever is 'new' in Boccaccio's vision, that vision
was produced out of an existing set of cultural and moral givens; the
second, if less convincing in its total premise than either of the other
two, at least has this much on its side: Boccaccio's art is more aware of
itself as an aim in itself and of the possibility of an art for mere delecta-
tion's sake than are most of its medieval precursors; the third, with
which I disagree most strongly because it leads to the most inhibiting
final perceptions, has on its side Boccaccio's palpable hostility to the
representatives of the social and religious institutions that are ostensibly charged with the maintenance of morality.
    Thus I would put forward a fourth possibility for a general under-
standing of the purpose of Boccaccio's *Decameron*, which I now see as a
text that offers

4 an exploration of humankind's inability to be governed by, or to
   govern itself in accord with, traditional morality or to find a har-
   monious way of living within nature; yet the work does envision humanity's ability to develop an aesthetic expression which
   is fully capable of examining its own corrupt and unameliorable
   being. (In this formulation one finds elements of Mazzotta and
   Seung.)[7]

If Boccaccio is 'new' in his *Decameron*, I think that some such combination of negative observations of human behaviour and the pleasing
development of the aesthetic means to portray such behaviour may
help to account for his novelty.

Boccaccio's presentation of his book as Ovidian text, with particular
relevance to the *Amores*, has received some brief notice.[8] What has
gone almost totally unnoticed, as far as I have observed, is the way in
which he carefully connects his own role, as a narrator who wishes to
ease the pains of love, to the Ovid of the *Remedia amoris*.[9] The textual
evidence for this rapprochement seems to me so inviting that one can

only wonder that it requires demonstration. There is a single likely reason for the existence of so crucial a lacuna in our understanding of the
Decameron. We have tended to decide two issues before we begin to
read the text: first, that Boccaccio, as champion of an erotic sensibility,
could not possibly uphold the values of a text which is anti-erotic; second, that the *Remedia* is in fact a seriously anti-erotic text. Both of these
assumptions, like the baseless (and still occasionally present) notion
that the phrase 'Iohannes tranquillitatum' [sunshine Johnny] means to
praise Giovanni's good nature (rather than condemn his fickle friendship), require better analyses.

It is true that in the Middle Ages the *Remedia* was generally understood as an anti-venereal text.[10] Those who knew it by its name alone, or
through the instructions of others, or by means of anthologized fragments, may well be excused this questionable assumption. But anyone
who reads the text with smiling attention realizes that it is a joke at the
expense of the foolish and vituperative detractors of the *Ars amatoria*. In
brief, I would describe this problem as follows: Ovid, in the *Ars*, had
meant to demonstrate (as he had frequently done in what is surely one
of the greatest first works ever written, the *Amores*) that lovers are foolish. Having assumed the role of *praeceptor Amoris*, Ovid allows us to
read him lasciviously if we are so inclined, but hopes that the wiser of us
will understand that his text is in fact a witty and devastating revelation
of the follies of lovers. The *praeceptor Amoris* is really the *magister de
amore*, an ironist, even a satirist.[11] If that is so, we can readily understand
the reaction of such a writer to what to him must have seemed the ludi-
crous reactions of Roman bluenoses. His polished, witty verses display
the nonsense of carnality; the bluenoses cry out against his prurience.
The only form of response to such unenlightened critics was to write a
companion piece which would apparently give them what they wanted:
the remedies of love.[12] The latter work was thus intended to take
revenge upon a critical response that showed neither grace nor acumen.

Where the earlier work pretended to praise the god of Love and
actually revealed his damaging effects, the *Remedia* pretends to counter
the god of erotic activity but actually tells lovers how to get what they
want. Lovers in the *Ars* are plangent losers; in the *Remedia* they are cool
and collected exploiters of the objects of their desires. Boccaccio, I
believe, not only carefully observed the reversals in Ovid's two com-
plementary works, but found them utterly germane to his own purposes. The *Decameron* is presented as a *remedium amoris* – in the root
sense of Ovid's title. Its task, as we must agree, if we read its *Proemio*
with any care, is apparently to offer ladies who are unhappily amorous

'utile consiglio' [useful counsel] by which they may understand what they should flee, what they should seek. But his unenlightened detractors, like Ovid's, do not understand (or even observe) this patent overall intention of the work, stamped clearly into its proem. The Introduction to the Fourth Day and the Author's Conclusion both spend considerable time trying to convince these *morditori* [critics] (whether these actually existed or are invented is of little moment to this argument) that the tales and the intentions of their author are, if not chaste, not libidinous either.[13] It seems that Boccaccio did not believe that the *Decameron* was acceptable to the outraged sensibilities of its real or imagined detractors. And thus the *Corbaccio* had to be put forward as the companion piece to the *Decameron* and as the overtly remedial text required by their small imaginations. (Some years ago I published a study that attempts to return to the notion that the *Corbaccio* was written soon after the *Decameron*, noting that it, like the *Decameron*, begins with a hitherto unnoticed citation of the *Remedia*, and that it, like Ovid's apparent palinode, mocks the opposers of love even more than lovers.)[14] Before we begin to examine the evidence for an Ovidian presence in the text of the *Proemio*, I would like to examine the binary arrangement which typifies its development.

The *Proemio* is divided into two parts, one of which is devoted to the 'autobiography' of its author as formerly unhappy lover, the second to the intended audience of his book. I do not think it is accidental that these two parts are of equal length, each being allotted seven periods, or sentences (the second, §2, though the fifteenth sentence, §15, of the *Proem*). What follows is a reductive paraphrase of this matter.

§2. It is humane to be compassionate to those who suffer pain; those who have been so comforted, as I have been, owe a special debt to others less fortunate than they.
§3. From my earliest youth until now I have been unhappily in love with a noble lady.
§4. I was perhaps saved from death by the good advice and consolation of a friend.
§5. It pleased God, who is infinite, to make my love finite when all else failed to do so, so that all that is left of my passion is a better regulated pleasure in loving, all unhappiness taken away.
§6. My gratitude to them [now plural] will last until I die.
§§7–8. Now that I am free, I offer this book in exchange, if not to those who are wise or lucky enough to have avoided love, then at least to those who are in need of my comforting.

§§9–11. Do not women require such aid still more than men? Their otiose, shut-in existence leaves them vulnerable to thoughts of love unless they have access to the sort of advice that men do not seem to require equally.

§12. For men have many escapes: birding, hunting, fishing, riding, gaming, or business.

§§13–14. Thus I have assembled these one hundred *novelle*, whether fables, parables, or histories,[15] told by seven ladies and three men in time of plague, along with the ladies' songs, stories concerning pleasing and harsh amorous incidents as well as other fortune-tossed events, so that the love-struck ladies may know what to flee and what to seek, thus abating their tribulation.

§15. If such should be the result – and may God grant that it be so – then let them give thanks to the God of Love, who, by freeing me from his chains, has granted me the power to wait upon their pleasure.

Wending its way through both parts of the *Proemio* is a series of antithetically related pairs.[16] These may be described as falling into two groups, one of which contains words for the malady of love and its results, the second the medicine which may be applied to the patient in hopes of restoring her or him. The resulting chain of metaphorically related entities is arresting:

Causes or Symptoms of Pain	Antidotal Measures
§2. afflitti	compassione, conforto, piacere
§3. amore, fatica, fuoco, appetito, noia	
§4. noia, morto	rifrigerio, piacevoli ragionamenti, consolazioni
§5. amore, faticoso, affano	consiglio, piacere, dilettevole
§6. pena, fatiche, morte	benefici ricevuti, benivolenza
§7.	libero, alleggiamento
§8.	sostentamento, conforto, utilità
§9.	[sostentamento]
§10. amorose fiamme	piaceri, pensieri allegri
§11. malinconia, focoso disio, noia	ragionamenti
§12. malinconia ... afflige, noioso pensiero, noia	consolazione

§13. quelle che amano,	cento novelle
pestilenzioso tempo,	
mortalità	
§14. noia	diletto, sollazzevoli cose, utile
	consiglio
§15.	liberandomi, piaceri

The connections and oppositions suggested by this table of some of the key words of the *Proemio*, are, I think, worth close consideration. Reading 'vertically' down through the first column of these concatenated terms, we note that the 'afflicted' suffer from a varied roster of ailments, ranging from those that lead to physical death to those more usually thought of as pleasant activities, such as sexual relations. The word which rises from the *Proemio* as making its most representative statement is *noia*, which occurs half a dozen times. Morally and aesthetically it is the demon of the *Decameron*. Here it is associated with love, death, and plague. Our traditional 'robust' reading of the *Decameron* has kept us from seeing the obvious parallels established in the text at its outset between sexuality and pestilence.[17] The word *noia* helps to make the implicit connections still more clear, as it moves from the pages of the Proem to those of the Introduction (§§2, 6, 67, 70, 77), into Panfilo's frame for the first tale (which echoes the first sentence of the Proem [I.1.3]), whence it makes its way into the first tale, where it is Cepparello's equivalent for the name of the mortal disease from which he suffers (I.1.32). *Noia*, one might begin to perceive, is something like the major preoccupation of the *Decameron*, one which runs the length of the text (the last time we encounter the word is in X.10.31, where it describes the anguish at heart felt by Griselda as she gives her baby daughter to her husband's servant to be killed – or so she thinks). Against the onslaught of sexual passion, plague, and death the text arrays a series of phonically related groups: *compassione-conforto-consolazioni-consiglio; piacere-piacevoli ragionamenti-pensieri allegri; sostentamento-sollazzevoli cose* [compassion-comfort-consolation-counsel; pleasure-pleasurable conversations-happy thoughts; support-enjoyable things]. Many of these words are used twice or more and constitute a sort of *materia medica* to be used against the disease of love. We should have recognized by now whose voice we should be hearing in the background: the Ovid of the *Remedia amoris*.

The Ovidian persona of the *Ars amatoria* is that of the pornographic poet ('ego sum praeceptor Amoris' [I am Love's teacher] at 1.17; 'lascivi praeceptor Amoris' [instructor in lascivious Love] at 2.497; 'nil nisi lascivi per me discuntur amores' [only lascivious loves are learned from me] at 3.27).[18] The first voice we hear, in the opening verses of the *Remedia*, claims to be that of an enemy of Cupid. What he in fact proposes as the purpose of his work is not the wars against Amor, which the god himself is imagined as foreseeing ('bella mihi, video, bella parantur' [wars, I see, yes, wars being prepared against me (1.2)]), but a police action on behalf of those lovers who are unhappy, while those who are joyful in their ardor are urged to continue in their pleasure (1.11–16). Those who, in the Middle Ages or today, take the title of the *Remedia* as indicating a sweeping indictment of the pleasures of the flesh are simply not readers of Ovid. The work has more in common with medical writings than with moral treatises. It is thus that he plays with his detractors, composing a treatise in verse which in fact is far more critical of them than it is of love. (Not that Ovid is ever uncritical of happy lovers, whom he rather presents as being brutish, trivial, and self-seeking.)

Boccaccio's own pose in the *Proemio* is not very different. The resemblances between his first beginning and the *Remedia* are numerous. The following series of resemblances is given in brief compass (see the Appendix for the Latin and Italian texts):

1 Both narrators have been and continue to be lovers (if Boccaccio seems a less enthusiastic one than Ovid claims to be).
2 Both texts have as their 'medical' purpose the saving from death those who suffer from unhappiness in love.
3 Both texts thus promise to liberate those who are in bondage.
4 In both texts *otium* is seen as a cause of unhappy amorous feelings.
5 Both texts suggest that activity will counteract that sickness, jointly specifying, among others, hunting, birding, and fishing.
6 Both texts offer instruction to those who would avoid the pains of love in what to flee and what to seek.
7 Both authors, having offered themselves as preceptors in how to learn the art of 'unloving,' conclude by referring to the gratitude that will be owed them by their auditors.

Even that rather skeletal series of resemblances will perhaps convince some readers who have not previously thought so that consultation of the *Remedia* is useful to an appreciation of Boccaccio's expressions of his intention in his *Proemio*. It may also suggest that we have at last discovered the identity of the unidentified 'amico' whose 'piacevoli ragionamenti' brought the author back from the brink of death in his unhappy love affair. He would rather seem to be the author of the *Remedia*, would rather seem to be the writer of a specific classical text than an unnamed fourteenth-century giver of solace.

Ovid himself would return to these concerns in the *Heroides* (19.5–16). We hear the words of Hero, addressed to absent Leander:

Urimur igne pari, sed sum tibi viribus inpar:
fortius ingenium suspicor esse viris;
ut corpus, teneris ita mens infirma puellis –
deficiam, parvi temporis adde moram!
Vos modo venando, modo rus geniale colendo
ponitis in varia tempora longa mora.
aut fora vos retinent aut unctae dona palaestrae,
flectitis aut freno colla sequacis equi;
nunc volucrem laqueo, nunc piscem ducitis hamo;
diluitur posito serior hora mero.
his mihi summotae, vel si minus acriter urar,
quod faciam, superest praeter amare nihil.

[We burn with equal fires, but I am not equal to you in strength; men, methinks, must have stronger natures. As the body, so is the soul of tender women frail – delay but a little longer, and I shall die! You men, now in the chase, and now husbanding the genial acres of the country, consume long hours in the varied tasks that keep you. Either the marketplace holds you, or the sports of the supple wrestling-ground, or you turn with bit the neck of the responsive steed; now you take the bird with the snare, now the fish with the hook; and the later hours you while away with the wine before you. For me who am denied these things, even were I less fiercely aflame, there is nothing left to do but love.][19]

In recent years a number of commentators have had recourse to this passage in their discussions of the otiose ladies of the *Proemio*.[20] Since it is certainly well considered an auto-citation, one wonders why no attention has been given to its sources in the *Remedia*. A working hypothesis might hold that, while the apparent compassionate atmosphere of the *Heroides* would not seem inappropriate as a source for the apparently compassionate Boccaccio, the reader who resorts to this text would not be as happy to consider the likelihood that Boccaccio was in fact more interested in the evidently ironic and distanced formulations of the *Remedia*.

Consideration of the closeness of Boccaccio's language to that of Ovid's self-presentation in a similar role, as my addendum suggests, is still more likely to convince us that the *Remedia*, more than any other work, is the governing precedent text which Boccaccio's beginning invokes. Our initial sense of disbelief, based on an understanding of the *Remedia* which does not do justice to its complexity, may yield to a more sympathetic attitude once we consider that Boccaccio's view of himself as a remedial Ovid includes the awareness that Ovid himself was writing ironically and that the persona he knows he has apparently assumed is that of Dante, whose fifth canto is resolute in putting even the most sympathetic of carnal sinners into the pit.

If Boccaccio is Ovid, he is also Dante. Beginning with its subtitle, which has it that the *Decameron* is 'cognominato Prencipe Galeotto,' an evident gesture towards *Inferno* V, Boccaccio makes it clear that no other literary text is as important to him as Dante's *Commedia*. This is not to forget how assiduously he perused – indeed copied out in his own hand – so much of the rest of the Dantean corpus, but only to reflect his own sense of priority. Boccaccio's opening gesture towards Dante rather establishes a problematic textual connection than it attempts to resolve a problem. It is my belief that a good deal of Boccaccio's traffic in the text of the *Commedia* has exactly such a task. And it seems to me that all of his moralizing readers, whether they hold that Boccaccio is a supporter of a conventional morality or the revolutionary proponent of a new one, make a similar mistake when they fail to account for the subversive and ironic relation between the author and his material, between the writer and his audience.[21] To read Boccaccio 'straight' puts us at risk, the same risk we undergo if we attempt a similar reading of the amatory Ovid. In an article,[22] I have attempted to demonstrate that the very phrase in the *Proemio* which would seem to anchor the *Decameron*'s purpose to a Horatian and traditional literary moralism (the familiar binome *utile/dulcis* [useful/pleasing]), 'diletto ... utile consiglio' [pleasure ... useful counsel] eventually undermines exactly such a conventional moral stance. In the world of the *Decameron* that which is *utile* is, far more often than not, merely that which brings profit or pleasure (or the avoidance of pain). Thus if the work begins as Horatian, it concludes by making the 'useful' entirely dependent upon the human impulses of the user.

Vittore Branca has opportunely reminded us that both the *Commedia* and the *Decameron* begin by referring to events or dates which mark the thirty-fifth year of the author's life.[23] And the sense of an author-protagonist who has recently escaped from a life-threatening situation pervades both proemial passages. In both texts this situation is referred to as *noia* (*Proemio* §§3, 4; *Inferno* 1.76: 'Ma tu perché ritorni a tanta noia?'). In their former difficulty each is aided by the counsel of a 'friend': in Dante, this was Virgil, sent by Beatrice; in Boccaccio, as I have just proposed, the adviser is Ovid. The playfulness of this inter-textual exchange may be still more sophisticated than even this much may suggest. In Dante, the appearance of Virgil to tell of Beatrice's *vita* in heaven is clearly reminiscent of the mournful passage in *Vita nuova* 23.6 in which 'alcuno amico,' [a friend], one who is further described in the accompanying verse (23.24) as 'omo ... scolorito e fioco' [a man ... pale and faint] comes to tell Dante that Beatrice is dead. This figure is nearly certainly in Dante's mind as he describes Virgil, bringing better news of Beatrice, in *Inferno* 1.[24] If Boccaccio drew a similar conclusion, his own 'alcun amico' reflects both the salvific Virgil in the first canto of the *Commedia* and his antithetic model in the *Vita nuova*. As the Italian Ovid, one who leaves the role of Virgil to Dante, he is likely to have been pleased by exactly such a recondite reference. We might further speculate that it is in a neighboring passage in the *Vita nuova* that Dante, for the only time in his *opere*, refers to the *Remedia amoris* by name (25.9): Ovid too, he says, speaks of Love as though he were a person when he has him say 'Bella michi, video, bella parantur' [Wars, wars are in store for me, I perceive] in the book, 'c'ha nome Libro di Remedio d'Amore.' Boccaccio's *Proemio*, which also shares two occurrences of hapax legomenon with the *Commedia* (*rifrigerio*, 4, and *Paradiso*, 14.27; *faticoso*, 5 and *Inferno*, 23.67), shares other elements in its vocabulary with its precursor (e.g., 'come a Colui piacque' [§5], 'ne' suoi più cupi pelaghi navigando' [§5],[25] in such a way as to indicate that, beginning with his subtitle, Boccaccio wanted his reader to entertain the possibility that the *Decameron* is to be read as Dantean moralization. It is my opinion that this gesture is made only to be withdrawn in favor of a more disconcerting and interesting claim, namely that the *Decameron* is to be dealt with as a text descended from the playful and mocking book which calls itself *Love's Remedy*, but is in fact a work which examines love's problematic, which knows that, whatever else human life encompasses, its major premise is appetite. Correction of that appetite may be a desirable, if not an easily achieved, goal. Compassionate study of it is the aim of those who are themselves most human.

Appendix

The *Remedia amoris* and Boccaccio's *Proemio*

1. The narrators as past and present lovers:

> ego semper amavi,
> Et si, quid faciam nunc quoque, quaeris, amo. (7–8)

... dalla mia prima giovanezza infino a questo tempo oltre modo essendo acceso stato d'altissimo e nobile amore ...; mi fu egli di grandissima fatica a sofferire, certo non per crudeltà della donna amata, ma per soverchio fuoco nella mente concetto da poco regolato appetito (§3) ... il mio amore ... si diminuì in guisa, che sol di se nella mente m'ha al presente lasciato quel piacere che egli è usato di porgere a chi troppo non si mette ne' suoi più cupi pelaghi navigando; per che, dove faticoso esser solea, ogni affanno togliendo via, dilettevole il sento esser rimaso (§§3, 5).

2. Unhappy love as leading to death:

> At siquis male fert indignae regna puellae,
> Ne pereat, nostrae sentiat artis opem. (15–16)

> Qui, nisi desierit, misero periturus amore est,
> Desinat ... (21–2)

Nella qual noia tanto rifrigerio già mi porsero i piacevoli ragionamenti d'alcuno amico e le sue laudevoli consolazioni, che io porto fermissima opinione per quelle essere avenuto che io non sia morto. (§4)

3. The need to be free of Love's sway:

> Publicus assertor dominis suppressa levabo
> Pectora: vindictae quisque favete suae. (73–4)

> Optimus ille sui vindex, laedentia pectus
> Vincula qui rupit, dedoluitque semel. (293–4)

... ora che libero dir mi posso ... (§7)

... a Amore [le donne] ne rendano grazie, il quale liberandomi da' suoi legami m'ha conceduto il potere attendere a' lor piaceri. (§15)

4. Otium as cause of unhappy love:

... fugias otia prima ... (136)

Otia si tollas, periere Cupidinis arcus ...
Tam Venus otia amat; qui finem quaeris amoris,
  Cedit amor rebus: res age, tutus eris. (139, 143–4)

Esse dentro a' dilicati petti, temendo e vergognando, tengono l'amorose fiamme nascose [cf. *Rem.* 105: 'tacitae serpunt in viscera flammae'] ..., e oltre a ciò ... il più del tempo nel piccolo circuito delle loro camere racchiuse dimorano e quasi oziose sedendosi ... (§10)

5. Activities which counteract lovesickness:

Rura quoque oblectant animos ...
... tu venandi studium cole ...
Lenius est studium, studium tamen, alite capta
  Aut lino aut calamis praemia parva sequi,
Vel, quae piscis edax avido male devoret ore,
  Abdere suspensis aera recurva cibis. (169, 199, 207–10)

[Gli uomini], se alcuna malinconia o gravezza di pensieri gli affligge, hanno molti modi da allaggiare o da passar quello ...; volendo essi, non manca l'andare a torno, udire e veder molte cose, uccellare, cacciare, pescare, cavalcare, giucare o mercatare. (§12)

6. Author's advice in what to flee, what to seek:

... quos [cibos] fugias quosque sequare, dabo. (796)

... parimente diletto della sollazzevoli cose in quelle [novelle] mostrate e utile consiglio potranno [le donne] pigliare, in quanto potranno cognoscere quello che sia da fuggire e che sia similmente da seguitare. (§14)

7. Both authors conclude in a similar vein (the thanks due them from their auditors):

Postmodo reddetis sacro pia vota poetae,
Carmine sanati femina virque meo. (813–14)

Il che [passamento di noia] se avviene, che voglia Idio che così sia, a Amore ne rendano grazie, il quale liberandomi da' suoi legami m'ha conceduto il potere attendere a' lor piaceri. (§15)

NOTES

An earlier and shorter version of this essay was given as the first *Lectura Boccaccii Americana*, in Washington, D.C. in December 1984. I thank Professor Elissa Weaver, the editor of this volume, for the permission that she granted some years ago to print an expanded version of that essay in *Miscellanea di Studi Danteschi in memoria di Silvio Pasquazi* (Naples: Federico & Ardia, 1993), I: 423–40. It was subsequently published, in a slightly abbreviated version of the above, in the volume of my essays on Boccaccio, *Boccaccio's Dante and the Shaping Force of Satire* (Ann Arbor: University of Michigan Press, 1997), 89–107. I thank both these publishers for their cooperation in making this publication possible.

1 For example, Gibaldi, 'The *Decameron* Cornice,' 349–57. Gibaldi is but one of the more recent students of the frame to spend all his attention on the second beginning of the work. For bibliography relating to the *Proemio* see that provided in the previously published versions of this study: R. Hollander, *Miscellanea Silvio Pasquazi*, 439–40; and *Boccaccio's Dante*, 104–7.
2 Di Pino, 'Il proemio,' 209–20; Getto, 'La cornice,' 1–33 (esp. 1–9); Russo, 'Proemio alle donne,' 9–15.
3 Kirkham, 'Allegorically Tempered *Decameron*,' 1–23. Rpt. in *Sign of Reason*, 131–71.
4 Bernardo, 'Black Plague As Key,' 39–64; Branca, *Boccaccio medievale*, (Florence: Sansoni, 1970³ [1956]); Kirkham, *Sign of Reason*.
5 Olson, *Literature As Recreation*; Singleton, 'On Meaning,' 117–24.
6 Di Pino, *La polemica del Boccaccio*; Getto, *Vita di forme*; Scaglione, *Nature and Love*; Baratto, *Realtà*.
7 Mazzotta, '*Decameron*: Marginality of Literature,' 64–81, and *World at Play*; Seung, 'The Sovereign Individual,' 207–16.

8 For discussion of the phrase 'senza titolo' of *Dec.* IV, Int. 3 as suggesting a generic resemblance between the two works (since the *Amores* was often referred to, and indeed twice by Boccaccio in the *Esposizioni*, as *Sine titulo*), see R. Hollander, *Boccaccio's Two Venuses*, 115–16, 235; see also Branca, 'Note' (*Decameron* 1976), 1197; Padoan, 'Sulla genesi,' 93–4.

9 Since I first advanced this hypothesis, Janet Smarr, who, I believe, was the first person ever to have made the suggestion that the *Remedia* is significantly linked to Boccaccio's strategy of self-presentation in the *Decameron* (Smarr, 'Symmetry and Balance,' 176–7), has repeated and developed her observation (Smarr, *Boccaccio and Fiammetta*, 166; Smarr, 'Ovid and Boccaccio,' 252); see also Kirkham, 'Boccaccio's Dedication,' 337. The latter, however, privileges the resonance of the *Heroides*. See note 18 below.

10 For a detailed account of the *Remedia* (considered alongside the companion *Ars*) as object of the medieval scholiast's attention see Hexter, *Ovid and Medieval Schooling*, 15–82.

11 Hexter points out that Ovid's phrase 'ego sum praeceptor Amoris' was simply too eloquently ambiguous for most of his readers. In Hexter's words (*Ovid and Medieval Schooling*, 21), 'it seems Ovid misjudged either the effectiveness of the image or the capacity of his readers.'

12 For Boccaccio's awareness that the *Remedia* was written early in Ovid's career and as a companion to the *Ars*, see R. Hollander, *Boccaccio's Two Venuses*, 114.

13 An article by Janet Smarr ('Ovid and Boccaccio: A Note on Self-Defense') demonstrates that Boccaccio's self-defence in the *Conclusione dell'autore* is modelled on Ovid's in the second book of the *Tristia*.

14 See R. Hollander, *Boccaccio's Last Fiction*.

15 For the descendance of these three terms from the traditional rhetorical triad *historia, fabula, argumentum* see Stewart, 'Boccaccio e la tradizione retorica: La definizione della novella come genere letterario,' in *Retorica*, 7–18; for their relationship to Dante see R. Hollander, *Allegory in Dante's Commedia*, 256–8.

16 See Davis, 'Boccaccio's *Decameron*,' for consideration of the binary structure of the work as a whole.

17 But see the brief appreciations in Mazzotta, 'Decameron: Marginality of Literature,' 65, and *World at Play*, 30. For Boccaccio's interest in the tradition of *aegritudo amoris* see Ciavolella, 'La tradizione dell'*aegritudo amoris* nel *Decameron*' and *La 'malattia d'amore' dall'antichità al medioevo*.

18 For the texts and English translations of Ovid's *Ars amatoria* and his *Remedia amoris*, see Ovid (Publius Ovidius Naso), *The Art of Love*.

19 Translation by Grant Showerman in Loeb Classic edition of Ovid (Publius Ovidius Naso), *Heroides and Amores*.

20 Branca, 'Note' (*Decameron* 1976), 979; Olson, *Literature as Recreation*, 209; Kirkham, 'Boccaccio's Dedication,' 335 (also adverting to the *Remedia*, 337); Muscetta, 'I modelli, il Proemio, l'Introduzione, i novellatori,' in *Giovanni Boccaccio*, 158; Potter, *Five Frames*, 126.

21 Luciano Rossi's recent revisionary study ('Ironia e parodia nel *Decameron*: Da Ciappelletto a Griselda,' in *La novella italiana: Atti del Convegno di Caprarola, 19–24 settembre 1988* [Rome: Salerno Editrice, 1989], 365–405), with which I find myself in essential agreement and which does much to undermine some of the 'certainties' in contemporary interpretation of the *Decameron*, offers welcome support to the ironic reading of the text proposed here. For an overview of the subject see Knox, *Ironia*. And now see Delcorno, 'Ironia/parodia,' in *Lessico critico decameroniano*, ed. Bragantini and Forni, 173.

22 See R. Hollander, '*Utilità* in Boccaccio's *Decameron*,' 215–33.

23 Branca, 'Note' (*Decameron* 1976), 981, remanding the reader to *Boccaccio medievale*, 34f.

24 See R. Hollander, *Il Virgilio dantesco*, 75–7.

25 The second resonance had been previously noted by Branca, 'Note' (*Decameron* 1976), 977, and both are listed by Bettinzoli, 'Presenze dantesche nel *Decameron*,' 269, 271.

The Place of the Title
(*Decameron*, Day One, Introduction)

THOMAS C. STILLINGER

The first person to appear on the First Day of the *Decameron* is 'l'autore' [the author] – if, that is, we consider the Day's rubric to be a part of the Day.

> Comincia la Prima Giornata del *Decameron*, nella quale dopo la dimo-
> strazione fatta dall'autore per che cagione avvenisse di doversi quelle
> persone, che appresso si mostrano, ragunare a ragionare insieme sotto
> il reggimento di Pampinea si ragiona di quello che più aggrada a ciasche-
> duno. (I Intro. §1)

> [Here begins the First Day of the *Decameron*, in which – after the author's
> explanation of why certain persons, who later appear, happened to meet
> together to converse – under the rule of Pampinea they speak of whatever
> most pleases each one.][1]

In medieval and Renaissance studies, no figure has recently attracted more attention than 'l'autore.' The historical emergence of the modern author – that is, the consolidation of modern institutions of authorship and authority – has been traced both in diachronic overviews and in close readings of idiosyncratic individual texts.[2] The *Decameron* deserves to be discussed in this context. It provides, in its 'autore,' an influential new characterization of the vernacular, secular author; at the same time, it seems to challenge any simple notion of *auctoritas*, old or new. Boccaccio simultaneously claims and disclaims authority for himself. As a brief emblem of this strategy consider his statement, in the Introduction to the Fourth Day, that the stories of the *Decameron* are negligible because they are, among other things, 'senza titolo' [without title (IV Intro. §3)]. 'Senza titolo' is itself a title: the phrase translates 'Sine titulo,' a medieval name for Ovid's *Amores*.[3] Thus in a single gesture Boccaccio disparages his own writing and puts it on a par with a canonical text.

In his later commentary on Dante, Boccaccio explains that Ovid's *Sine titulo* is so called because it has no 'materia continuata' [continuous subject matter]; rather, it is made up of 'pezi' [pieces.].[4] A title, then, is the index of a unitary work. The play on 'senza titolo' in the *Decameron* suggests that a title is also a sign of value: in marking a text as a unitary work, it confers a certain authority. In fact the problem of identifying and naming works is closely linked to the problem of establishing authorship.[5] According to medieval literary theory, the meeting-place of work and author is the *titulus*: Conrad of Hirsau writes that every book has a title, and every title indicates an author.[6] The 'titulus,' for Conrad, is a rubric providing at least a pair of proper names, like the 'titolo' that Boccaccio approves for the *Divine Comedy*: 'Here begin the *cantiche* of the *Comedy* of Dante Alighieri, Florentine.'[7]

But 'titulus' could also mean title in the modern sense, the proper name of the work by itself. Even the short title may imply an author. A more recent theorist, Paul de Man, suggests as much when he writes that 'any book with a readable title page is, to some extent, autobiographical.'[8] De Man may be drawing on the fact that a modern title page usually includes the author's name, but I take his statement in a stronger sense: the book's construction of itself as a knowable totality, signalled in the title, is inseparable from its projection of an extra-textual author. For de Man, the projection of an author is always a figure of language, a prosopopoeia in that it presents a mask or face.[9] The naming of the work is another kind of personification.

Conrad of Hirsau and Paul de Man, premodern and post-structuralist, provide ahistorical formulations of an ideal link between work and author. In the centuries that separate these critics, however, 'work' and 'author' have complex and intertwined histories. The detailed investigation of *auctoritas* now underway might usefully be supplemented by a study of the notion of the literary work. Broadly speaking, the modern author emerges alongside a new definition of the work as, among other things, original, self-contained, and organically whole; if our own age is seeing 'the death of the author' and a transition 'from work to text,' to cite two well-known titles, in Boccaccio's time the author and the work are both ascendant. Certainly the *Decameron* is a landmark in the rise of the autonomous work. Its title is modelled on that of Saint Ambrose's *Hexameron*, a book of Latin sermons on the six days of Creation. In the *Hexameron*, as later in Bernardus Silvestris's *Cosmographia*, the analogy between the human writing of a book and the divine creation of the world is implicit but powerful.[10] Boccaccio borrows this analogy for his vernacular story collection. The shift from six days to ten may be understood as amplification, as secularization, or as parody; whatever its tonality, the title 'Decameron' designates a human creation, a world of fiction.[11] Yet the Introduction to the First Day shows, I shall argue, that Boccaccio's attitude towards the idea of a literary work is as complex as his attitude towards authority.

The rubric to the First Day includes the proper name of the book and the designation 'l'autore.' Yet its image of authorship is double. The sentence begins by announcing an 'author's explanation,' and ends on another kind of discourse, the communal storytelling of the First Day. The transition from explicit authorial control to 'il reggimento di Pampinea' [the rule of Pampinea] is, in effect, a transfer of authority. A transfer of authority is visible again in the Introduction as a whole. The body of the Introduction is conspicuously divided into two contrasting halves: a general description of the 1348 plague in Florence, and then the beginnings of the storytelling game in the church of Santa Maria Novella and in a villa outside the city. One difference between the two halves is a shift in authorial perspective. The plague description is offered by Boccaccio as his own eyewitness testimony; the initial chance meeting of seven ladies in church is narrated second-hand. Boccaccio says that he later heard about the conversation of the ladies 'da persona degna di fede' [from a person worthy of faith (I intr. §49)]. This person – evidently one of the ladies – is herself a kind of author: Boccaccio is echoing a standard derivation of 'autore' from a Greek word meaning 'degno di fede e d'obedienza' [worthy of faith and obedience].[12] Boccaccio will later describe himself as the scribe of the *Decameron* stories rather than their 'inventore' (Concl. §§16–17); he declines both credit and blame for the efforts of the seven ladies and the three noble youths. In the rubric to Day One, the contrast between Boccaccio's authorship and the world of self-authoring storytellers is reflected in the pairing of two cognates: Boccaccio makes a conscious 'dimostrazione' [explanation], while the characters, more simply, 'si mostrano' [appear]. The syntax seems to limit the authority of the single author: 'l'autore' is confined to a subordinate clause, and the main verb of the sentence is the collective speech act, 'si ragiona' [they speak].

Rubrics are not usually read as complex, carefully structured texts. In attempting such a reading of the rubric to Day One, I may seem to be denying its evident status as a mere signpost: a rubric's referent is, after all, the much longer text that it heads. Yet the relationship between the two texts, little and big, has a complexity of its own. In my own reading, I assumed a parallelism between the two, and invoked 'the body of the Introduction' to support a claim about the meaning of its rubric. To assimilate the rubric entirely to its text, however, would be to foreclose the possibility that the head and the body may have different things on their mind. This minor problem of interpretive authority, of the government of meaning, is raised on a larger scale by the Introduction in its relation to the *Decameron*.

The Introduction to the First Day has received an extraordinary amount of critical commentary, yet this commentary has rarely treated the Introduction as a distinct, integral text. Rather than attempting a separate *lectura*, of the sort routinely afforded individual *Decameron* stories, critics have treated the Introduction as an entry to larger textual structures. The second half of the Introduction, the encounter between the young aristocrats, typically becomes an occasion for discussing the *cornice* of the *Decameron*, the continuing narrative that frames the hundred stories. The central question about the *cornice* has been its function within the book: does it constitute the story collection as a unitary work, and does it provide a gloss on the whole? The first half of the Introduction, the plague description, is sometimes included in the definition of the *cornice*, but it is usually treated as a separate problem – and considered, again, in its relationship to the whole *Decameron*.[13] Vittore Branca is unusual in his insistence (in a chapter entitled 'Coerenza ideale e funzione unitaria dell'Introduzione') on the wholeness and balance of the Introduction.[14] His topic is still, however, the fit between the Introduction and the book as a whole: he argues that the Introduction maps out, in small, the 'ideal itinerary' of Boccaccio's 'human comedy.' All of these readings treat the Introduction as an elaborate rubric to the *Decameron*.

Such an approach is not hard to justify. If the *Decameron* is a unified work, an organic whole that embraces and transcends the division into stories, then the Introduction to the First Day must be an important manifestation of this totality. Indeed, the first sentence after the rubric speaks of 'la presente opera' [the present work (I Intro. §2)], and goes on, as we shall see, to give the work a metaphorical face. Yet the Introduction is not *merely* a rubric or an introduction. (The name *Introduc-*

tion is, of course, an editorial convenience.) It is a text with designs of its own, and one of its aims is to complicate, even as it asserts, the very notion of 'the book as a whole.' The Introduction, I shall argue, is a meditation on titles, a meditation on the relations between texts and persons. It offers a critique of the gesture that would transform a stretch of writing, or a stretch of history, into a self-present and self-presenting totality, an entity like a person; yet it moves beyond critique to imagine a new writing inextricably bound up with the personal, the social, the historical.

The face of the work appears when Boccaccio cautions his female readers not to be overly alarmed by his account of the plague – 'la dolorosa ricordazione della pestifera mortalità trapassata ... la quale essa porta nella sua fronte' [the painful memory of the recent deadly plague ... which it carries on its brow (I Intro. §2)]. The opening of the book is potentially misleading precisely because it leads somewhere; it is a 'grave e noioso principio' [arduous and painful opening (I Intro. §2)], but the reader who perseveres will take a journey that will turn out to be delightful – and all the more delightful for its 'orrido cominciamento' [horrid beginning (I Intro. §4)]. The image is employed again, however, to make a very different statement, at the end of the entire book: in the Author's Conclusion, Boccaccio guarantees that each story has its true nature plainly written on its face: 'tutte nella fronte portan segnato quello che esse dentro dal loro seno nascose tengono' [each of the stories bears marked on its brow that which it hides within its bosom (Concl. §19)].

The brow of a text can thus be read in two quite different ways. The two statements do not contradict each other outright, since the rules for individual stories may well diverge from the rules for the work as a whole. Still, this is a kind of 'bifrontality,' to appropriate a term from Branca:[15] we are offered two different models for how a 'fronte' might work. In one case, each story has a rubric that gives a true image of what is inside the story: the rubric is attached as a distinct text, a small reflection of the larger story. In fact the story rubrics are, as Antonio D'Andrea has pointed out, little narratives themselves;[16] if they are not quite as reliable as Boccaccio claims, they are nonetheless clearly legible signs, standing for their referents as miniatures or metaphors. In the other case, the 'fronte' of the book is its beginning; it is connected to the rest of the book by contiguity, as it is only the first stage in the book's larger journey. This is a metonymic relationship but not an accidental one: Boccaccio says that he begins his book this way 'quasi da necessità' [almost of necessity (I Intro. §7)], since the plague is connected to the storytelling by another kind of metonymy, the metonymy of cause and effect.

These two versions of the textual face are answered, within the Introduction, by two powerful images of the human face made textual through the addition of an instantly legible sign. The phrase 'manifesto segno' [manifest sign] appears twice. In the first instance we are told that when the plague began in the East, bleeding from the nose was a 'manifesto segno' (I Intro. §10) of certain death; as the plague moved west, its characteristic symptoms shifted to other parts of the body, the groin and armpits. In the second instance, Filomena places a laurel garland on the head of Pampinea to serve as a 'manifesto segno' of her 'real signoria e maggioranza' [royal sovereignty and authority (I Intro. §97)]. This sign too will move, as the reign passes in orderly fashion from one storyteller to another. The double appearance of 'manifesto segno,' like the double appearance of 'fronte,' points to a contrast between two modes of signifying; once again, the theoretical opposition between metaphor and metonymy provides a useful tool for describing the contrast.[17] The plague symptom, an involuntary overflow from within the body, betokens death metonymically, through inescapable association. The laurel crown is conventional and metaphoric, fit for a praiseworthy ruler because its own branches are thought to be worthy of praise.[18]

These signifying faces, textual and human, evoke the problematics of the literary title. A title is the manifest sign of a work – its heading or front or face. And the relationship of title to work can be understood as both metonymic and metaphoric: the title is part of the work, its beginning as a text, yet it is the term that stands in for the totality of the work.[19] (Hence my initial hesitation about whether the rubric to the First Day should be included within the day.) The fronts and signs that I have just assembled seem to play out both possibilities in a symmetrical fashion. The rubrics to the stories and the crown of the storytellers are metaphoric titles: they are imposed on a whole text, a whole person, from outside, and they display the inner qualities of the bodies they grace. The introductory plague description and the early plague symptom are also signs affixed to bodies – the body of the *Decameron*, the body of the plague victim – but they are not imposed from outside; they emerge from within, becoming visible on the face. Moreover, the 'manifesto segno' of death is, like Boccaccio's plague description, a beginning: it is the first step in a process, and it is surrounded in the text by explicit references to the idea of beginning. If the plague description is a 'grave e noioso principio,' an 'orrido comminciamento' [arduous and painful opening, horrid beginning (I Intro. §§2, 4)], the plague itself 'quasi nel *principio* della primavera ... orribilmente *cominciò* i suoi dolorosi effetti ... a dimostrare' [around the *beginning* of spring ... horribly *began* to show its painful effects (I Intro. §9)].[20] Both the signs of plague and the passage describing the plague are like the metonymic title, the incipit.

The contrast between these two versions of the title serves, I shall argue, as a structuring principle for the bipartite Introduction: the two 'manifesti segni' are balanced as paradigmatic signs for two modes of signification and two discourses. I shall treat them separately, beginning with the title as metaphor. As Jonathan Culler has pointed out, metaphor and metonymy rarely receive a balanced treatment in literary theory or in literature: metaphor is routinely privileged over metonymy and other figures, because of the cognitive value inherent in the discovery of resemblances.[21] Not surprisingly, medieval discussions of titles tend to stress their totalizing, metaphoric quality. The most common etymology derives 'titulus' from 'Titano, id est a sole' [from Titan, that is from the sun]. This etymology is elaborated in an anonymous *accessus* to Sedulius: 'According to Servius the term *titulus* (title) comes from Titan, that is, the sun, either by a process of diminishing (*diminutio*) or by comparison. It is said to come through diminution because the light of that work is small in relation to the whole sun; by comparison [because], just as the rising sun gives light to the whole world, so the title illuminates the work that follows.'[22] The first explanation, through diminution, is somewhat cryptic, but I read the implicit logic thus: the work gives a smaller light than 'the whole sun,' and hence it is a diminution; this diminution matches the verbal diminution of 'Titan' in 'titulus.' To express this as an analogy, *work* is to *sun* as *title* is to *Titan*. But since Titan *means* the sun, the analogy implies an identity between work and title. The title is more than a designation or heading; it is a synonym for the work, as though one could write 'titulus, id est opus.' As the diminutive of *Titan*, the very word *titulus* is an oxymoronic yoking of the gigantic and the miniature; likewise, the title is a small version of a large totality. The second explanation, through similitude, quite clearly sets forth a different analogy: *title* is to *work* as *sun* is to *world*. Now it is the title that illuminates, and the word *totum* [whole] is transferred from the sun to the sphere that is illuminated.

The title confers wholeness on the work even as it provides the authoritative gloss. The contrast between the two explanations is not, however, a contradiction. Both explanations are similitudes, and point to a principle of similitude – the operating principle, one might add, of the medieval science of etymology, which explicates a word by assuming a likeness between its meaning and the visible trace of its origin.[23] In this particular etymology, method and content are congruent: both etymology and title illuminate through similitude.

To observe this theory of the title in critical practice, we might briefly consider Peter Lombard's influential commentary on the book of Psalms. The titles of the individual Psalms are said to have been appended by the prophetic scribe Esdras as a kind of inspired but ancillary gloss to David's text; they are 'keys to the Psalms.'[24] The titles generally specify the Psalms' historical context, but their real significance is allegorical: Peter Lombard reads the Old Testament story typologically to find the true meaning of the Psalms. For example, when a title contains the word *titulus* (as in 'In finem, Pro populo ... David in tituli inscriptionem,' Ps. 56.1), this word is never merely self-reflexive. Rather, it draws us away from the life of David and points to the *titulus*, or superscription, that Pilate imposed upon the Cross.[25] Yet the first Psalm is said to lack a title because it *is* a title. As 'the head of the book,' 'the title and prologue of the work which follows,' the first Psalm contains within itself 'the sum of the subject matter of the entire book,' namely 'the whole Christ.'[26] Peter Lombard's commentary assumes the title's metaphoric power, along with its status as the miniature embodiment of a totality.

I have suggested that the *Decameron* offers two different models of the title. The model favored by medieval literary theory, the title as totalizing metaphor, seems appropriate to the rubrics of the individual stories, and to the storytellers' laurel crown. Beyond this, I would suggest that the entire second half of the Introduction – the passage that features the laurel crown as a 'manifesto segno,' and that leads up to the first of the story rubrics – is a privileged site of metaphorical signs.

The names of the storytellers are introduced as transparent allegories: Boccaccio says that he is suppressing the real names and supplying 'nomi alle qualità di ciascuna convenienti o in tutto o in parte' [names appropriate to the qualities of each one, either as a whole or in part (I Intro. §51)]. And the numbers of the storytellers – seven women and three men, adding up to the ten of the 'Decameron' – carry obvious numerological force. As it happens, the storytellers have inspired a range of rather different symbolic interpretations; what is clear, in the words of Victoria Kirkham, is that 'they create a situation charged with allegorical resonance.'[27] Moreover the *brigata* constitutes itself as an orderly totality, a society under the rule of a figurative monarchy.[28] Names, persons, community, crown: all are signifiers that point along a vertical axis; they are like the 'titulus' in its solar aspect. Indeed, the storytellers gather under the sign of the sun. Throughout the *cornice* their daily activities are coordinated to the motion of the sun, and the speech in which Pampinea proposes the storytelling game begins, 'Come voi vedete, il sole è alto ...' [As you see, the sun is high (I Intro. §110)].

The storytellers carry another kind of significance as well. It has long been observed that their fictional names refer to earlier writing by Boccaccio and other writers in Boccaccio's tradition; what has not been remarked is the predominance of literary titles in the cast of characters. Before considering the group, I want to focus on 'Filostrato' as a kind of experimental limit case for a certain mode of titling.

Boccaccio's earlier career as a writer reveals an analytic curiosity about every aspect of the form of a book; not surprisingly, his interest in titles is long-standing. In the early poem, *Filostrato*, the name Filostrato is presented as a transparent signifier. The opening rubric begins: 'Filostrato è il titolo di questo libro, e la cagione è questa ...' [*Filostrato* is the title of this book and the reason is this ...]. The name is immediately and sufficiently explained by its etymology, 'a man conquered and laid prostrate by love.'[29] Yet it achieves a certain complexity through its range of applications. It appears, always in rubrics, as the proper name of the poem, as an epithet for the hero Troiolo, and as the poet's pseudonym. In its very transparency, 'Filostrato' makes possible a specular identification among author, work, and protagonist.

Such an identification had long been visible, of course, in the Bible. As we have seen, Peter Lombard reads Psalm 1 as a *titulus* that establishes the 'summam et materiam totius libri' [sum and subject matter of the entire book] – namely 'Christus integer' [the whole Christ]. The book embodies the authoring Word. The *Filostrato* is original in adapting this totalizing identification to a secular author, a modern work, a human protagonist. I have elsewhere discussed the *Filostrato* as the staging of a poet's self-creation and self-authorization.[30] But the book is equally a fantasy of the book as autonomous totality. The choice of Troiolo as protagonist suggests another kind of totalization: Troiolo encapsulates and personifies the city Troy as a part for the whole, as a metaphoric image, and as a verbal diminutive.

The Filostrato of the *Decameron* may recall Troiolo: Filostrato presides over the fourth day of storytelling, as if to commemorate Criseida's betrayal of Troiolo on the fourth day of her promised ten-day absence. But this later Filostrato points more clearly to the authorial persona of the earlier work. Filostrato has a special privilege within the frame-story; as he reveals in the Conclusion to the Third Day, he knows the fictional name he will be assigned (Filostrato), understands its meaning, and accepts it as all too appropriate (III Concl. §6). Moreover, like the poet Filostrato, the storyteller is only interested in stories that contain images of himself, stories of unhappy lovers. For this he is gently mocked by the other storytellers.[31] But this mocking only emphasizes a critical distance that is built into the form of the *Decameron*. Filostrato, once the sole author of an autonomous textual world, is now one storyteller among ten; he evokes a certain kind of author and a certain kind of work within a very different kind of work that projects a very different kind of author. The frame-story of the *Decameron* refers to the fantasy expressed by the earlier poem *Filostrato*, but places it, as it were, within a frame.

A similar claim can be made for the narrators as a group. Each of the ten alludes to a character from an earlier work, but at the same time embodies a text or a set of texts. Five of the ten evoke titles. Panfilo is a character in several of Boccaccio's works, but he is also an earlier Pamphilus, believed by Boccaccio to be one of his Italian predecessors. In this second sense, 'Panfilo,' like 'Filostrato,' fuses author, character, work: Pamphilus is the author of a dialogue between Pamphilus and a lady, entitled *Pamphilus de Amore*.[32] 'Pampinea' is the title, and the title character, of an early Latin eclogue by Boccaccio.[33] 'Emilia' is part of *Teseida delle Nozze d'Emilia* – the title for the *Teseida* chosen by its dedicatee, Fiammetta.[34] Fiammetta is, of course, Boccaccio's frequent dedicatee – he says that the *Filocolo* bears her name written on its 'fronte' [brow (V 97 §2)] – and she is also the authorial persona who gives her name to the title of *L'Elegia di Madonna Fiammetta*.[35] The other five storytellers evoke, in more general ways, whole literary projects. Filomena is the recipient of the *Filostrato*. Lauretta is clearly Petrarch's Laura, the beloved of the *Canzoniere* whom Boccaccio himself described as a fiction, an allegory for the laurel crown.[36] Neifile probably represents, as Branca states, the *dolce stil nuovo* and Dante's early love-poetry.[37] More generally, Dioneo, whose name derives from an epithet for Venus, can stand for love and love poetry; Elissa, or Dido, evokes tragic love and the complaints of *Aeneid* 4 and Ovid's *Heroides*.

Each of the ten narrators has presided over a textual universe – Elissa
has literally been a queen – but in the *Decameron* each has the rule of
one day out of ten.

The *brigata* of the *Decameron* is thus an assembly of titles: half of the
storytellers have had an earlier life as title characters, and the other
half may be understood as designations for texts, as headings or
rubrics. What does Boccaccio accomplish by gathering these personified titles in the second half of the Introduction? If the title is a sign of
totality, a guarantee of textual unity and identity, then we can read the
staging of this assembly as an emphatic declaration of the *Decameron*'s
own status as a unitary work. In this reading, Boccaccio commences his
collection of stories by insisting on the possibility of textual wholeness;
the second half of the Introduction is a kind of super-title for the book,
an authorizing rubric with the force of ten titles. Yet I believe that this
reading must coexist with another equally plausible reading: these
embodied titles paradoxically stand for disembodiment, fragmentation, death.

To see this, we might begin by considering another royal title character, a figure who could fittingly be grouped with the ten storytellers:
'Prencipe Galeotto' [Prince Galeotto]. The *Decameron*'s cognomen or
subtitle has generated rather more critical discussion than 'Decameron.'[38] For my purposes, it is enough to point out a formal feature of
the name. 'Galeotto' is another term that fuses character, work, and
author. Boccaccio is alluding, of course, to Francesca's next-to-last line
in *Inferno* 5: 'Galeotto fu 'l libro e chi lo scrisse' [A Gallehault was the
book and he who wrote it].[39] Yet Galeotto is originally a character
within the Arthurian romance that Paolo and Francesca have been
reading. In his later commentary on *Inferno*, Boccaccio describes Galeotto as both a prince and a giant: as the go-between for the early stages
of Lancelot and Guinevere's love, he physically stands in front of the
two to screen their first kiss from the view of the court.[40] The person
and the book dissolve into each other: Galeotto is the occasion for one
kiss, and the book dubbed 'Galeotto' is the occasion for another.

The figure of Galeotto in turn provides a link between the personified titles of the *Decameron* frame-story and the first half of the Introduction – for the first page offers another clear allusion to *Inferno* 5. I
have quoted the sentence in which Boccaccio worries about the terrifying effect of the memory that the book bears on its face. Here is the next
sentence: 'Ma non voglio per ciò che questo di più avanti leggere vi
spaventi, quasi sempre tra' sospiri e tralle lagrime leggendo dobbiate

trapassare' [But I do not want this to frighten you away from reading further, as if in reading you were going to pass forever among sighs and tears (I Intro. §3)]. The verb phrase 'più avanti leggere' [reading further] points to the sentence that immediately follows Francesca's imposition of the title 'Galeotto' – her last sentence, 'quel giorno più non vi leggemmo avante' [that day we read no farther in it (5.138)].[41] The echo is reinforced by the reference to eternal sighs and tears, which recalls the eternal lamentation of the Circle of Lust, as well as the sympathetic tears produced by the pilgrim Dante and the 'time of sweet sighs' (5.118) he asks Francesca to recall.

The threat of an interruption to reading, which Boccaccio mentions in his Introduction so as to avert it, can take several forms. The explicit fear is that female readers, being naturally 'pietose' [piteous], may be overcome by the remembered horrors of the plague. This is to say that they may respond to the plague narrative as Dante responds to Francesca's brief autobiography: he swoons 'di pietade,' [for pity (5.140)], abruptly ending his conversation with her. He is figuratively reading no more. Yet the allusion to *Inferno* 5 must evoke, at the same time, the literal cessation of reading in Francesca's story, as if readers of the *Decameron* might put down the book for more carnal reasons. This carries a paradoxical implication: the choice of 'Galeotto' as a subtitle seems to concede an immoral content that Boccaccio elsewhere denies, yet the reader of a Galeotto has a moral obligation not to stop reading. At least one other kind of interruption is possible, this one carrying an opposite moral force. Any citation of Dante's 'più non vi leggemmo avante' [we read no further] may also evoke a text to which Dante alludes, Augustine's 'nec ultra volui legere' [I did not wish to read further]: that is, the moment in the *Confessions* when Augustine, reading the Bible, is converted and closes his book.[42] I have travelled far from Boccaccio's explicit statement, but there is a certain logic to the idea that an immediate conversion to higher thoughts, caused by the spectacle of human mortality, would short-circuit the extended reading Boccaccio desires.

Whatever its moral valence, the allusion to *Inferno* 5 points to a formal problem, the relationship between interruption and totality. The two terms would seem to be antithetical. Interpretive models that assume an organic correspondence between form and meaning tend to privilege the ending of a text as the moment when total form and total meaning become fully visible at last. By this logic an interrupted reading should be incomplete, approximate. Yet for Francesca and for Augustine it is the abrupt interruption of reading that signals a full grasp of the whole. It is as though poetic closure could be discovered or imposed by the physical closing of a book. Francesca and Paolo stop reading because they have arrived at an understanding, and an understanding of their book. '[S]olo un punto fu quel che ci vinse' [one point alone it was that conquered us (5.132)], says Francesca: that point is the represented fulfilment of desire in a kiss, and to read any further would be to miss the point. If this seems a bad way of reading, a jumping to conclusions, we have the example of Augustine to show us that Francesca and Paolo's reading may be wrong in content but it is not wrong in form. Augustine achieves the sense of an ending in the middle of his book: 'For instantly, even with the end of this sentence, as if by a light of security infused into my heart, all the darkness of doubt dispersed' (8.12).[43] The interruption of reading can be an experience of totality. For Francesca, the gesture of closing the book, the gesture that closes her speech, is all but simultaneous with the rhetorical gesture of placing a title (or cognomen) on the book.

A title can be the sign of totality, of presence, of a kind of personhood for the text. Yet Francesca's bitter dismissal of her book as a Galeotto, informed by whatever new understanding she has achieved in Hell, suggests that a title can also impose a negative closure. Just as the cessation of reading can amount to a totalization, totalization can never be absolutely distinguished from annihilation. The title can also be a sign of death. The medieval dictionaries recognize this: the French theologian and Latinist Alain de Lille, among others, states that *titulus* can mean 'a memorial epigram or epitaph that is inscribed on the tombs of the dead.'[44] And Uguccione da Pisa and Guillielmus Brito, who give the etymology from 'Titan,' also record an alternative etymology. As Brito explains:

'Vel dicitur titulus a theta, figura sic facta, Θ scilicet, que olim in frontibus dampnatorum imprimebatur.' Unde quidam ait,
  O multum ante alias infelix littera theta.
Habet enim telum per medium, quod est signum mortis. 'Sicut autem per illam figuram reddebatur homo noscibilis, sic per titulum cognoscitur liber.'

['Or title is so called from theta, the figure made thus, Θ, which was once imprinted on the foreheads of the condemned.' Whence a certain writer says,
  O letter unhappy far above others, theta.

For it has a spear through the middle, which is a sign of death. 'Just as by this figure a man was made knowable, so by the title a book is known.']⁴⁵

This version of the title is still metaphoric – the theta is a sign that frames a miniature emblem – but it is inscribed on the human face as a death sentence. It has more to do with the plague than with the game of storytelling.

The storytellers themselves, however, may also betoken annihilation. 'Filostrato' means 'one struck down by love,' and the hero who receives that epithet, Troiolo, is struck down fatally. Filomena and Fiammetta are tragic heroines in Ovid's myth and Boccaccio's *Elegy*; Virgil's Elissa dies on a funeral pyre, and Emilia in the *Teseida* weeps at her husband's pyre. Neifile evokes Dante's 'new love,' and thus the mourning for Beatrice in the *Vita nuova*; Lauretta evokes the Laura who died – according to Petrarch – in the plague of 1348. Thus at least seven of the storytellers carry an association with death. Now, in the *Decameron*, all ten are alive and well. Their very health, in a time of plague, seems to support an optimistic theory of allusion: allusion revives an anterior meaning, makes it present to a new text. In the *cornice*, according to this theory, figures from literature and figures *of* literature have become living persons: Laura lives on as Lauretta. But the reappearance of a proper name can carry other connotations.

In the social practice of Boccaccio's Florence, as Christiane Klapisch-Zuber has described, children were often named after departed relatives; the dead were thereby said to be 'remade.'⁴⁶ The living were not 'remade'; there was 'a sort of taboo' on the duplication of a name currently employed within a family (305). But a new death could prompt the rebaptizing of a child, in order to 'remake' a nearer rather than a more distant relative (301–3). Now, Boccaccio says that he is naming, in fact renaming, his storytellers. In his claim to be imposing names ('intendo di nominarle' [I intend to name them (I Intro. §51)]) he is like a Florentine father writing a 'family book,' who typically 'stressed his own responsibility ... in the choice of a child's given name' (288). The new names of the storytellers together constitute an image of a literary lineage, from Virgil and Ovid to Boccaccio's own career before the plague. But such a 'remaking' may signal a recognition of death and discontinuity within the tradition. Laura can be remade as Lauretta because she has died within Petrarch's book. Dioneo, an idealized figure of love in Boccaccio's *L'Ameto*,⁴⁷ may stand for love, but he may equally stand for the death of love described in the Proem to the

Decameron. In this reading, the storytellers gather to form an elegy, an 'ubi sunt?' For Pampinea, one of the horrors of the plague is the unexpected appearance of 'l'ombre di coloro che sono trapassati' [the shades of those who have passed away (I Intro. §59)]. My suggestion is that Pampinea herself, and her nine companions, may be understood as shades, as memorial apparitions.

Even the sun has a darker side. It is true that the storytellers gather at noon; Muscetta writes of 'il pieno sole che illumina la scene' [the full sun that illuminates the scene].[48] But the storytellers gather in the shade. As they have left Florence to evade the plague, so they now seek out a spot where '[non] poteva d'alcuna parte il sole' [the sun could not enter (I Intro. §109)]. The parallel between plague and sun is not accidental, and not unique to this text. The epidemic was represented iconographically as a rain of mortal arrows from above;[49] many believed that it proceeded, in Boccaccio's own phrase, 'per operazione de' corpi superiori' [through the working of heavenly bodies (I Intro. §8)]. The sun was not usually one of the heavenly bodies held responsible for the outbreak of the plague. But a certain Simon de Covino, writing in France in 1350, notes that the sun is 'the king and prince of all planets, and the heart of heaven, according to the sayings of philosophers.'[50] Accordingly his hexameter poem is entitled 'De judicio solis in convivio Saturni' [Concerning the judgment of the sun at the banquet of Saturn]; Simon associates the plague with an unusual conjunction of Saturn and Jupiter, but imagines this conjunction as a celestial debate over the fate of humanity, with the sun rendering a fatal verdict. Again, there was no eclipse of the sun in the years before 1348, yet such an eclipse appears in a poetic dialogue on the plague involving Boccaccio himself. Cecco di Meletto addresses a sonnet to four Italian contemporaries concerning the relationship between terrifying heavenly signs and the plague's 'saette / avvelenate' [poisoned arrows], and the omen he mentions last is precisely a 'solare eclisse' [solar eclipse] in Boccaccio's reply.[51]

The sun can stand for the heavens more generally, and for God; hence it is a powerful emblem for the plague understood as a punishment from above. Just as important, however, is the sun's association with the world as a whole. As Simon de Covino writes, it is 'the light of the world, the eye by which all things are seen.'[52] As an image of totality, the sun can express the threat of total loss. Moreover, the sun makes the world present to itself but it is endlessly caught up – through its diurnal cycle and its ominous eclipses – in a dialectic of presence and absence.[53] The midday sun evokes a more specific cultural tradition: Nicholas J. Perella writes that the sun at noon 'has symbolical associations with the Divinity and ... with the "destruction that wasteth at noonday" – the raging pestilence from which [Boccaccio's] *lieta brigata* has sought to escape.'[54] But the association of the sun with both universality and universal death does not depend on this tradition. It is equally visible in the matter-of-fact phrasing of a contemporary English chronicler: 'this cruel death spread on all sides, following the course of the sun.'[55]

The title in its solar aspect is thus profoundly double. As the diminutive metaphor for a work, the proper name of a totality, the title promises full presence but opens the way to loss, dismissal, annihilation. At this point, we might observe that the second half of the Introduction does for the literary work what Boccaccio elsewhere does for the author. Just as Boccaccio simultaneously claims and disclaims a Dantean authority, so the play of totalizing metaphors in the Introduction both constitutes the text as work and questions that constitution. Boccaccio encourages such a double reading by balancing the second half of the Introduction – the illuminated scene of personified titles – against the dark spectacle of the first half. Yet the first half of the Introduction offers more than an implicit critique of the solar title; it explores an entirely different way of understanding titles.

I have suggested that a title is both a metonym and a metaphor for its work. The first possibility is rarely theorized, but the signifying faces that open the Introduction – the 'fronte' that is merely a misleading beginning, the 'manifesto segno' of death from the plague – signify metonymically, as parts taken from the whole. They point to a mode of signification that is played out in the plague description. The journey of the disease from east to west might be described in terms of the sun's path, but the sun is not mentioned. Instead, there is merely a horizontal progression, and it is matched by the relentlessly metonymic quality of the writing, which accumulates symptoms and incidents without finding a centre or a principle of order. As Giuseppe Mazzotta writes, 'The world of the plague is transformed into an ominous text, with its signs proliferating, shifting and only decipherable as presages of death.'[56] I understand 'text' here in its deconstructive sense – an unbounded writing, text rather than work. Signs are radically contingent, and contingency itself is figured as physical contact, as contagion. Boccaccio's narrative features no individual characters; as Mazzotta points out, the disease itself has no proper name.[57]

Consider the list of actions taken by various groups in response to the plague:

1 Almost everyone flees the sick and their belongings (I Intro. §19).
2 Some try to live moderately and avoid excess (§20).
3 Others try to live as luxuriously as possible (§§21–2). (At this point, a comment on the breakdown of all law [§23].)
4 Others seek a middle way between §2 and §3 (§24).
5 And others flee (§25).

The logical difficulties here – the idea of trying to moderate moderation, and the double mention of flight as both the nearly universal choice and one option among many – give the list the distinct feel of an associative improvisation; the breakdown of law is also a breakdown of any clear overview.

Yet, just as the second half of the Introduction features metaphoric presences that bespeak absence, so the metonymic writing of the first half ultimately forms an image of absoluteness and wholeness. The plague's devastation approaches a negative totalization. With the breakdown of social order, the hierarchical distinctions internal to the city are erased, replaced by a meaningless factionalization as the people choose between equally ineffectual hygienic plans. Salvatore Battaglia provides an eloquent brief reading of this loss of structure, which he describes not as a fragmentation but as a universalization and abstraction.[58] (He thus anticipates René Girard's more general claim that 'The plague is universally presented as a process of undifferentiation, a destruction of specificities.'[59]) Battaglia's 1936 essay on Boccaccio's 'lyric schemes' is primarily concerned with frame-stories depicting idealized courtly circles; the term 'lyric' is appropriate both because of the refined amorous preoccupations of these groups and because of their non-narrative formal quality, their abstract and circular atemporality. His analysis leads him to view the plague description of the *Decameron* as, in effect, a negative lyric. The shifting textuality of the plague description, the naming of parts, adds up to a totality – and this totality in turn calls forth its antithesis, the articulated and illustrious city before the plague, the lost world evoked in an explicit *ubi sunt* lament at the end of the plague description (1 Intro. 48).[60]

In the Introduction, then, metonymy and metaphor are the two faces of a single sign. Boccaccio has taken pains to distinguish between two ways of understanding the literary title, the textual 'fronte,' and has played out these two possibilities in two distinct sections. But under either interpretation the title is a marker of totality, and the distinctive mode of each half ultimately delivers an image of totality: an image of a city lost and found, an expansive text bound into a book.[61] The place of the title, therefore, is not merely the second half but the entire Introduction.

My aim in this essay, however, has not been to mend the division in the Introduction by inscribing a single rubric above the text. If the Introduction is unified by a double tendency towards unification, its doubleness remains the most salient fact about it. How are we to read the split? Mazzotta has suggested that the two moments of the Introduction, the plague and the storytelling, nearly make a chiasmus: the plague description is presented as a digression within the book, and the storytelling is a temporary diversion from the experience of plague.[62] I would add that each half of the Introduction contains a reflection of the other: Pampinea's own description of the plague (I Intro. §§56–62) recapitulates Boccaccio's, and the escape of the ten young people seems to be anticipated unsympathetically in Boccaccio's mention of a group that fled the city (I Intro. §25). But Mazzotta describes this relationship as a *near* chiasmus because the two moments of the Introduction frame each other 'without ever intersecting as in a chiasmus, though they well might.'[63] For all their mutual reflection, their mutual framing, the two passages seem to remain disjunct.

The disjunction between the plague description and the storytellers' story is not simple or absolute, however. If there is no intersection, no overlap or fusion, there is something else more unexpected: Boccaccio brings his two texts together in such a way as to create a space between them, a space for a text not yet written. A single long sentence both divides and links the two halves.

A me medesimo incresce andarmi tanto tra tante miserie ravolgendo: per che, volendo omai lasciare star quella parte di quelle che io acconciamente posso schifare, dico che, stando in questi termini la nostra città, d'abitatori quasi vota, addivenne, sì come io poi da persona degna di fede sentii, che nella venerabile chiesa di Santa Maria Novella, un martedì mattina, non essendovi quasi alcuna altra persona, uditi li divini ufici in abito lugubre quale a sì fatta stagione si richiedea, si ritrovarono sette giovani donne tutte l'una all'altra o per amistà o per vicinanza o per parentado congiunte, delle quali niuna il venti e ottesimo anno passato avea né

era minor di diciotto, savia ciascuna e di sangue nobile e bella di forma e
ornata di costumi e di leggiadra onestà. (I Intro. §49)

[To me myself it is painful to reflect so deeply upon so many miseries:
therefore, wishing at last to let stand that part of them which I can suit-
ably omit, I say that, our city being in this condition, almost empty of
inhabitants, it happened, as I later heard from a person worthy of faith,
that in the venerable church of Santa Maria Novella, one Tuesday morn-
ing, there being almost no one else there, having heard the divine services
in mournful attire which such a season required, seven young women
found themselves together, each connected to the other either as a friend
or as a neighbor or as a relative, of whom none had passed her twenty-
eighth year nor was younger than eighteen, each one wise and of noble
blood and beautiful of form and fair of manners and of graceful modesty.]

This sentence draws a line between two discourses, two worlds; yet in
its length and its elaborate syntax it creates a space of confrontation, a
space where two fronts face each other. The textual encounter is cast as
a meeting of persons. The plague narrative has lacked a protagonist,
and critics agree that the storytellers of the *cornice* are barely characterized[64]; yet the sentence begins emphatically with the authorial
persona ('me medesimo') and concludes with the personal qualities of
seven young women. We have seen this transition from author to storytellers before, in the rubric to the First Day; indeed, this is the sentence that announces the transfer of authority I mentioned earlier, by
introducing the idea of an informant among the women. The transition
sentence repeats and amplifies the rubric from within the text.

In its opening, the sentence makes a protagonist of the author. The
particular horrors of the plague, so painfully enumerated in the preceding pages, are here summed up and abstracted; they appear in the
text as 'so many miseries,' and then a part that can be omitted, and
then a condition of emptiness. What is vivid is the subjectivity that
encompasses such memories. This is the point at which the authorial
persona of the *Decameron* most resembles the earlier persona Filostrato;
Filostrato also uses the verb 'rivolgere,' when he describes his own
mental search for an ancient story to embody his misery.[65] The phrase
'stando in questi termini la nostra città, d'abitatori quasi vota' [our city
being in this condition, almost empty of inhabitants] recalls the opening of the book of Lamentations: 'Quomodo sedet sola civitas plena
populo!' [How doth the city sit solitary that was full of people].[66] In the

Vita nuova, Dante cites this verse at the beginning of the chapter announcing Beatrice's death (28.1), later explaining that he has employed it as the 'entrata' [heading or entry] to his new material (30.1);[67] it is cited again in the Proem to the *Filostrato* (13). In those texts, the devastation of a city is a metaphor for personal loss, a figure of closure that opens the way to new writing; in the *Decameron* the sudden insistence on authorial subjectivity reframes the plague description as a bitter lyric indeed.

In the first half of the sentence, then, an open-ended metonymic discourse is closed off as a totality. The plague has no ending in the *Decameron*, but it finds here instead a destination, a resting place in memory: it is situated in a person, the author himself, who becomes a metaphorical embodiment of loss. This process is reversed in the second half of the sentence. Earlier I totalized the second half of the Introduction as a place of totalities and allegorical signs; taken by itself, however, this sentence seems to be presenting naturalistic characters and the beginning of a story. Some of the details in the sentence, such as the numbers, might be read allegorically; in this first appearance, however, such details look like specifications rather than symbols. Whatever the women later come to mean, their first associations are social relationships with each other. The sentence begins with a complex of subordinate clauses; it ends in a trail of 'ands' and 'ofs,' accumulating qualities in a list that could go on indefinitely. The metaphoric frame is here presented under the heading of metonymic open-endedness. The sentence as a whole is a miniature version of the chiasmus Mazzotta describes: it enacts an interchange between the Introduction's two modes of signification, its two faces.

But the sentence also encompasses a fleeting third moment: 'sì come io poi da persona degna di fede sentii ...' [as I later heard from a person worthy of faith ...]. This subordinate clause belongs to neither half of the Introduction. Yet it points to a real social encounter between the persons that embody the two halves.[68] What is most striking is the lack of specification, the disembodied quality of a meeting which is mentioned but not described. We may presume that the 'persona degna di fede' is one of the seven ladies, but this is mere presumption; in any case we cannot know which lady is meant, or her real identity.[69] The *time* of the encounter is equally vague. Both halves of the Introduction contain clear temporal markers: the plague arrives in 1348 (I Intro. §8), and the meeting in church occurs on a Tuesday. These markers point to two different systems of time, corresponding to the Introduction's two modes of signifying: for the metonymic plague, the linear sequence of world history; for the metaphoric *brigata*, the endless cycle of the week. But the meeting between Boccaccio and his reliable source is located in a purely relative 'poi' [later]. The transition sentence opens a space for social encounter and for the 'and then' of narrative.

This space, briefly glimpsed in the Introduction, is the space of the *Decameron*'s *novelle*. The hundred stories resurrect, as Battaglia says, 'all those differentiations and individual tendencies that constitute the personality of individuals'[70] – the contingent touches that are erased, in different ways, by the plague and by the story of the storytellers. This requires a new logic of signification. It is not surprising, then, that the phrase 'manifesto segno' reappears, textually reversed, in the first story of the First Day, when the two Florentine brothers worry that turning away a dying Ciappelletto would be, to the neighbors, a 'segno manifesto di poco senno' [manifest sign of little wisdom (I.1.23)]. In the Introduction, the 'manifest sign' pointed to the certainty of death or the certainty of praise, but now it is caught up in an economy of social appearances. This transition is theorized by the narrator Panfilo at the end of his own brief introduction: he says that the significance of his story will appear 'manifestamente' [manifestly], and then modifies the adverb: 'manifestamente, dico, non il giudicio di Dio ma quel degli uomini seguitando' [manifestly I say, not according to the judgment of God but that of men (I.1.6)]. The Introduction's absolutes have been replaced by the provisional arrangements of human society.

I have argued that the Introduction to the First Day is both a powerful totalizing rubric for the *Decameron* and a critique of such rubrics. The *titulus* in its solar aspect appears in full force, in the second half, yet the plague description urges a deconstructive reading of the very signs that guarantee textual presence and unity. But the Introduction *also* offers a second positive theory of titling, and stages a meeting between one theory and the other. This meeting allows Boccaccio to move beyond rhetorical self-critique. In the Introduction as a whole, the plague reveals the doubleness of the personified text, but the personification of texts redeems the defeated naturalism of plague writing, laying the groundwork for a world of stories. The Introduction is thus a heading that stands in marked contrast to the text that it heads. Ultimately the dialectic between the Introduction's two signifying modes – between metaphor and metonymy as two ways of constructing textual totality – is less important than the dialectic between the Introduction and the stories, which is a dialectic between totality and unboundedness, between rhetorical personification and social life. Recent criticism of the *Decameron* has tended to stress *either* the systematic wholeness of the book *or* the slipperiness of the signs within it. This body of criticism, in its disjunctiveness, elaborates a double perspective generated by the two-faced Introduction, which seals the *Decameron* as a paradoxical object, both a mathematically complete totality and a space of boundless play.[71]

The meeting of textual faces in the Introduction is recast, in the body of the text, as conversation and storytelling. The *novelle* make use of metonymy and metaphor and all the figurative resources of language, including the power to totalize. We can see a play of totalities in the first story, for example: its plot is founded on the choice between two extreme readings of Ciapelletto, as a saint or as the 'worst man alive.' Again, the author's defence in the Introduction to the Fourth Day is a rhetorical tour de force that derives much of its humor from the contradictions in the things people say about women – the social group most likely to be totalized as a single entity and absolutized as good or evil. This authorial intervention, strategically located between Filostrato's self-absorbed self-portrait and the tragic day he rules, offers a view of the *Decameron* quite different from that of the Introduction. From this new perspective, the book as a whole does not exist; there is a work in progress, being read and enjoyed and attacked as it is written. This is not merely a provisional vantage point, but a comic and liberating annihilation of the book. It is the Introduction, in its framing of the title, that makes possible a seemingly endless writing 'senza titolo.'

NOTES

1 Quotations from the *Decameron* are drawn from the edition of Vittore Branca, in *Tutte le opere di Giovanni Boccaccio*, vol. 4, hereafter cited parenthetically in the text. All translations are my own. Here, and in my later discussion of I Intro. §49, I have tried to follow Boccaccio's syntax as closely as possible, since it is important for my argument; the translations of McWilliam and of Musa and Bondanella are equally faithful to Boccaccio's meaning and make far better English than mine.

2 A good collection of critical essays, with a cogent introduction, is *Discourses of Authority in Medieval and Renaissance Literature*, ed. Brownlee and Stephens.

3 See Branca's note at IV Intro. §3, and R. Hollander's discussion in *Boccaccio's Two Venuses*, 114–16.
4 Boccaccio, *Esposizioni sopra la Comedia di Dante*, IV litt. §119.
5 See Foucault, 'What Is an Author?' 118–19.
6 Conrad writes that 'the title briefly indicates the author and his subject-matter ... Finally, the title prefaces all books' ('Dialogue on the Authors,' in *Medieval Literary Theory*, ed. Minnis and Scott, 43).
7 *Esposizioni sopra la Comedia di Dante*, Accessus §13.
8 De Man, 'Autobiography as De-Facement,' 70.
9 Ibid., 76.
10 Ambrose's *Hexameron* is divided into six books, corresponding to the six days of Creation. The analogy between Ambrose's work and God's becomes explicit at the end: 'But now we seem to have reached the end of our discourse, since the sixth day is completed and the sum total of the work of the world has been concluded ... Surely we should now make our contribution of silence, since God has rested from the work of the world' (*Hexameron, Paradise, and Cain and Abel*, 6.10.75). On the *Cosmographia* see Linda Lomperis, 'From God's book to the Play of the text in the *Cosmographia*,' *Medievalia et Humanistica* 16 (1988), 51–71.
11 See Almansi, *Writer as Liar*, 1–18.
12 In *Convivio*, ed. Simonelli, Dante gives two alternative roots for 'autore.' The second (for which he rightly credits Uguccione da Pisa) is 'uno vocabulo greco che dice "autentin," che tanto vale in latino quanto "degno di fede e d'obedienza." E così "autore," quinci derivato, si prende per ogni persona degna d'essere creduta e obedita' [a Greek word, 'autentin,' which means in Latin 'worthy of faith and of obedience.' And thus 'autore,' derived from this, is used for any person worthy of being believed and obeyed (4.6.3–5)]. On authority in the *Convivio*, see Ascoli, 'Vowels of Authority.' Boccaccio has already alluded to this definition in establishing his own personal authority for the plague description: he says that he would not have written it had he merely heard it from another person, no matter how 'fededegna' (I Intr. §16).
13 The critical literature on the *Decameron* is so extensive that I can offer only very selective (and not very descriptive) citations of the works that have seemed to me most helpful. Many of of these works provide, of course, further bibliography. On the meaning of the *cornice*, see Marino, *Decameron 'Cornice'*; Potter, *Five Frames*; Cerisola, 'Questione delle cornice.' On the relationship of the plague description to the *Decameron*, see Bernardo, 'Plague as Key'; Olson, *Literature as Recreation*; Mazzotta, *World at Play*, 39–64; Levenstein, 'Out of Bounds.'

14 Branca, *Boccaccio medievale*, 31–44.

15 Ibid., 93.

16 D'Andrea, 'Le Rubriche del *Decameron*.' For a good brief treatment of the story rubrics, and the entire paratextual apparatus of the *Decameron*, see Battaglia Ricci, *Boccaccio*, 141–9.

17 On metaphor and metonymy in contemporary literary theory, see, e.g., Culler, 'Turns of Metaphor.' Briefly, theorists drawing on the work of the linguist Roman Jakobson have treated metaphor and metonymy as the two 'poles' of language: metaphor is 'based on the perception of an essential similarity,' and metonymy is 'based on a merely accidental or contingent connexion' (Culler, 190). Like some other contemporary theorists, Culler seeks to complicate this too-neat opposition. My own aim in invoking the terms is not to ground Boccaccio's text in the universal practices of language, but rather to point out relationships between the signifying modes Boccaccio himself describes.

18 Filomena chooses the laurel because 'assai volte aveva udito ragionare di quanto onore le frondi di quello eran degne e quanto degno d'onore facevano chi n'era meritamente incoronato' [she had frequently heard it said that laurel leaves were especially worthy of veneration and that they conferred great honour upon those people of merit who were crowned with them (I Intro. §97)].

19 This general and elementary observation is my own, but I have been educated on titles by several sophisticated essays. For a brief but detailed historical survey of titles, see Levin, 'Title as a Literary Genre.' On medieval titles in particular see Dembowski, 'Quelques considérations.' More theoretically, John Hollander, '"Haddocks' Eyes."' Genette, 'Title in Literature.' Derrida, 'Title (to be specified).'

20 In addition, forms of the verb 'cominciare' (begin) appear four other times in the first paragraph describing the plague: 'incominciata' (§8), 'cominciamento' (§10), 'cominciò' (§11), 's'incominciò' (§11).

21 Culler, 'Turns of Metaphor,' 198–9.

22 Minnis and Scott, eds., *Medieval Literary theory*, 19. For the Latin text see Huygens, *Accessus ad Auctores*, 29: 'Titulus autem Servio adtestante a Titano, id est a sole, per diminutionem vel per similitudinem dicitur: per diminutionem dicitur, quia parva lux est istius operis respectu totius solis, per similitudinem autem, quia sicut sol oriens illuminat totum orbem, sic titulus sequens opus.' I should stress that the word 'titulo' does not appear in Boccaccio's Introduction; I refer to the etymology as an important indicator of the medieval thinking about titles, since part of my argument is that this thinking lies in the background of the Introduction.

23 See Bloch, *Etymologies and Genealogies*, 53–63.

24 Peter Lombard, *Patrologia Latina* 191.60; Minnis and Scott, eds., *Medieval Literary Theory*, 111.

25 See for example the comment on Psalm 56: 'Hanc historiam tangit titulus, sed hoc ab historia nos retrahit quod de tituli inscriptione dicit. Nullus enim titulus legitur fuisse inscriptus David ... sed Christo qui de David natus est, inscriptus est titulus' [The title touches upon this history, yet the mention of the title's inscription draws us away from the history. For we do not read of any title inscribed for David; but a title is inscribed for Christ who is born of David (Peter Lombard, *Patrologia Latina* 191.527)].

26 *Patrologia Latina* 191.60; Minnis and Scott, eds., *Medieval Literary Theory*, 111.

27 Kirkham, 'Allegorically Tempered *Decameron*,' 170.

28 The community of storytellers is imagined as a body in need of a head when Elissa argues that the seven women must have men to guide them: 'Veramente gli uomini sono delle femine capo' [Truly men are the head of women (I Intro. §76)]. The ladies soon find male companions, and the natural gender hierarchy is transmuted into the ludic government of the *brigata* when Pampinea speaks of the need for 'alcuno principale, il quale noi e onoriamo e ubidiamo come maggiore' [some leader, whom we may honor and obey as superior (I Intro. §95)], and is herself immediately crowned queen of the First Day.

29 Boccaccio, *Filostrato*.

30 Stillinger, *Song of Troilus*, ch. 4: 'The Form of *Filostrato*.'

31 This is Filostrato's own claim in the introduction to his story of the next day (V.4.3); he is referring to comments like Lauretta's at IV.3.3. On Filostrato as a tyrant in Day Four, see Marcus, *Allegory of Form*, 54–6. I have discussed the relationship between the two Filostrati in *The Song of Troilus*, 209–10.

32 See Garbaty, '*Pamphilus, De Amore*,' for an English translation and for the citation of Boccaccio's letter referring to Pamphilus as an Italian poet.

33 Boccaccio, *Eclogues*, trans. Smarr, 13–21.

34 Boccaccio, *Teseida delle nozze di Emilia*, 'Risposta delle Muse.'

35 On the figure of Fiammetta, see Smarr, *Boccaccio and Fiammetta*.

36 Ibid., 3.

37 *Decameron*, note to I Intro. §51.

38 See, e.g., R. Hollander, *Boccaccio's Two Venuses*, 102–6 (with bibliography); Mazzotta, *World at Play*, 56–7.

39 Dante, *The Divine Comedy*, 5.137. Further citations of *Inferno* will be identified parenthetically in the text; I modify Singleton's translation at one point below. The critical literature on Francesca and her 'Galeotto' is of course vast; see, e.g., Noakes, 'Double Misreading.'

54   Thomas C. Stillinger

40 *Esposizioni sopra la Comedia di Dante*, V litt. §183.
41 R. Hollander, *'Boccaccio's Dante'* (1997), 55–7.
42 Augustine, *Confessions*, vol. 1, 464 (Book 8, chap. 12); trans. mine.
43 Augustine, loc. cit.: 'Statim quippe cum fine huiusce sententiae, quasi luce securitatis infusa cordi meo, omnes dubitationis tenebrae diffugerunt.'
44 *Patrologia Latina* 210.974.
45 Brito, *Summa Britonis*; trans. mine. Brito ends his entry on 'titulus' by citing Uguccione's *Derivations* as the source for 'omnia ista.' The two interpolated sentences derive from Isidore of Seville's discussion of the theta (*Etymologiarum*, I.ii.8), which does not mention titles.
46 Klapisch-Zuber, 'The Name "Remade."' Page references will be given parenthetically. Klapisch-Zuber gives many examples of the practice, including 'the tax declaration of a humble sharecropper, explaining to the tax officials, who may have been surprised to encounter a three-year-old Antonio whom they could see listed as older in a previous survey: "He died and I remade him"' (300). Klapisch-Zuber focuses on the period 1360–1530, but notes that 'These practices seem to have been ancient' (302). Boccaccio uses the verb 'rifare' in this sense (*Esposizioni sopra la Comedia di Dante*, XVI §43).
47 *Comedia delle ninfe fiorentine*, XXVI §72 ff.
48 Muscetta, *Giovanni Boccaccio*, 64.
49 Polzer, 'Fourteenth-Century Iconography.'
50 Littré, 'Opuscule,' 207, trans. mine. This text is discussed in Campbell, *Black Death*, 30–1.
51 Boccaccio, *Rime*, 88–94.
52 Littré, 'Opuscule,' 216, trans. mine.
53 Derrida, writing on the sun as at once the prototypical referent of metaphor and the prototypical metaphor *for* metaphor, comments that 'The very opposition of appearing and disappearing, the entire lexicon of the *phainesthai*, of *aletheia*, etc., of day and night, of the visible and the invisible, of the present and the absent – all this is possible only under the sun' ('White Mythology,' 251).
54 Perella, *Midday in Italian Literature*, 38.
55 Gottfried, *Black Death*, 58–9.
56 Mazzotta, *World at Play*, 30.
57 Ibid.
58 Battaglia, 'Schemi lirici nell'arte del Boccaccio,' in *La Coscienza*, 641–4.
59 Girard, 'The Plague,' 136.
60 Mazzotta, *World at Play*, 22–3.
61 Some theorists associate totalization with metaphor as against metonymy. De Man writes, 'The inference of identity and totality that is constitutive

of metaphor is lacking in the purely relational metonymic contact: an element of truth is involved in taking Achilles for a lion but none in taking Mr Ford for a motor car' (*Allegories of Reading*, 14). But a metonymic sign can be *taken* as an emblem of totality – as when Lisabetta identifies her lover with her lover's head, and then with the basil pot that contains it (*Decameron* IV.5). According to some definitions, the metonymic sign would then *also* become metaphoric. My own stress is on the way the Introduction shows two contrasting modes of totalization.

62 Mazzotta, *World at Play*, 16.
63 Ibid., 45.
64 Markulin, 'Emilia.'
65 *Filostrato*, Proem §27.
66 Branca notes the allusive presence of Lamentations slightly earlier in the Introduction, at I Intro. §47, and makes the connection with *La Vita nuova*.
67 Dante, *Vita nuova*.
68 In its textual form, this clause is a microcosm of the whole sentence: 'io' refers back to the first-person pronouns of the beginning of the sentence, while the epithet 'degna di fede' would fit comfortably in the list of attributes at the end of the sentence, 'di sangue nobile e bella di forma' and so on. My point is that the persons which are segregated in the sentence as a whole, and the Introduction as a whole, are here joined by a single verb describing a speech act.
69 This encounter, or another one like it, is mentioned again in the *Valle delle Donne* episode at the end of the Sixth Day, when the seven ladies go off by themselves to explore an idyllic landscape: Boccaccio says that he describes the place 'secondo che alcuna di loro poi mi ridisse' [according to what one of them later told me (VI Concl. §20)]. Here the informant is explicitly one of the ladies. It is striking that the encounter between author and storytellers is mentioned *only* at moments when the seven female storytellers are separated from the three men. Boccaccio's relationship to his *brigata* thus parallels his relationship to a female readership: one man and a community of women. For more on the relations Boccaccio constructs between women and (his) writing, see my 'Language of Gardens,' 301–21.
70 Battaglia, *Boccaccio*, 643–4, trans. mine.
71 Noteworthy efforts to describe the book as a systematic whole (what we might call a 'Decameron') include Barolini, 'Wheel of the *Decameron*'; Kirkham, 'An Allegorically Tempered *Decameron*'; Smarr, *Boccaccio and Fiammetta*, 165–204. For the text as an uncentred play of mediations (a 'Galeotto'?), see e.g., Almansi, *Writer As Liar*; Marcus, *Allegory of Form*; Mazzotta, *World at Play*; Markulin, 'Emilia.' Two essays which treat the dialectic

between systematic totality and narrative unboundedness in the *Decameron* – and which I take as congenial precedents for my own argument – are Padoan, 'Mondo aristocratico' (which associates the frame-story and the unity of the *Decameron* with the aristocratic Naples of Boccaccio's youth, the sphere of the stories with the communes of Florence); and D'Andrea, 'Struttura e costruzione del *Decameron*,' in *Il Nome della storia*, 126–34 (which describes a 'bifrontalità' between the didactic-structural perspective belonging to the storytellers and the narrative perspective inherent in the stories). Similarly, Pier Massimo Forni writes, 'The tension between the exigencies of closure and those of possibility is one of the principal sustaining forces of this remarkably complex textual edifice' (*Adventures in Speech*, 28), though Forni's own study emphasizes 'the exigencies of closure.'

The Stories

The Tale of Ser Ciappelletto (I.1)

FRANCO FIDO

Poised at the threshold of the *Decameron*, the figure of Ciappelletto seems excessive and elusive, on the one hand, and endowed with a curious referential power, a kind of anthropological plausibility, on the other. Here is what Stendhal, almost five centuries later, would write of an odious preceptor he had as a child:

> Abbé Raillane was in the strictest sense of the word a sinister rascal ['un noir coquin']. It would be hard to find a drier soul, more inimical to all that is honest, more perfectly devoid of any human feeling. He was short, thin, very pinched with a green complexion, a false stare, and an abominable smile ... That Jesuit was missing only one defect: he was not dirty. On the contrary, he was very clean and extremely well-groomed ['fort soigné et fort propre'] ...[1]

– exactly like our notary, who is small in stature and very neat ('piccolo di persona era e molto assettatuzzo,' I.1.9).

Writing about Ser Ciappelletto again puts the critic in a situation analogous to the one governing another equally eloquent but far more likable sinner: Dante's Francesca. In both cases we must revisit, competently and perceptively, places that have already been described many times and yet to a certain extent remain enigmatic, even less amenable than other literary creations 'to yielding their final secret,'[2] as a great contemporary of ours once said. In dealing with characters and texts such as these, we must once again ask the simplest and most naïve questions, as though we were reading *Decameron* I.1 and *Inferno* V for the first time.

But before asking these questions – or rather, to ensure that they are truly ingenuous – it would be wise to revisit the principal landmarks along the path that modern criticism has followed in its ever-renewed inquiry into the disquieting notary from Prato. The modern history of a *lectura Ciappelletti* begins, perhaps, like so much else, with Croce, who in 1933 defined Ciappelletto as an artist who ends up winning admiration for his artistry from both author and readers.[3] Croce was probably reacting to and attempting to play down Momigliano's too severe, scandalized reading, which had spoken of the tale's 'sinister pages' and of the 'towering moral monstrosity' of its protagonist.[4]

Following Croce's lead, Luigi Russo in 1938 accepted the idea of a Ciappelletto, who, in his religious indifference and near innocence, elicits our admiration as an ingenious and disinterested artist. But Russo surpasses Croce with precise and acute stylistic observations, such as when he writes that the portrait of Ciappelletto is characterized by an 'unexpected and sudden dissonance between the premise and the consequence': recall, for example, that 'essendo notaio, avea grandissima vergogna quando uno de' suoi strumenti ... fosse altro che falso trovato' [being a notary, he felt great shame whenever one of his deeds was found to be anything but false (I.1.10)].[5] Several other readers have repeated this point, among them Enrico de' Negri, for whom the whole story is 'a joke and, above all, a stylistic joke.'[6]

Another point made by Russo, on the commonplace Machiavellism and the purely economic logic of the whole novella – whereby from Musciatto to the usurer brothers to the Burgundian friars, all are concerned solely with their business affairs – may have provided an early suggestion for Vittore Branca's more complex interpretation. After recognizing in Ciappelletto the champion of the new and inexorable power of money, Branca stresses the link between *ragion mercantile* – a mercantile ethos – and rhetorical competence. For Branca too the key to the story lies in the figure of inversion or distortion, which works at all levels: from the psychological (hypocrisy of the main character) to the narrative (metamorphosis from monster to saint) to the syntactic – as Russo had already seen – with sentence endings often reversing their beginnings.[7]

In the late 1950s, Giovanni Getto published *Vita di forme e forme di vita nel* Decameron, with a chapter on Ciappelletto that remains one of the tale's most detailed and acute readings.[8] One could call it a structuralist reading *avant la lettre*, inasmuch as it distinguishes three successive portraits of Cepparello, each with a different narrative function. The first, faithful to the original, slips easily into the memory of messer Musciatto in search of a collector tough enough to deal with the wickedness of his Burgundian debtors. The second, in dialogue form, takes shape through the performance that the dying con artist enacts on two levels, for the holy friar and the two Florentine usurers, respectively. This portrait, which reverses the first as its photographic negative, provokes an exchange of roles between confessor and penitent: when you spit in church 'voi fate gran villania' [you commit a great act of villainy (I.1.64)], Cepparello explains to the friar. Later it leads to a new reversal, from the two brothers' fear that the notary's corpse would be 'gittato a' fossi a guisa d'un cane' [thrown into a ditch like a dog's (I.1.24)] to the solemn pomp with which that same body will be worshipped and entombed. Getto calls these the two opposite ends of a single grand narrative. The third portrait, 'preached' by the holy friar – who thus becomes a sort of unknowing executor of Cepparello's will – brings about the notary's definitive metamorphosis from infernal creature to saint. This is our story's final variant of the medieval theme of 'the world turned upside down.'

My summary cannot do full justice to the hermeneutic wealth of Getto's reading, which influenced later critics also by stimulating discussion of its less acceptable points, such as the remark, along the lines of Croce and Russo, that 'the prime mover of the whole story is not a religious interest, but a merely literary concern.'[9] In fact, the most significant critical contributions of the 1960s sought precisely to find a possible religious meaning in the story of Ciappelletto. In 1964, Giorgio Padoan saw the novella in the historical context of that medieval religiosity according to which God, being the real author of all miracles, can perform them not only through the 'false and lying gods' of classical times, but even through the damned.[10] In this light, the story's conclusion entails one last reversal: Ciappelletto easily wins his duel with the friar but loses the one with God, because his blasphemous performance ultimately becomes an instrument of the Church's greater triumph, so that his apparent victory is actually a posthumous defeat.

Marga Cottino-Jones finds this same principle of reversal confirmed, at the linguistic-stylistic level, by the alternation of augmentatives and diminutives that runs throughout the tale.[11] More generally, in the 'perfectionistic craving for evil that [Ciappelletto] enjoys to the highest degree,' Cottino-Jones recognizes the mark of a certain ethos, a 'black sanctity' that is symmetrically opposed, at the other end of the book, to the real, radiant holiness of Griselda. But the paradox remains comic, because our *saint noir*, thanks to his rhetorical expertise, secures his triumphal admission *post mortem* into the bosom of the community – a community that consists of the dead buried in the friary, the believers, and perhaps even the saints. Such a return to the group typifies the happy ending of comedy.

Mario Baratto also speaks of comedy, but in a simultaneously more concrete and more subtle way, in his 1970 book, *Realtà e stile nel Decameron*.[12] On the one hand, Baratto insists on the powerful theatrical effect of the speeches that grow in concentric circles around the bed of the dying, and then dead, notary. First we have the conversation between the two brothers, then between them and Ciappelletto, then between Ciappelletto and the friar, and finally between the friar and the crowd gathered in the church. On the other hand, Baratto notes the protagonist's twofold motivation. The first is utilitarian, inasmuch as he seeks a certain result – to get his hosts out of a difficult situation – and the second histrionic, since he is concerned with the quality of his performance. To this ambivalence there corresponds another, more general and profound ambiguity. Ciappelletto's irreverence is an act of defiance prolonged for his own narcissistic satisfaction, but it also betrays his impotence in the face of death. So in one sense the story of the notary is that of a bourgeois Capaneus, who brandishes eloquence rather than invective, and in another sense – and herein lies its originality – this same story puts between God and man the wholly secular exercise of theatrical art, usually reserved for 'relationships among men.'[13]

When Baratto published his book, European and American critics were already becoming passionately involved with narratology and meta-literature – with the theory and history of the narrative process on the one hand, and with the self-reflexive character of literary texts, which in a way always talk about themselves, on the other. A year earlier, in 1969, Todorov's *Grammaire du Décaméron*, Neuschäfer's *Boccaccio und der Beginn der Novelle*, and the Italian translation of Sklovsky's *Lettura del Decameron* had all been published.[14] No wonder the *Decameron* as a whole, and certain stories in particular, like those of Ciappelletto and Oretta (VI.1), soon became choice ground for the most sophisticated narratologists and meta-critics.

In America, one of the first intelligent applications of these approaches to Boccaccio's masterpiece may be found in an essay by Giuseppe Mazzotta, 'The *Decameron*: The Marginality of Literature' (1972), where the work is seen as the author's protracted meditation on the gap between historical truth and artistic fiction.[15] Literature is always a lie, and Ciappelletto stands out as the first illustrious example of 'creative lying' in the book. For Guido Almansi too, in *The Writer As Liar* (1975), Ciappelletto's confession is a work of art: its deceitful elaboration exhibits an obvious analogy to literary production, equally founded on falsehood. A writer named Boccaccio invented a narrator named Panfilo, who invented a character named Cepparello, who reinvents his own biography. If literature is by definition false, then all of its possible interpretations are legitimate and equivalent. The process of reading thus becomes transgression and sacrilege, an infinite descent into scandal and indecency. No wonder the author entrusts the task of opening his book precisely to this character, a kind of perverse Virgil ready to guide the reader through every level of his own fictional hell.[16]

Following on the work of Mazzotta and Almansi and also of Italian critics like Battaglia and Mazzacurati,[17] but with original and persuasive insights, Millicent Marcus published *An Allegory of Form: Literary Self-Consciousness in the* Decameron in 1979.[18] According to Marcus, Boccaccio frees the narrative process from any absolute interpretive system, thus creating a non-dogmatic and radically new 'literary space.' In a story like that of Ciappelletto, the author, discrediting the tradition of the exemplum, instructs his readers not to expect any ideological or ethical message. This desacralizing of literature must extend to the author himself, who questions his own authority by opposing, to the humanly plausible hypothesis of Cepparello's damnation, the inscrutable justice of God: 'The arrogance of any pretension to incarnate divine providence in literature is really the subject of this story.'[19] Ciappelletto, who through words has created an identity for himself that is the opposite of his real one, and has so brilliantly done so that this linguistic fiction will be canonized, is a go-between not only in the obvious sense that Panfilo attaches to the expression, of true or supposed intermediary between God and the believers, but also in the very 'meta-sense' according to which the whole book is a go-between or Galeotto. Our notary too is a vehicle of literature, or to phrase it better, the source of a process at the other end of which, as consumers of his fiction and representatives of the reader, the two Florentine brothers stand hidden and eavesdropping behind their screen.

More recently, some interesting remarks on Ciappelletto were made by a scholar of English literature, Walter Davis, in his essay 'Boccaccio's *Decameron*: The Implications of Binary Form' (1981), and by Joy Hambuechen Potter, in *Five Frames for the* Decameron: *Communication*

and Social Systems in the 'Cornice' (1982).[20] Davis sees in our story a case
of 'rhetoric in the service of suspense,' and he links it to the two tales
that immediately follow, inasmuch as all three explore the ways in
which a story becomes credible, and the effects of such credibility on
the listeners. According to Potter's anthropological perspective, the
deliberate desacralizing of the rituals and hierarchy of the Church in
I.1, as well as in other stories, comes not from any irreligiosity on Boccaccio's part, but from his awareness of a crisis in these institutions,
which have lost their power to certify and sanctify.

The recent contribution that seems to me to be most original and
stimulating is Robert Hollander's essay on Ciappelletto and Fra
Cipolla, 'Boccaccio's Dante: Imitative Distance.'[21] In this study Hollander seeks, in the *Decameron* or at least in certain of its moments, a
palimpsest of the *Divine Comedy.* While such a hypothesis may seem
surprising or daring, it shows its fruitfulness by leading the critic to
point out, for the first time, significant analogies and oppositions
between Ciappelletto and Brunetto Latini. Ser Cepparello da Prato is a
notary and homosexual like Brunetto (and these are the only differences with respect to Cepparello Dietaiuti, Boccaccio's supposed historical model),[22] and likewise a paradoxical master of the art 'of how
man makes himself eternal'; he thus offers an inverted representation
of Brunetto's virtues. In this way he participates in the *Decameron's*
general plan of reverent parody, so to speak, of the *Comedy,* understood
as a calling into doubt of Dante's judiciary optimism, his desperate
faith (if I may be permitted an oxymoron) in a justice that transcends
man but can be intuited by him, at least in the *tempi lunghi* [the long
run], in which divine providence manifests itself on earth.

Hollander's essay may be taken as well as a positive illustration of
the need, acutely felt these days by Boccaccio's readers (I am thinking,
for example, of Antonio D'Andrea, Michelangelo Picone, and Paolo
Valesio)[23] to move, or better to descend, from the text to its 'subtexts.'
This need must not be confused with the well known, and often ingenuous, interest of the positivists in the 'sources.' Rather, it reflects the
lesson of the historical school about reading a text in the literary frame
of a *tradition,* and specifically in the historical-geographical frame of
Romania.

Up to this point I have sought to provide, without any pretence of
completeness, an idea of the hermeneutic process that has developed
around this tale. My examples all fall under the rubric of 'author criticism,' consisting of original and recognizable, or 'signed,' contribu-

tions. But there exists as well a 'vulgate criticism' for Ciappelletto, a set of more obvious but useful annotations that are difficult to assign to one or another reader. From one observation to the next, they have come to constitute a first standard description of our text, like those with which each one of us begins the analysis of a novella for our own students. Before turning to the most problematic part of my essay, I want to close this review with an image of the novella of Ciappelletto gleaned precisely from the 'vulgate criticism,' limiting myself to just a few of its features. There is the exceptional presence of an edifying discourse at the beginning and then at the end of the story; a historical background evoked with great precision—the descent into Italy of Charles of Valois in 1301; the importance of the Florentine banking and commercial institutions in France and Burgundy, as exemplified primarily by Musciatto Franzesi; and the background of the Christian world of the Duecento and Trecento, teeming with popular saints, people who died with the odor of sanctity and were directly canonized by the faithful on the basis of their miracles. No geographical precision corresponds to the exactness of the historical reconstruction: we are in Burgundy, but we do not know which city, perhaps Dijon. Finally, there is the masterful construction of the novella according to a double tripartition. First part: religious preamble, historical context, portrait of Cepparello in Musciatto's mind. Second part: the adventure, or real action of the tale, also presented in three moments or 'acts' (the text's own theatrical provocations encourage my terminology): the conversation between the two brothers interrupted by their sick guest Cepparello; Cepparello's speech to the friar overheard by the two brothers; the friar's sermon in church. Third part: Ciappelletto's apotheosis and the narrator's pious commentary.

Among the questions that the novella intentionally asks its readers, two, coming towards the end, address the story itself, its 'content': (1) Are the miracles attributed to San Ciappelletto true? Panfilo answers: they may be true, depending on the answer to the second question. (2) Is our hero in hell or in paradise? Panfilo, and through him the author, obviously urges us to ask such a question, but as some scholars, and Marcus in particular, have observed, he enjoins us not to look for an answer, which only God may know.

A third question comes instead from the novella's religious preamble. On the one hand, Panfilo deduces from our weakness that we need 'procuratori,' celestial advocates like Mary or the saints, so that our poor prayers may get to God; but our very weakness can induce us to choose the wrong advocate. Here the forensic or legal analogy ends. If while on earth we entrust ourselves to a lawyer who is not up to the job and may not even be admitted into the courtroom, our interests will surely be in danger. But God, 'piú alla purità del pregator riguardando che alla sua ignoranza o allo essilio del pregato, così come se quegli fosse nel suo cospetto beato, essaudisce coloro che 'l priegano' [heeding more the sincerity of the supplicant than his ignorance or the eternal exile of the person (i.e., the advocate or pseudo-saint) to whom prayer is directed, exactly as if the latter were in his blessed presence, answers those who pray to him (I.1.5)]. Therefore, (3) is the mediation of saints necessary or not in the commerce between God and men? This time Panfilo does not answer, nor does he say that one need not try to respond. Indeed, to ensure that this contradictory theory of the necessity and efficacy of an advocate, even a wrong or absent one, is not lost on his listeners, he insists pleonastically at the end of the story, exalting God's kindness, that 'faccendo noi nostro mezzano un suo nemico, amico credendolo, ci essaudisce, come se a uno veramente santo per mezzano della sua grazia ricorressimo'. [when we make his enemy our go-between, believing him to be a friend, He (God) answers us, as if we were making recourse to one who is truly saintly as a go-between of His grace (I.1.90)]. I shall return to this point later. For now I shall simply observe that formulas like those of idealist criticism about Boccaccio's religious 'innocence' do not seem the most apt to clarify such an insistent aspect of our text.

Finally, there is an even more general question that comes from considering the story in the context of the work to which it belongs and of its declared poetics, the textual project to which it refers: (4) Why begin with a story and a character like this, in a book of stories offered to delicate ladies, indeed written in aid of and as refuge to ladies in love, who having read the stories 'parimente diletto delle sollazzevoli cose in quelle mostrate e utile consiglio potranno pigliare, in quanto potranno cognoscere quello che sia da fuggire e che sia similmente da seguitare' [can take in equal parts delight and useful advice in the enjoyable things shown in them, because they will be able to know what is to be avoided, and, similarly, what is to be followed (Proem.14)]? There is no love in I.1, there are no female characters, and four principal characters in five are wicked and corrupt.

With regard to Ciappelletto and his story, Dante's *Inferno* has often been cited, in particular for the sacrilegious confession of Guido da Montefeltro to Boniface VIII, the blasphemous attitudes of Capaneus and Vanni Fucci, and, as we have seen more recently and subtly, for the possible anti-model of Brunetto Latini. And surely one may see this story, set among quarrelsome and disloyal people like the Burgundians and dominated by protagonists who are even worse, as an extension of the infernal situation created by the plague, just as, fifty tales later, the story of Oretta recalls the pastimes of the ten young people in the countryside. But the hypothesis of a 'comic' hell, in the medieval and Dantesque sense of the word (see the 'Letter to Can Grande,' *Epist.* XIII), is already delineated in the first novella, where to the negative series:

> evil of the Burgundians
> evil of Musciatto
> evil of Ciappelletto
> evil of the two brothers
> illness of Ciappelletto
> death of Ciappelletto
> his probable damnation,

there corresponds a positive series:

> art of Ciappelletto
> his absolution
> relief and entertainment of the brothers
> contentment of the friar
> good deal made by the friary
> canonization of Ciappelletto
> triumph of the Church.

A possible thematic link of an 'infernal' nature between the Introduction and the first story must not therefore be rejected, if for no other reason than that it constitutes the first 'Dantesque palimpsest,' as Hollander would say, across which the distress of the horrible beginning, or, to cite Dante, of the 'materia a principio horribilis et fetida,' is quickly redeemed by entertainment. But the question that we have asked ourselves – Why this story precisely *at the beginning* of the book? – induces us to reflect on Ser Ciappelletto's liminal and privileged position with respect to all the stories *that follow.*

Using a ballistic simile that would not displease a lover of violence like Ser Cepparello, one could say that flashes of light emanate from his story, illuminating other *Decameron* characters and stories like long-, medium-, and short-range tracers aimed at strategic targets. The most obvious of these 'thematic bridges' regard the last two tales of the last day and the last of the sixth. We have the inverted symmetries, often emphasized by critics, between Ciappelletto the false saint after his death and Griselda the true saint in life, and between the debauched, blasphemous, and homosexual Ciappelletto and the courteous Torello, crusader, happy husband, and father. This latter correspondence finds further reinforcement in the fact that these are Panfilo's first and last stories in the *Decameron*. Indeed, the same antithetic and chiastic structure of the rubric or subtitle to I.1 could be a foreshadowing or early indication not only of the reversals already observed within the story, but also of the 'macro-trope' of inversion that frames the hundred stories, binding Ciappelletto to Griselda and Torello:

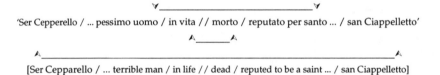

'Ser Cepperello / ... pessimo uomo / in vita // morto / reputato per santo ... / san Ciappelletto'

[Ser Cepparello / ... terrible man / in life // dead / reputed to be a saint ... / san Ciappelletto]

No less evident, and this has been frequently noted as well, is the relationship between Ciappelletto and Cipolla, though in this case it is one of analogy more than opposition. That connection lies in the details that sustain the narrative: an embarrassing situation, a church sermon, the credulity of the faithful, the cult of relics. But above all it takes shape in the disproportion between great art at work and the ease with which the result is obtained. Ciappelletto's and Cipolla's rhetorical overkill thus comes definitively to reflect their histrionic and, as Croce and Russo have already noted, appealing narcissism. The parallel between the two tales holds as well for the characters' particular narrative technique, a type of minimal art of lying, according to which a certain affirmation can be true and very banal on the one hand, extraordinary and wonderful on the other. Thus the notary, who (since he is as fond of women as dogs are of clubs) surely never knew a woman carnally, can rightfully proclaim himself technically to be a virgin, sending the friar into ecstasies. So too can Cipolla turn a walk along well-known Florentine streets into a fabulous voyage in the Orient, or describe the simple operation of stuffing sausages as 'rivestendo i porci delle lor busecchie medesime' [dressing pigs with their own intestines (VI.10.40)], or list among the wonders of the land of the Basques the fact that 'tutte l'acque corrono alla 'ngiù' [all the waters there run downhill (VI.10.41)].

So far we have traversed well-charted terrain. But the relationship between Ciappelletto and Martellino, the protagonist of II.1, has been less frequently noted. Aside from the analogous frame – church full of people, canonization by popular acclaim of a layman who has just died – the game of reversals turns up here too. The notary of Prato offers the holy friar, and then through him all the Burgundians, a radical, new, and better counterfeit of his soul, and in so doing reaches his goal and becomes the occasion for miracles that may be true. The Florentine entertainer and con artist, by creating an uglier counterfeit of his physical person before the faithful of another church, fakes a miracle and is unmasked and punished.[24]

This comparison of the two first tales of the first two days draws our attention to a more ample and complex sequence in which both participate: stories 'di cose catoliche' [about religious matters], as Filostrato will say at the beginning of II.2. The sequence includes the first three stories of the First Day (Ciappelletto; Abraham the Jew, who goes to Rome and converts; Melchisedech, who tells Saladin the fable of the three rings); the first two of the Second Day (Martellino; Rinaldo d'Asti, repaid by the widow for his devotion to St Julian); and the first of the Third Day (Masetto di Lamporecchio, happy in both youth and old age for having put horns upon Christ's hat). If we examine the arrangement of the six stories over the three days, respectively Days Three, Two, and One, it may turn out to be proper, a *convenevole cosa*, that at the apex of this theological wedge there returns, in reference to Masetto, the hat-garland-crown pun with which, at the base of the same wedge, Panfilo had begun the story of Ciappelletto. To be sure, the arrangement of the six stories, as well as the recourse to the hat-garland exchange from the beginning of the first to the end of the last, could be unintentional. Indeed, the First Day contains some other tales that one could easily include in this chapter 'about religious matters.'

What cannot be accidental is the articulation, through the six stories to which I am referring, of a discourse of moral theology:

- Impossibility of knowing whether a man is saved or damned, and how God intends to make use of him (Ciappelletto)
- Impossibility of judging a religion by the behavior of its ministers (Abraham)

- Conversely, respectability of every religion as long as it is sincerely believed and inspires by its precepts honest and generous behaviour (Melchisedech)
- Miracle of St Arrigo shown to be false only by the chance presence in the church of two Florentines who recognize the 'miraculously healed cripple' (Martellino)
- Presumed compliance of St Julian, who procures for his devotee not only lodging and dinner but also a pleasant night of love, thus making himself a *mezzano* or go-between in the most common sense of the word (Rinaldo d'Asti)
- Joyful bigamy of the nuns, spiritual spouses of Christ and carnal companions of the clever gardener (Masetto)

The thematic and tonal movement from the beginning to the end of this series seems likewise clear to me. If Ciappelletto's great art can and must entertain, the novella that immediately follows it retrospectively illuminates its serious side, the underlying moral of the first, by means of the strong analogy between the corruption of the notary of Prato and that of the clerics of Rome. Like Musciatto and the two usurious brothers when they consider Cepparello's character, Abraham cannot help but recognize in the Roman Church 'lussuria, avarizia e gulosità, fraude, invidia e superbia e simili cose e piggiori, se piggiori essere possono in alcuno' [lust, avarice, and gluttony, fraud, envy, and pride and the like and worse, if any of them could be worse (I.2.24)]. The priests and friars who should uphold the Christian religion undertake to destroy it just like Cepparello, the blasphemer addicted to false oaths. But God 'corrects' the course of things so that Abraham converts willingly, and miracles may happen in San Ciappelletto's name.

Cepparello and the Roman Curia are therefore the paradoxical signifiers of a referent that is at once indubitable and inscrutable: divine providence. Only later in the sequence does there appear what will be, along with ingenuity, the book's great theme: love, or rather desire. The narrator underscores this transition as well: 'Belle donne, a raccontarsi mi tira una novella di cose catoliche e di sciagure e d'amore in parte mescolata' [Lovely ladies, I am drawn to tell you a story about religious matters, mixed in part with misfortunes and love (II.2.3)], Filostrato says in the preamble to the story of Rinaldo. From here on, nature and humor become more overt and 'crude,' leading up to the story of Masetto. But a joking and good-naturedly irreverent closing line like Filostrato's, about the horns that the fake mute Masetto put on Christ's cap, is finally more innocent than the compunctious reflections of Panfilo and Neifile at the end of the stories of Ciappelletto and Abraham. One could indeed observe that the possibility of freely playing with religious matters (or, in Masetto's case, with pious bodies) without incurring accusations of irreligiosity, is correlative with the cautious distinctions that we have heard between the judgment of men and that of God. The unbridgeable distance between the two leaves us on our own and in the power of our more or less reasonable initiatives.

In putting his own narrative under the protection, so to speak, of St Ciappelletto, St Arrigo, and St Julian, three advocates as diversely plausible as they are equally efficacious in their own way, the *Decameron*'s author is free – according to what the most recent scholars have acutely intuited – to set aside, or put between parentheses, religion as a sure and omnipresent daily guide for our actions. In the space that thus opens up between the two moments of the earthly voyage, the *nunc*, and the *hora mortis nostrae*, it becomes possible, indeed is for a time necessary, to apply to the former a wholly human axiology based on economic and aesthetic criteria. This is a discourse that naturally is valid *also* (and in Boccaccio's case, *above all*) for literature.

We have seen that the other interesting question raised by some of the most perceptive contemporary criticism is that of Ciappelletto as narrator or pseudo-autobiographer, and, therefore, of the novella's self-referentiality – both fashionable notions, as we know. In this case too, it seems to me that in order to add some useful observations (at least I hope) to the many that have already been formulated, one must consider I.1 for its intertextual connections with the other tales, or, if we prefer to adopt Maria Corti's terms, in the macro-text of the *Decameron*. As we all well know, the book is full of characters who are *ben parlanti*, and who in this sense compete in eloquence with the ten narrators of the frame. But the clear, unmistakable cases of stories within which another story is narrated are three, significantly two in the First and one in the Sixth Day: Melchisedech, who tells Saladin the tale of the three rings, Bergamino, who tells Can Grande della Scala the novella of Primas and the Cluny abbot; and the bungling knight who wants to make Madonna Oretta's travels pleasurable with a story of his own. In the first two cases the enclosed tales are clearly allegorical. They work to bring the external or containing novella to a resolution, and they apply perfectly to its circumstances: three rings *like* the three monotheistic religions; Primas poorly received by the abbot and reduced to eating three loaves of bread *like* Bergamino, whom Can Grande had reduced to pawning his three garments.

More unique, and from our point of view more interesting, is the third story, that of Madonna Oretta, especially if we compare it to the other two cases (again in the First and Sixth Days) in which, without offering a true and proper internal novella, the external story contains a long narrative discourse that the protagonist directs at a certain circle of listeners who are also characters in the story. I am thinking naturally of Ser Cepparello, who narrates the holy life of Ciappelletto to the friar, and of friar Cipolla, who recounts his wondrous travels to the people of Certaldo. Cepparello and Cipolla lie constantly as they talk, but they invent pleasant and effective fictions. In both cases, on the receiving end, or that of the narratee, there are two different listeners. The first is more important (in terms of authority, like the holy friar, or in terms of quantity, like the people of Certaldo) and also more gullible: he *believes* the story to be true, taking the fiction for reality. The second, less important and hidden listener (the two Florentine brothers, the two pranksters who stole the parrot feather), recognizes the story as fiction, that is, as literature. The devotion of listeners of the first type leads to miracles, the lucidity of listeners of the second type to admiration of art and to entertainment. To be sure, that admiration is of an opposite kind in the two cases, because the fearful usurers are reassured while the pranksters from Certaldo are deluded by friar Cipolla's genius. One could also say that in both cases the two different audiences embody on the one hand the confusion between religion and literature, and on the other the capacity to distinguish between religion and literature.

The relationship between Ciappelletto and Madonna Oretta is more complex, inasmuch as the same two terms, religion and literature, are presented this time 'in the negative': I.1 is the story of an absent saint, and VI.1 is the story of an absent novella. To go from the first to the second of these two tales (and the move is legitimized by their position in the book, numbers one and fifty-one, respectively) means to go from a fiction that radically upends reality – the photographic negative of himself that Cepparello offers to the holy friar – to the reality of an absent fiction offered by the knight to Oretta, like a photographic plate that is completely white – 'una delle belle novelle del mondo' [one of the beautiful novellas of the world (VI.1.7)] – or completely black – 'fieramente la guastava' [he was brutally spoiling it (VI.1.9)]. We know nothing about the knight's story, aside from the fact that he does not know how to tell it, nor will Oretta ever know its ending: 'Il cavaliere ... mise mano in altre novelle e quella che cominciata aveva e mal seguita senza finita lasciò stare' [The knight ... set about telling other stories, and the one he had begun and badly developed he let stand without an ending (VI.1.12)] Likewise, if we accept Panfilo's proposal to read I.1 as a *Vita sancti Ciappelletti*, we will never know the ending, celestial or infernal, of this one either. In this regard, I might add, it may or may not be significant that the book's only other unfinished story is number 101, or if you prefer number 100½, regarding Filippo Balducci and the goslings, about which the narrator, speaking in a rare instance in the first person, declares that he does not want to reveal its conclusion.[25]

But let us return to the discourse at hand, the relationship between religion and literature. Divine providence, in and of itself and by definition, is doubtless a producer of truth, but because we are weak such a truth can escape us. Before arriving at the first terrace of purgatory we (and along with us Dante himself) do not hear the visible speech of God's statuary, and we cannot therefore distinguish *His* sculptures from human ones. Now, if we cannot be certain about the endings to God's stories, is it not then perhaps true that the ambiguities of human stories are redeemed or 'forgiven'?

This is the argument that Boccaccio – a Boccaccio whom we cannot accuse of intellectual libertinism – will bring to bear in the fourteenth book of the *Genealogie*, chapter 12, 'Damnanda non est obscuritas poetarum':

> Nonne divinum eloquium, cuius ipsi professores haberi cupiunt, a Spiritu Sancto prolatum, obscuritatum atque ambiguitatum plenissimum est? (2.714)

> [Is it not true perhaps that the Holy Scripture, of which they (the enemies of poetry) pass themselves off as true interpreters, while coming from the Holy Spirit, is replete with obscurities and ambiguities?]

Our subjective semiosis is imperfect, inasmuch as it relies on the precarious human means that we have at our disposal. As Prospero will say in the Epilogue to the *Tempest*: 'Now my charms are all o'erthrown, / And what strength I have's mine own, / Which is most faint ...' But it is precisely in the inadequacy of our strength, from which comes our uncertainty about our judgments, where the force of literature paradoxically lies. In a passage from the Conclusion to the *Decameron*, the

narrator repeats almost to the letter the observation made about Ciappelletto by Panfilo, who inferred from the transience of worldly things
the scarce trustworthiness of human reasoning:

> Confesso nondimeno le cose di questo mondo non avere stabilità alcuna
> ma sempre essere in mutamento, e così potrebbe della mia lingua essere
> intervenuto ... (Concl. 27)

> [I confess nonetheless that the things of this world have no stability at all,
> but are always changing, and so it could have happened to my tongue ...]

But before prescribing to his companions the magnificent theme of the
last day, the very same Panfilo had said in the Conclusion to the Ninth
Day:

> Queste cose e dicendo e faccendo senza alcun dubbio gli animi vostri ben
> disposti a valorosamente adoperare accenderà, ché la vita nostra, che altro
> che brieve esser non può nel mortal corpo, *si perpetuerà* nella laudevole
> fama, IX. (Concl. 5, italics mine)

> [Both saying and hearing these things will doubtless fire up your well-
> disposed souls to behave valorously, so that our life, which cannot be any-
> thing but brief in its mortal body, *will be perpetuated* with praiseworthy
> fame]

Given the lack of an immutable frame of reference, we cannot always
make ourselves guarantors of the truth of words, but we know their
power through experience. Brunetto taught Dante how man makes
himself eternal. Ciappelletto makes himself eternal too, in his own
way, in the cult of the good Burgundians, thanks both to God's goodness and to his own genius as an artist. And the seven young Florentine women of the *Decameron*, by speaking and listening to one
another, will perpetuate their brief lives beyond the mortal body in
praiseworthy fame. This is no small feat, if for the moment we are not
allowed to know any better.

At this point, it should be clear why, in my opinion, the formula of
the 'marginality of literature' proposed for Boccaccio not many years
ago can be both accepted and overturned, considered alongside the
opposite formula about the 'centrality of literature.' Each of us will
have to decide if this second proposition implies a corollary on the

marginality of religion. In this connection it may be proper to recall that at the end of *The Name of the Rose* the blind ex-librarian Jorge da Burgos burns his abbey in order to keep the second book of Aristotle's *Poetics* from circulating among men, providing a philosophical justification for comedy, satire, and mime, and helping readers laugh lucidly, when necessary, even at the truth. If the reading of the novella of Ciappelletto that I have here proposed is plausible, we may at least suspect that Umberto Eco's terrible obscurantist monk arrived too late, or, better, destroyed his immense library for nothing, since just a few decades later the *Decameron* would be saved from the fire.

NOTES

This essay was translated by Michael Sherberg.

1 Stendhal, *Vie de Henry Brulard*, 97, 104.
2 Montale, 'I limoni,' l. 24.
3 Croce, 'Boccaccio e Franco Sacchetti,' 81–91.
4 *Decameron: 49 novelle* (1968 [1924]), 38, 41.
5 *Decameron. Venticinque novelle scelte e ventisette postille critiche*, ed. Luigi Russo (Florence: Sansoni, 1939); later in Russo, *Letture critiche*, 60; on Ciappelletto, 51–68.
6 De' Negri, 'Legendary Style.'
7 Branca, *Boccaccio medievale*, 93–101, 156–60.
8 Getto, *Vita di forme*, 34–77.
9 Ibid., 77.
10 Padoan, *Il Boccaccio, le muse*, 55–9.
11 Cottino-Jones, 'Ser Ciappelletto.'
12 Baratto, *Realtà*, 293–301.
13 Ibid., 300.
14 Todorov, *Grammaire du* Décaméron; Neuschäfer, *Boccaccio*; Šklovskij, *Lettura del Decameron*.
15 Mazzotta, '*Decameron*: Marginality of Literature'; see also his '*Decameron*: Literal and Allegorical'; both revised in *World at Play*.
16 Almansi, *Writer as Liar*, 28, 36.
17 Battaglia, *Giovanni Boccaccio*, 1–81; Mazzacurati, 'Alatiel.'
18 Marcus, *Allegory of Form*, 11–26.
19 Ibid., 14.
20 Davis, 'Boccaccio's *Decameron*'; Potter, *Five Frames*, 50–2, 60–1.

21 R. Hollander, 'Boccaccio's Dante: Imitative Distance,' now in *Boccaccio's Dante and the Shaping Force of Satire*, 21–52. Hollander's comparison between Ciappelletto and Brunetto was again suggested by Rossi, 'Ironia e parodia.'

22 On the question of Ciappelletto's possible 'models' see Branca's note in his edition of the *Decameron* (Turin: Einaudi, 1984), 49.

23 See for instance D'Andrea, 'Uno asino per isciagura,' in *Il Nome della storia*, 120–5; Picone, 'Dal fabliau alla novella.' I am also referring to an unpublished paper by Paolo Valesio entitled 'Federigo degli Alberighi e i fabliaux,' read in 1985 at the New England Inter-University Seminar in Italian Studies, Cambridge, Mass.

24 On false miracles and their frequency in the Middle Ages, see the magnificent page of Lodovico Antonio Muratori's *Antiquitates italicae Medii Aevi*, reprinted in the author's own Italian translation in L.A. Muratori, *Opere*, 1: 731–2.

25 On the 'half-story' of Filippo Balducci see D'Andrea, 'Esemplarità, ironia, retorica.'

The Tale of Abraham the Jew (*Decameron* I.2)

MARGA COTTINO-JONES

The second novella of the *Decameron*, the story of 'Giannotto di Civigni' and 'a Jew named Abraham,' has received little critical attention. According to Mario Baratto, one of the few contemporary scholars to study the novella in some detail, it presents themes and patterns that are hardly new in medieval literature. Baratto summarizes them as 'the invective against the corruption of the Roman church ... the typology of the wise and shrewd Jew ... the language of a simple man infused with the power of the Holy Spirit, the manner of his conversion (which proves by contrary logic the presence of Divine Providence), and so on.'[1] These themes are common to the early medieval narrative genre of the exemplum, considered by critics such as Salvatore Battaglia, Vittore Branca, and Carlo Delcorno to be the forerunner of the novella.[2]

It is not surprising, then, that both Letterio Di Francia, and Pietro Toldo indicate an exemplum belonging to the collection of Etienne de Bourbon as the most likely source of this novella. For Di Francia Etienne de Bourbon's short tale is probably the oldest rendition of a lost 'primitive form' that might have been the archetype of Boccaccio's tale of religious conversion (I.2) and others like it, of which we find examples in the anonymous *Avventuroso ciciliano* and in John Brunyard's *Summa predicantium*.[3] Even though these tales differ considerably in narrative development, characterization, and tone, there is a textual correspondence between Bourbon's exemplum and *Decameron* I.2 that points to Boccaccio's acquaintance with the earlier text.

Etienne's exemplum, as quoted by Toldo, begins: 'Fides est firmum et stabile *fundamentum* Ecclesie.'[4] I emphasize the word 'fundamentum,' since it is also found in *Decameron* I.2, in the expression 'fondamento e sostegno' [foundation and support], repeated twice in Abraham's account of his experience at the Roman court, first referring to the highest officials of the Church hierarchy (§25) and then to the Holy Spirit (§26). Apart from this textual reference, however, and that of the Jew, featured as one of the two main characters, there would seem to be no other connection between Boccaccio's tale and Etienne de Bourbon's text. It is my contention that we must search elsewhere for better connections, and precisely in Boccaccio's own novellas I.1 and I.3 of the *Decameron*. These tales provide, as we shall see, several convincing textual associations – both verbal and thematic – with novella I.2, as Franco Fido also suggests in his study of I.1 (see pp. 69–70).

The tale of Giannotto and his Jewish friend Abraham has close verbal and thematic correlations to the Ser Ciappelletto story, which precedes it, and to the tale of Saladin and Melchisedech, which follows. Indeed, I would argue that these two novellas serve as the subtexts of our story. The reading I propose, therefore, is one that would reveal the correlations among these first three novellas of the *Decameron* and the central message that together they convey concerning the mutual relations of man, God, and the Church. Each of the three stories deals with these relationships, though each underscores a different aspect and approaches the subject from a different perspective.

Decameron I.1 both offers a model of human depravity in the character of Ciappelletto,' the worst man that ever lived' (I.1.15), and raises questions about the institution of the Church, in particular its authority to attribute sainthood to an individual post mortem. Through the comments of the storyteller, Panfilo, the novella proposes a direct connection between man and God through prayer, and questions the role of the Church and the intercession of its saints in the relationship between man and God.

Many *Decameron* stories present the institution of the Church as the proper site of popular ritual, that is, of traditional celebrations, ceremonies, and religious rites such as baptisms, funerals, weddings, and special feast days. Two rituals sanctioned by the Church, both of which encourage 'miracles,' are key to the story of Ser Ciappelletto: the sacrament of confession and the religious funeral. The rogue makes a brilliant false confession, which is taken by the saintly priest and his parishioners to be the verbal signifier of a truly saintly life; his grand Church funeral, celebrated with all the solemnity of a religious feast, serves to confirm this belief. The narrator's ironic view of the Church as an institution is revealed through his playful rendition of the deceptive language used by Ciappelletto, the sinner, in perpetrating his confession at the expense of the 'holy friar,' who hears and believes it.[5] Ciappelletto, by falsely portraying himself in his confession to be a perfect man, convinces his confessor, and, through him and the authority of the Church, ultimately transforms the reality of his sinful life into the fiction of sanctity (see Fido, p. 61).

Decameron I.3, the story of Saladin and Melchisedech, through the comments of the storyteller Philomena in its exordium, establishes a close connection to the preceding two tales. Philomena notes that the previous storytellers have already spoken very convincingly 'about God and the truth of the Christian faith' (I.3.3); she then extends the discussion in a debate concerning which of the three main religions is the 'true one,' an issue that in the second tale included only two: Judaism and Christianity.

In addition to staging an ideological debate about religion, both tales I.1 and I.3, like I.2, also present characters who are involved in business matters. In particular, I.1 carefully portrays a mercantile world as the social background for the action whose main characters are motivated by, to use Vittore Branca's words, their 'mercantile logic.'[6]

Even from this brief overview, it becomes clear that the second novella of the *Decameron* has still more connections to the first and third tales. As in the first, also in the second novella the role of the Church as an institution is questioned. The second story highlights the sinful behaviour of the highest members of Church hierarchy. Abraham turns out to be an intelligent individual observer who judges the Roman Curia to be unqualified to represent Christianity, and yet, ironically, to be the best guarantor of its continuing superiority over the Jewish faith. The novella clearly encourages the individual to choose his religion and to do so using his individual resources, especially his intelligence and business experience. Like the third novella, the second also represents a contest of religions; in this case it is again the question of the superiority of the Jewish or the Christian faith. The 'wise' Jew, Abraham, resolves the question in favor of the latter based on strictly personal observations. His reasoning differs from Melchisedech's in the third tale, because it cannot be applied to a general debate on the issue of religion. As in both I.1 and I.3, also in I.2 the Church as an institution is acknowledged only as the site for ritual – in this case, for the celebration of the sacrament of baptism. In regard to social context, the second novella deals with the mercantile world in much more detail than the first by making its main characters two rich merchants

and by stressing the ideological impact of 'mercantile logic' on characters and situations. The social context also connects one of the two
merchants of the second novella – the 'wise ... Jew' – to the 'wise' Jew
Melchisedech of the third novella.

These many correspondences of themes and characters among the
first three tales contribute importantly to a meaningful reading of the
second novella. Once its text is juxtaposed to those of the other two
tales, novella I.2 can indeed be seen to function in the larger narrative
context as both a preparation for the third novella, and, even more significantly, an extension of the first. The remarks that follow will high-
light some of the most significant textual elements of the second
novella which gain relevance when compared to the texts of the other
two novellas, and especially to the first.

Neifile, who tells the second story, underscores in several ways its
continuity with the first in her brief exordium. There she openly states
her intention to imitate Panfilo, the storyteller of I.1, by showing in her
tale, as he had done in his, that 'la benignità di Dio' [God's mercy
(I.2.3)] patiently tolerates human deficiencies, even when, as in her
story, the sinners are precisely 'coloro li quali d'essa ne deono dare e
con l'opere e con le parole vera testimonianza, il contrario operando'
[those who should bear true witness to His mercy through their actions
and words and yet do just the opposite (§3)]. The human errors of Panfilo's tale, Ser Ciappelletto's sins, are here extended to the sins of a
larger group consisting of the highest ranking clergy, including the
Pope and the Roman cardinals. The first novella, then, with its ironic
interactions among an individual sinner, the Church, men, and God,
becomes the essential subtext for this story of eminent yet sinful representatives of the Church, their connections with the Christian religion
and with God, and their influence on an individual human being.

The sins committed by the characters in both novellas provide an
important area of pertinent correspondence between I.1 and I.2 (see
also Fido, p. 70). In I.2 Abraham first observes the sins of the Roman
Curia during his stay in Rome, and once back in Paris he recounts
them to his friend. The angle from which Abraham scrutinizes the conduct of the Roman clergy is clearly set by novella I.1's presentation of
the sins – particularly lust and gluttony – of the 'disorderly' life of Ser
Ciappelletto which led to his 'fatal illness.' As far as lust is concerned,
Ser Ciappelletto is guilty of the 'unnatural' kind, as he 'delle femine era
così vago come sono i cani de' bastoni; del contrario più che alcuno
tristo uomo si dilettava' [was as fond of women as dogs are of sticks; of

the opposite (sex, males) he took greater pleasure than any other wicked man (I.1.14)]. At the Roman court the sin of lust is rampant, and Abraham finds that 'dal maggiore infino al minore generalmente tutti disonestissimamente peccare in lussuria, e non solo della naturale ma ancora nella sogdomitica.' [generally all members of the Curia, from the highest to the lowest, dishonestly practised the sin of lust, not only the natural kind, but also the sodomitic (I.2.19)] As for gluttony, Ser Ciappelletto was described as 'gulosissimo e bevitor grande, tanto che alcuna volta sconciamente gli facea noia' [an uncontrollable glutton and drinker who would often get sick because of his intemperance (I.1.14)] while his counterparts in Rome are characterized by Abraham as 'universalmente gulosi, bevitori, ebriachi e più al ventre serventi a guisa d'animali bruti ... che a altro' [universally gluttons and drunkards, and, like brute animals, subject to their bellies more than to any other rule (I.2.20)].

Among his other sins, Ser Ciappelletto has an immense fascination for anything that could be considered false, including legal documents, and eventually in his own confession he gives a masterful rendition of this sinful proclivity through the clever use of deceptive language. Abraham sees a similar penchant for deception in the devious activities of the Roman court, particularly in their attempt to fool God through deceptive language, ('ntentione,' I.2.21) 'avendo alla manifesta simonia "procureria" posto nome e alla gulosità "substenazioni."' [calling their conspicuous simony 'mediation' and their gluttony 'sustenance' (§21)]. If we look at the sinful life of the Roman prelates with Ser Ciappelletto's sinful life and false confession in mind, we see that the sins of the Pope and cardinals, as Abraham enumerates them, conform generally to the sequence of mortal sins on which the saintly friar carefully questions Ciappelletto at his confession. Beginning with lust, Abraham proceeds to list gluttony, avarice, and anger, and he concludes with fraud. Even the narrative form of these sections of the two novellas are similar – in both cases we have a dialogue.

Finally, the confessional mode of the first tale comes here to its natural conclusion; that is, we have in I.2 a judgmental, moralistic conclusion that seems to refer to both texts; in the words of Abraham, 'il vostro pastore e per consequente tutti gli altri si procaccino di ridurre a nulla e di cacciare del mondo la cristiana religione, là dove essi fondamente e sostegno esser dovrebber di quella' [your shepherd and consequently all of the others as well, are trying to reduce the Christian religion to nothing and to banish it from the world, while instead they should be its foundation and support (I.2.25)]. It seems important to note that the contextual significance of the wicked and filthy lives of the clergy in Rome, with its effects on men and the ethical questions it raises, is strengthened by its subtext, the story of the 'evil and sinful life' of 'the worst man that ever lived' (I.1.15). The criticism of sinful behaviour is here clearly extended from a private, individual level (Ser Ciappelletto) to an institutional one (the Roman clergy). Ironically, Ciappelletto reinforces the religious belief of others through his example;[7] in his false confession he carefully keeps his true sinful nature concealed from those he wishes to influence. In the same way, in I.2, the Roman clergy, through their own example, displayed here in all of its depravity and sinfulness, succeed, albeit unknowingly, in strengthening an individual's (Abraham's) belief in the superiority of the Christian over the Jewish faith. The ironic tone of the story grows out of this unexpected interpretation of the papal court's sinfulness, put forth by Abraham as unshakeable proof of the superiority of the Christian religion. The message embedded in both novellas gains in significance through the juxtaposition of Abraham's conversion and Ser Ciappelletto's reinforcement of the religiosity of the Burgundians.

Sinfulness embodied, as in the first novella, in one individual and deceptively hidden from public domain, may have positive effects on a Christian congregation; on the other hand, once extended to the institutional level and openly acknowledged by all, it loses its positive effects on the group and can only be dealt with on a personal basis, according to the intelligence, good judgment, and moral convictions of the individual. The danger, therefore, of institutional sinfulness seems much more serious for the Christian community of this novella than Ser Ciappelletto's false sanctity for the Burgundians. For this reason, much more careful attention is paid in I.2 to the social background that nurtures the characters and to the qualifications of the characters themselves, as we will see later in our discussion. Furthermore, by reproposing, within its own parameters as a subtext, the issue of Ser Ciappelletto's 'evil and sinful life,' novella I.2 opens a dynamic of narrative correlations and oppositions that raise wider ethical and social questions which might have been lost without those references, as the following chart attempts to demonstrate.

According to table 1, Ciappelletto directly correlates with the Roman clergy as to sinfulness and inversely as to awareness; the Christian community of I.1 directly correlates to Abraham, as object affected positively by A, while it relates inversely to the Roman clergy of I.2 as to

Table 1 Chart of Correlations and Oppositions

A. Agents (The Sinful)	B. Objects (The Affected)	C. Goal	D. Outcome
I.1: Ciappelletto: Positive effect on: INDIVIDUAL KNOWING DECEPTIVELY SINFUL	Believers COMMUNITY UNKNOWING	Deceiving friar DECEIVING GOD	Successful Doubtful
I.2: Roman clergy: Positive effect on: COMMUNITY UNKNOWING OPENLY SINFUL	Abraham INDIVIDUAL KNOWING	Deceiving God	Unsuccessful

awareness. In his deceptive relationship with God (see C. Goal) Ser Ciappelletto corresponds to the Roman clergy, while the outcome of their deception perpetrated against God differs. In Ser Ciappelletto's case, according to Panfilo, the outcome is still pending, while instead the Roman clergy does not succeed in deceiving God, as Abraham unequivocally states: 'quasi Idio, lasciamo stare il significato di vocaboli, ma la 'ntenzione de' pessimi animi non conoscesse e a guisa degli uomini a' nomi delle cose si debba lasciare ingannare' [as if God did not know the intention of evil souls, besides the meaning of their words, and would let Himself be deceived like human beings are by the mere names of things (I.2.21)]. The juxtaposition of novellas one and two, then, in this particular context, provides a moralistic epilogue to both novellas and broadens the area of moral responsibility for both the individual and the collectivity who are sinful and guilty of attempting to deceive God. The enlarged context, however, would also seem to question Abraham's highly intellectualized affirmation of the superiority of the Christian over the Jewish faith by correlating his intellectual awareness with that of Ciappelletto, the model of all depravity. Indeed novella I.3 will repropose this debate in openly critical terms.

In order to clarify this apparently contradictory implication, let us consider at this point the attention novella I.2 pays to the mercantile world that makes up the social background of its main characters. As previously noted, the importance of the mercantile ideology is also put into relief when I.2 is juxtaposed to I.1, in which the mercantile world is presented as a system of mediated exchange, that is, in terms of loans (messer Musciatto), usury (the two Florentine brothers), and brokerage (Ser Ciappelletto). This representation, from a medieval Christian standpoint, thus clearly suggests that the narrator of I.1 is critical of his characters and of the society they represent, and that mediation controls not only financial affairs but also most human relationships in the story. For example, Musciatto uses the mediation of Ser Ciappelletto in his dealings with the Burgundians, Ser Ciappelletto uses the friar to save the brothers' reputation as well as his own, the friar in turn uses Ser Ciappelletto to influence his congregation, and eventually the congregation uses Ser Ciappelletto to influence God. In the second tale, instead, the accent is on the personal qualities and talents of the two wealthy merchants who are the protagonists of the novella, and particularly those qualities which, according to Sergio Zatti, are typical of the mercantile system of life, that is, directness, initiative, mutual advantage, rational calculation, sense of measure, and desire to pursue mutual advantage.[8]

Indeed, all matters presented in the story, even those that are not business-related, are expressed in terms that embody the ethos and logic of the mercantile system. In his attempts to convince Abraham to accept the 'Christian truth,' Giannotto proclaims the ethical superiority of Christianity over the Jewish faith and he does so in economic terms, which he suggests his friend will have the rational ability to see and to understand. Giannotto contrasts the prosperity and growth of Christianity to the decadence and weakening of Judaism:

> [la] *verità cristiana* la quale *egli poteva vedere,* sì come *santa e buona, sempre prosperare e aumentarsi;* dove la sua, in contrario, diminuirsi e venire al niente *poteva discernere.* (I.2.6; emphasis mine, here and below)

> [*the Christian truth,* which he (Abraham) *could see prosper and grow constantly,* since it was *holy and good,* whereas, *he could observe* that his (Jewish religion), in contrast, was diminishing and coming to naught]

Here several parallelisms work to convey ethical values in economic terms. Abraham clearly shares this perspetive. On his return from Rome he reports:

> io veggio non quello avvenire che essi procacciano, ma continuamente la vostra religione *aumentarsi e più lucida e più chiara divenire,* ... mi par discerner lo Spirito Santo esser d'essa, sì come di *vera e di santa* più che alcuna altra, fondamento e sostegno. (I.2.26).

[I see not the results they (the sinful prelates) deserve, but instead (see) your religion *increase and become more illustrious and renowned* ... I seem to discern the presence of the Holy Spirit in it, as it is *truer and holier* than any other]

Both friends view the world in economic terms, in which 'prosperare e aumentarsi' [prospering and growing] are understood to be ['io veggio ... mi par discernere' (I see ... I seem to discern)] manifestations of the good.

The narrator presents Giannotto as a simple, uneducated man, whose language is unrefined, like that of most merchants (I.2.8). The Jew is instead endowed with intellectual qualities, and Giannotto reinforces this idea by praising Abraham's ability to 'see' and 'perceive.' Neifile calls Abraham 'valente e savio e buono uomo' [valiant, wise, and good (§5)] and 'diritto e leale uomo' [an honest and dependable person (§4)]. He shows his honesty and personal initiative in business-like, practical, rational, terms when he decides to travel to Rome in order to make an informed decision about the Catholic religion:

io voglio in prima *andare* a Roma e quivi *vedere* colui il quale tu di' che è vicario di Dio in terra e *considerare* i suoi modi e i suoi costumi, e similmente de' suoi fratelli cardinali; e se essi *mi parranno tali, che io possa* tra per le tue parole e per quegli *comprendere* che la vostra fede sia miglior che la mia ... io farò quello che detto t'ho.' (§§11–12)

[first I want *to go* to Rome in order *to see* him who you say is God's vicar on earth and *to examine* his ways and customs as well as those of his cardinals; and if, by your words and their actions, *I find myself able to perceive* that your faith is better than my own ... I will do what I told you I would do.]

In this passage, Abraham demonstrates his practical nature: he will go ('andare'), see ('vedere') and examine ('considerare') for himself. The paragraph describing his actions in Rome reveals his decision-making process, based once again on direct observation and intelligent consideration, as the text clearly shows in its use of lexicon:

Il giudeo ... se n'andò in corte di Roma dove ... *cautamente cominciò a riguardare* alle maniere del Papa e de' cardinali e degli altri prelati e di tutti i cortigiani; e tra che egli *s'accorse*, sí come uomo che *molto avveduto*

era, e che egli ancora da alcuno fu informato, egli *trovò* dal maggiore
infino al minore disonestissimamente peccare ... Oltre a questo ... *cognobbe
apertamente* ... (§19)

[The Jew ... went to the court of Rome where ... *he began cautiously to consider* the behaviour of the Pope, the cardinals, and the other prelates and
all the courtiers; and, whether *he realized it himself* – as he was a *very wise
and perceptive* man – or whether he was informed by others, *he found* them
all unscrupulously committing sin ... Besides this ... *he recognized clearly* ...]

Eventually he decides to return to Paris, 'parendogli assai aver veduto'
[as it seemed to him that he had seen enough (§22)].

In Abraham's own account to Giannotto of his Roman experience – his
witnessing of a spectacle of corruption and depravity – the stress is again
on his personal initiative and rational consideration. The expressions
'seems'/ 'seemed to me' ('parmene' / 'mi parve') recur five times in
these sequences, twice connected with seeing: 'niuna santità, niuna
divozione, niuna buona opera o essemplo di vita o d'altro in alcuno che
chierico fosse *veder mi parve*, ma lussuria, avarizia e gulosità, fraude,
invidia e superbia e simili cose e piggiori ... *mi vi parve* ... *vedere*' [it
seemed to me I saw no holiness, no devotion, no good deed or exemplary
life, but only lust, avarice, and gluttony, fraud, envy, pride, and the like,
and even worse, it seemed to me I saw there (§24)]. '*Parmene male* ... *mi
pare* che il vostro pastore e per consequente tutti gli altri si procaccino di
ridurre a nulla ... la cristiana religione ... *mi par discernere* ...'. Three times
they are connected with thinking: *It seems bad to me ... It seems to me* that
your shepherd and, consequently, all of the others as well try to destroy
... the christian faith ... *I seem* rightly *to perceive* (§§24–6).

The outcome is Abraham's determination to become a Christian and
his action to that effect: 'andiamo adunque alla chiesa, e quivi secondo
il debito costume della vostra santa fede mi fa' battezzare' [let us go to
church, and there, according to the rightful custom of your holy faith,
have me baptized (§27)]. Direct experience, careful observation, intelligent decisions, and consequent action are then the characteristic mercantile traits of the 'valiant, wise, and good' Abraham, who, as 'rich
man' and 'great merchant,' intelligently applies his merchant approach
and mentality to extra-mercantile matters, such as the choice of a religious faith; and he does so with equally successful results, at least from
Giannotto's point of view and from that of the mercantile ideology that
clearly inspires the novella.

The immediate effect of the novella is, therefore, the opposite of that created by the previous tale, since its mercantile logic would be viewed positively by the Florentine society of Boccaccio's times, and would attest to a sympathetic attitude on the narrator's part towards the characters and situations of novella I.2. Yet, at the same time, the highly intellectualized and business-oriented approach displayed by Abraham towards what should be an exclusively spiritual matter, such as religious faith, gains ironic implications from the textual interconnections of the tale. This textual ambiguity is underscored by the correlation our chart suggests between the wise Abraham and the champion of all vices, Ser Ciappelletto. Within these narrative parameters, therefore, even the solution in favor of Christianity that Abraham proposes to the debate assumes problematic connotations, and this reading of intentional ambiguity is corroborated by the fact that Abraham's conclusion will be challenged by the tale that follows, as the following brief consideration of that text will show.

The main characters of novella I.3 are Saladin, 'il valore del quale fu tanto, che non solamente di piccolo uomo il fé di Babillonia soldano ma ancora molte vittorie sopra li re saracini e cristiani gli fece avere' [whose worth was such that, not only did he go from being an insignificant man to becoming Sultan of Babilonia [Egypt], but he even won many victories over Saracen and Christian kings (I.3.6)], and Melchisedech, 'un ricco giudeo ... il quale prestava a usura in Alessandria' [a rich Jew ... a usurer who loaned money in Alexandria (§6)]. Saladin poses the question of the superiority of one religion over the other at the onset of the novella as a pretext; he plans a trick hoping to win needed financial support from the unsuspecting Jew. Saladin disguises his motives, asking Melchisedech an apparently friendly and respectful question which reproposes the religious debate:

'Valente uomo, io ho da più persone inteso che tu se' savissimo e nelle cose di Dio senti molto avanti; e per ciò io saprei volentieri da te quale delle tre leggi tu reputi la verace, o la giudaica o la saracina o la cristiana' (§8)

[My good man, I have heard from many people that you are very wise and very learned in religious matters; because of this I would very much like to learn from you which of the three Laws you believe to be the true one: the Jewish, the Saracen, or the Christian]

While in I.2 the rich and intelligent Abraham unselfconsciously applies his business-oriented approach to an ethical question, in I.3 a similar question concerning religion is posed purposely by Saladin. At the same time, the other character, Melchisedech, a double of Abraham – that is, a 'very rich' and 'wise ... Jew' – in response to Saladin's question about which of the three laws, the Jewish, the Saracen, or the Christian, is superior, provides a completely different solution from that of Abraham. He refuses to choose which of the three should be considered the one true religion.

In regard to the religious debate, then, the implicit comparison of the conclusion of novella I.3 to that of our novella questions the brilliant solution to the problem given by Abraham. Consequently, the juxtaposition of the second and third novellas provides a larger perspective on this particular issue, just as the juxtaposition of the first and second novellas does with regard to the question of sinfulness. The internal correlations among the novellas stress their textual interdependence and their thematic importance at the opening of the *Decameron*. They strongly suggest that the second novella plays a key role in the sequence with which the *Decameron* storytelling begins, even if it has been and still is far less well appreciated than the other two tales.

NOTES

1 Baratto, *Realtà*, 205–6; translation mine.
2 Battaglia, *La coscienza*; Branca and Degani, 'Studi sugli *exempla*'; and Delcorno, 'Studi sugli *exempla*.' These studies are also important for their rich bibliographies.
3 Di Francia, *Novellistica*, 103. See also his discussion of 'Abraam giudeo' in his article, 'Alcune novelle del *Decameron* illustrate nelle fonti.'
4 Toldo, 'conversione di Abram,' 355–9, esp. 358.
5 Giuseppe Mazzotta uses the expression 'the deception of language' in his discussion of I.1 in *World at Play*, 58. For Millicent Marcus's perceptive reading of the same novella, see her *Allegory of Form*.
6 See Branca, *Boccaccio medievale*, 158–60; also Padoan, 'Mondo aristocratico,' 129 (rpt. in Padoan, *Il Boccaccio, le muse*, chap. 1).
7 See Padoan, 'Mondo aristocratico.'
8 Zatti, 'Federigo.'

The Tale of the Three Rings (I.3)

PAMELA D. STEWART

Boccaccio has come very close, in recent times, to becoming a fashion-able writer, or, as the French would say, *un auteur à la mode* – but only for reasons of a purely intellectual and rather abstract nature – that is, for methodological considerations. The *Decameron*, in particular, has provided an exceptionally valuable corpus to narratological inquiry in all its varieties. I do not intend to detract from the importance of the results thus achieved or to minimize the merit of having conferred on Boccaccio studies something of the glamour of the limelight. But my approach will be different. In studying the tale of Melchisedech and Saladin, and the related criticism, I have come across a number of in-accuracies, oversights, and misunderstandings, all of which obscure the meaning of Boccaccio's treatment, in this tale, of the parable of the three rings. Through a close reading of the text and a fresh look at the context, I simply wish to call attention to one of the most intriguing, but also most interesting, pages of fourteenth-century Italian literature.

The parable of the three rings was widely known during the Middle Ages. It gained new notoriety at the end of the eighteenth century with Gotthold Lessing's play *Nathan der Weise*. In the second half of the nineteenth century the medieval versions of the parable attracted the attention of such scholars as Alessandro D'Ancona and Gaston Paris.[1] The 1884 lecture delivered by Paris to the Société des Études Juives provided the starting point for subsequent studies. Of these I will only mention here Mario Penna's book – the most extensive treatment of the subject – published in 1953: *La parabola dei tre anelli e la tolleranza nel Medio Evo*.[2]

The versions of the parable that circulated in Europe during the thirteenth and fourteenth centuries can be divided into two groups:

confessional and non-confessional. The confessional versions have the express purpose of exalting the supremacy of the Christian faith and are to be found in exemplary literature: in Etienne de Bourbon's *Tractatus de diversis materiis praedicabilibus*; in the anonymous *Dis dou vrai aniel* (both belonging very likely to the middle of the thirteenth century); in the *Gesta romanorum* (end of the thirteenth, beginning of the fourteenth century); and in John of Bromyard's *Summa praedicantium* (first half of the fourteenth century).[3] In all these versions but one there is a father, three sons, and three rings, of which one is authentic and the others copies. Etienne de Bourbon has an undefined number of daughters, only one of whom is legitimate, and consequently an undefined number of rings. In Etienne de Bourbon and in John of Bromyard, the false rings are· procured by the sons (or daughters) when they learn that the authentic ring has been given by the father to his preferred child. In the *Dis dou vrai aniel* and in the *Gesta romanorum*, it is the father who has the replicas made and distributes all three rings to the sons. In all four versions, upon the father's death the rings are produced and compared. Only the authentic one passes the test, showing its miraculous healing power.[4] With the exception of the *Gesta romanorum*, the true ring identifies the father's only heir. In the tale as recorded by Etienne de Bourbon, the ring goes to the only legitimate daughter; in the *Dis dou vrai aniel*, and in the account of the parable given by John of Bromyard, it goes to the youngest son – justified, in the *Dis*, because the two older sons are wicked: 'qui sont tenu/ A mescreant et a felon,/ cascun vau pis de Guennelon' (11, vv. 146–8) – and in John of Bromyard because the youngest is the wisest and most diligent of the sons: 'sapientior et diligentior.'[5] In the *Gesta romanorum* the father's inheritance is divided into three parts: his lands (*hereditas*) go to the eldest, his riches (*thesaurum*) to the second born, and the most valuable of all, the precious ring, to the youngest.[6] In every instance the authentic ring symbolizes the Christian faith.

The three non-confessional versions that form the second group (I leave aside stories presenting analogies or partial similarities)[7] are all from Italy and are to be found in *Il Novellino*, the *Avventuroso ciciliano*, and the *Decameron* (I. 3). They are all intended to show human inability to prove conclusively which of the three religions – Christian, Moslem, or Jewish – is the true religion. In all these versions there is a framing tale: the parable is told by a rich Jew (not otherwise designated in the *Novellino*, Ansalon in the *Avventuroso ciciliano*, Melchisedech in the *Decameron*), in response to the insidious question concerning the true religion put by the Sultan (mentioned only as 'il Soldano' in the *Novellino*, identified as Saladin in the *Avventuroso ciciliano* and in the *Decameron*). As for the parable itself, in each case the rings are three – one authentic and two replicas – it is the father who is responsible for the counterfeiting, and it is he who distributes the rings to the three sons, separately and in secret. For the rest the three versions present significant differences, which, strangely enough, have usually been overlooked or minimized.[8] While in the *Novellino* and in the *Decameron* it is not said which of the sons gets the authentic ring, in the *Avventuroso ciciliano* the father makes sure that it goes to his eldest son, "al maggiore.'[9] Moreover, much stronger emphasis is placed on the fact that the two counterfeit rings are totally worthless,[10] as are the two corresponding religions:

'... al mondo ae tre leggi notaboli, una la vostra; una la mia, una i cristiani. L'una è buona e salva, l'altre non sono niente. Quale sia quella non so. Ma ciascheduno di quelli di questa legge, si crede di avere la diritta al modo di quelli tre figliuoli.' (Nott, 456)

[... there are three notable Laws, the one yours, another mine, the third that of the Christians. One is the real one and the others nought; which is which I do not know, but each of the adherents of these three religions believes his to be the only true one, as the three sons each believed he possessed the true ring.][11]

The preference of the father for his firstborn is stated only in the *Avventuroso ciciliano*, and could be interpreted as an allusion to the Jewish religion on the part of the Jewish teller of the story, who would thus implicitly affirm the truth of his own faith, bringing this version of the parable very close to a confessional version in disguise.[12]

In the *Novellino* and the *Avventuroso ciciliano* no mention is made that the authentic ring should designate the heir,[13] and, consequently, contrary to what happens in the confessional versions, there is no need, after the father's death, to stage a comparison of the three rings so as to establish which is the original. Each son keeps his own ring, convinced he has the true one. And thus it is with the three religions. The account in the *Novellino* is particularly striking. With its extreme concision it manages to gloss over the complexities of the parable:

... elli fu un padre ch'avea tre figliuoli, e avea un suo anello con una pietra preziosa la migliore del mondo. Ciascuno di costoro prega[va] il padre ch'alla sua fine li lasciasse questo anello. El padre, vedendo che catuno il voleva, mandò per un fino orafo, e disse: – Maestro, fammi due anella così a punto come questo, e metti in ciascuno una pietra che somigli questa. – Lo maestro fece l'anell[a] così a punto, che niuno che conoscea il fine, altro che 'l padre. Mandò per li figliuoli ad uno ad uno, e a catuno diede il suo in secreto. E catuno si credea avere il fine, e niuno ne sapea il vero altri che 'l padre loro. E così ti dico ch'è delle fedi, che sono tre. Il Padre di sopra sa la migliore; e li figliuoli, che siamo noi, ciascuno si crede avere la buona.

[... there was a father who had three sons. He had a ring with a precious stone the most valuable in the world. Each of the sons besought his father to bequeath to him this ring; the father, seeing that each of them was desirous of having it, sent for a skilful goldsmith and said: 'Master, make me two rings like this one and set in each a gem similar to this one.' The goldsmith made the rings so like the original that no one but the father could recognize the authentic ring. The father sent for his sons in turn and gave them a ring, each in secret, and each of the sons believed he had the authentic one and none of them knew which was the true ring except for their father. And thus it is with the faiths that are three. Our Father on High knows which is the best; and each of us, who are his sons, believes he has the good one.][14]

The possible contradictions between the inability to identify the true religion and the perseverance of the faithful is avoided. Thanks to the brilliant use of the narrative technique of *abbreviatio*, the *Novellino* ably steers its course between the jeopardy of scepticism and that of confessionalism.

Unlike the *Novellino* and the *Avventuroso ciciliano*, in the *Decameron* (1) the ring designates the heir (I.3.11);[15] (2) the reason why the inheritance and the ring are not necessarily willed to the eldest son is carefully explained (it has to do with a longstanding family tradition [I.3.11–12]); and (3), at the end, after the father's death, once again just as in the confessional versions of the parable, a comparison is made of the three rings, but with the opposite result, since the comparison provides proof that it is impossible to establish which is the true ring, and the true religion. Moreover, Boccaccio adds that the three sons are equally meritorious and equally beloved of their father,[16] something which is not mentioned in the *Novellino* or the *Avventuroso ciciliano* and is of course excluded by the confessional versions of the parable. Boccaccio is obviously concerned to suggest an explanation for the deceitful stratagem of the father (God in the metaphor). Such an explanation is all the more appropriate since the false rings – that is, the false religions – are not discovered as such at the end of the parable, as in the confessional versions, and the deceit devised by the father appears to cast a permanent shadow over the future (for the Italian text, see note 17):

> The young men knowing the usance of the ring, each for himself, desiring to be more honored among his folk, besought his father, who was now an old man, to leave him the ring, whenas he came to die. The worthy man, who loved them all alike and knew not himself how to choose to which he would rather leave the ring, bethought himself, having promised it to each, to seek to satisfy all three, and privily let make by a good craftsman other two rings which were so like unto the first that he himself scarce knew which was true. When he came to die, he secretly gave each one of his sons the ring, wherefore each of them, seeking after their father's death to occupy the inheritance and the honor and denying it to the others, produced his ring in witness to his right; and the three rings being found so like unto one another that the true might not be known, the question which was their father's very heir abode pending and yet pendeth. And so say I to you, my lord, of the three Laws to the three peoples given of God the Father, whereof you question me; each people deemeth itself to have His inheritance, His true Law, and His commandments; but of which in very deed hath them, even as of the rings, the question yet pendeth.[17]

Boccaccio may well have had direct knowledge of the *Novellino*. More doubtful is the case of the *Avventuroso ciciliano*, whose date of composition is uncertain and could be as late as the middle of the fourteenth century, very close to that of the composition of the *Decameron*. But the points of contact with the confessional versions suggest that he also knew at least some of these. The network of contacts between the *Decameron* and the body of medieval exemplary literature has been illustrated by Vittore Branca and other scholars. Branca has remarked that the term 'essemplo' (in the technical sense of exemplum, an edifying exemplary tale) is used by Filomena in presenting her tale (I.3.5).[18] Melchisedech's words – 'Se io non erro, io mi ricordo aver molte volte udito dire ...' [Unless I am mistaken I recall having frequently heard ... (§11)] – seem to echo the frequent references to an oral tradition at the beginning of the exempla.[19] Furthermore, various similarities and analogies have been pointed out between several tales in the *Decameron* and certain exempla in Etienne de Bourbon's *Tractatus*.[20]

The differences between the *Decameron* and the *Novellino* (as well as the *Avventuroso ciciliano*) can certainly be traced to the narrative technique adopted by Boccaccio. The technique of *amplificatio* leads him of necessity to add circumstantial details that the opposite procedure of *abbreviatio* disallows. The relationship between the *Novellino* and the *Decameron* is usually discussed in these terms: as a question of rhetoric and style. It would be a mistake to underestimate the importance of this approach and the work of several scholars of undisputed merit who have adopted it.[21] But this approach can account only to a certain extent for the differences I have been pointing out. The actual procedure of *amplificatio* cannot be reduced simply to a rhetorical device.[22] The developments and additions required can be of diverse tenor and the choices made by the writer may be revealing of his attitude. Now it cannot be overlooked that in his amplifying elaboration of the parable, Boccaccio stresses elements that allow one to read the three religions as equivalent. To this end – paradoxically enough – he may well have also drawn on the confessional versions. In fact, as we have seen, the *Decameron* text is the closest, as regards many of the details, to those versions, but is the furthest away as to the overall significance of the parable. The inconclusive comparison of the three rings pushes to the brink of contradiction any religious commitment of a confessional type. Any such commitment makes sense only on condition we attribute an intrinsic value to the very act of believing, to faith itself. This seems to be, in the last analysis, the meaning the parable acquires in the *Decameron*. And from this point of view, Melchisedech can successfully conclude his answer, rising above Saladin's invidious question.

The general tendency in the criticism to assimilate the *Decameron* version of the parable with the other two non-confessional versions seems, therefore, unacceptable. The difference is not only a matter of detail, but of the overall meaning of the parable, and it reflects on Boccaccio's different treatment of the framing tale, often stressed by critics without perceiving the interdependence of parable and framing tale. In the *Novellino*, as well as in the *Avventuroso ciciliano*, the two protagonists of the framing tale, the Sultan and the Jew, are two figureheads, two schematic one-dimensional characters, mere vehicles of a verbal exchange. They are not individually characterized at the beginning, and suddenly disappear at the end. Only the bare circumstances – the richness of the Jew, the Sultan's need for money and his strategy for obtaining it – are prefaced to the parable in the *Novellino*:

Il Soldano, avendo bisogno di moneta, fo consigliato che cogliesse cagione a un ricco giudeo ch'era in sua terra, e poi gli togliesse il mobile suo, ch'era grande oltre numero. Il Soldano mandò per questo giudeo, e domandolli qual fosse la migliore fede pensando: s'elli dirà la giudea, io dirò ch'elli pecca contra la mia. E se dirà la saracina, e io dirò: dunque, perché tieni la giudea? El giudeo, udendo la domanda del signore, rispuose ...[23]

[The Soldan, being in need of money, was advised to find some fault with a rich Jew who was in his territory and take from him his property, which was immeasurably great. Accordingly the Soldan sent for the Jew and asked him which was the true faith, designing, should he reply 'The Jewish,' to say 'You are blaspheming against my Faith,' and should he say 'The Moslem,' to reply 'Why are you then a Jew?' The Jew, when he heard the Soldan's demand, answered ...]

The *Avventuroso ciciliano* adds the remark that Jews are universally hated ('And you must know that Jews are hated the world over, and have no homeland').[24] In both cases, after the Jew has finished telling the parable, the Sultan's admission of defeat is summarily mentioned and the tale abruptly ends: 'Then the Soldan, hearing him so skilfully redeem himself, knew not how to find fault with him, and thus decided to let him go' (*Novellino*)[25] and 'Saladin, hearing this, changed his mind, and freed the Jew' (*Avventuroso ciciliano*).[26] In the *Decameron*, instead, the framing tale is amply elaborated, the two antagonists appear carefully characterized, and at the end a relationship based on friendship and mutual trust is established between them.[27]

Saladin appears in all his grandeur, as a valorous and splendid ruler, at the very opening of the tale. He is similarly presented by Boccaccio in *Decameron* X.9 and in his commentary to the *Divine Comedy* (IV.i.243–4), where mention is made of Saladin's unorthodox approach to religion: 'And he was among the followers of Mohammed, although some would have it that he was not very observant of his laws and commandments.'[28] Boccaccio's presentation faithfully echoes the legend of Saladin widespread in the Christian Middle Ages – which, it must be said, bears little relation to historical truth.[29] Saladin's decision to call on the Jew for money is not introduced as a sudden, inexplicable whim, counter to his character, as is instead the case with the avarice of

Can Grande della Scala or that of the abbot of Cluny in *Decameron* I.7 – a tale in some respects analogous to ours. His need for money is explained as the result of his glorious military exploits and his extraordinary munificence – and his device to satisfy this need as an attempt to avoid resorting to force (I.3.6–7). Saladin's character does not undergo any development. He is a fixed star in the firmament of medieval legend: a standard of greatness and nobility. The change in his attitude towards Melchisedech at the close of the tale can be ascribed to the shifting perspective in which the Jew is seen. The initial presentation, according to the disparaging cliché of the rich but miserly Jew engaged in usury, is hardly corrected by the flattering and insinuating, if not ironic, words of Saladin: 'Valente uomo, io ho da più persone inteso che tu· se' savissimo e nelle cose di Dio senti molto avanti ...'(§8)[30] [Worthy man, I have understood from divers persons that thou art very wise and well versed in religious matters ...]. But the allusion to his wisdom is taken up shortly afterwards by the narrator, Filomena, in a quite different tone ('Il giudeo, il quale veramente era savio uomo ...' [The Jew who was indeed a wise man ...]), and is developed in what follows:

> Il giudeo, il quale veramente era savio uomo, s'avisò troppo bene che il Saladino guardava di pigliarlo nelle parole per dovergli muovere alcuna quistione, e pensò non potere alcuna di queste tre più l'una che l'altre lodare, che il Saladino non avesse la sua intenzione.[31] (§9)

> [The Jew, he perceived but too well that Saladin looked to entrap him in words, with the intention of picking a quarrel with him, and that if he were to praise any of the three (religions) more that the others, Saladin would have his way.]

His wisdom acquires a loftier meaning indirectly through his account of the parable. Here he demonstrates not only his skill in side-stepping the trap set for him, but also gives evidence of the superior approach he brings to bear on the question, by considering it from a vantage point from which it loses much of its relevance. For his skill and noble-mindedness he now emerges as the moral equal of Saladin:[32]

> Il Saladino conobbe costui ottimamente esser saputo uscire del laccio il quale davanti a' piedi teso gli aveva, e per ciò dispose d'aprirgli il suo bisogno e vedere se servire il volesse; e così fece, aprendogli ciò che in

animo avesse avuto di fare, se così discretamente, come fatto avea, non gli avesse risposto. Il giudeo liberamente d'ogni quantità che il Saladino il richiese il servì, e il Saladino poi interamente il sodisfece; e oltre a ciò gli donò grandissimi doni e sempre per suo amico l'ebbe e in grande e onorevole stato appresso di sé il mantenne (§§ 17–18).[33]

[Saladin perceived that the Jew had excellently well contrived to escape the snare which he had spread before his feet; wherefore he concluded to disclose to him his need and see if he were willing to serve him; and so accordingly he did, confessing to him that which he had it in mind to do, had he not answered him on such discreet wise. The Jew freely furnished him with all that he required, and the Sultan afterwards satisfied him in full; moreover, he gave him great gifts, and still had him to friend and maintained him about his person in high and honorable estate.]

The surprise ending is a common narrative device. In particular, apropos of the First Day of the *Decameron*, it has been remarked that all the tales end with a reversal of the initial situation.[34] There is indeed a reversal in our tale, but the dénouement is in no way arbitrary.[35] It is carefully prepared. The apparent contradiction between the initial presentation of the Jew as a usurer and a miser and the image we are left with at the end is dissolved in the gradual unfolding of his character. The indirect presentation of Melchisedech through his telling of the parable – precisely because of the deeper meaning the parable has in the *Decameron* – is decisive in creating the new climate of cordiality and friendship in which Saladin openly declares his true intentions and his need for money, and Melchisedech, in turn, gladly provides him with the funds requested.

If the narrative significance of the tale is to be found in the evolving portrait of the Jew – a narrative portrait rather than a descriptive one – namely, in the progressive revelation of the Jew's character along with the progress of the narration, the ideological significance is centred on the parable, and more specifically on the notion of the overriding importance of faith above and beyond the diversity of religious institutions (this of course extends only to the three biblically based religions). The parable articulates in more general, though metaphorical terms, the lesson to be drawn from the previous two tales, as presented by their narrators, Panfilo and Neifile. As Panfilo says, in God's eyes, the value of our faith is in no way diminished or impaired by the sinful condition of the intercessors, of the supposed saints, to whom we address our prayers, or even, as Neifile adds, by the scandalous corruption of the church and its ministers, who on the contrary should set an example. The protagonist of the first tale, Ser Cepparello da Prato, usually known as Ciappelletto, '... egli era il peggiore uomo forse che mai nascesse' [perhaps the worst man who ever lived (I.1.15)] thanks to his false deathbed confession, is venerated as a saint after his demise, and to him the faithful resort for help in addressing their prayers to God. Yet, as Panfilo explains at the outset and close of the tale, God, looking only at the sincerity of our faith, answers their prayers:

> ... grandissima si può la benignità di Dio cognoscere verso noi, la quale non al nostro errore ma alla purità della fé riguardando, così faccendo noi nostro mezzano un suo nemico, amico credendolo, ci essaudisce, come se a uno veramente santo per mezzano della sua grazia ricorressimo. (I.1.90)

> [... we may recognize how very great is God's mercy towards us, in that it takes account, not of our error, but of the purity of our faith, and grants our prayers even when we appoint as our emissary one who is His enemy, thinking him to be His friend, as though we were appealing to one who was truly holy as our intercessor for His favour.]

In Neifile's tale, a Jew called Abraham goes to Rome, and seeing with his own eyes that the papal court is a veritable den of iniquity, paradoxically decides to convert to Christianity, having convinced himself that it is the true religion, for only the direct intervention of God could possibly explain its continuing glory and expansion. According to Neifile's introductory words, the tale should induce us to disregard the corruption of the church and strengthen our faith (I.2.3). The first three tales seem, therefore, closely connected. They carry a similar message, though not the one attributed to them by Viktor Šklovskij: 'The old religion is thrown on the fire, just as during the plague old rags were burned for sanitary reasons.'[36] What is in question is not a revolutionary rejection of the traditional religions, as Šklovskij would have it, nor even an attitude of scepticism or religious indifference.[37] Strategically situated in a position of prominence, the three tales form rather a triptych on the paramount value of our faith in God.

This would make a fitting close to my reading of Boccaccio's tale of Melchisedech were it not for Filomena's opening words, which seem to be in direct contradiction with my interpretation of her tale:

'La novella da Neifile detta mi ritorna a memoria il dubbioso caso già avvenuto a un giudeo. Per ciò che già e di Dio e della verità della nostra fede è assai bene stato detto, il discendere oggimai agli avvenimenti e agli atti degli uomini non si dovrà disdire: a narrarvi quella verrò, la quale udita, forse più caute diverrete nelle risposte alle quistioni che fatte vi fossero. Voi dovete, amorose compagne, sapere che, sì come la sciocchezza spesse volte trae altrui di felice stato e mette in grandissima miseria, così il senno di grandissimi pericoli trae il savio e ponlo in grande e in sicuro riposo.' (I.3.3–4)

[The story told by Neifile reminds me of the perilous bind in which a Jew once found himself. And since God and the truth of our faith have already been well dealt with among us, it will not seem inappropriate to descend now to the deeds and adventures of men. So I will tell you a story which, when you have heard it, will possibly make you more cautious in answering questions put to you. It is a fact, my sweet companions, that just as folly often destroys men's happiness and casts them into deepest misery, as prudence extricates the wise from dreadful perils and guides them firmly to safety.]

These words from the storyteller herself have indeed helped steer critics away from the ideological import of the parable and towards an interpretation of the tale as simply a celebration of cunning, prudence, and savoir faire.[38] But Filomena's statement is not altogether convincing. Its inherent difficulty has quite rightly been pointed out by Millicent Marcus, who writes: 'What distinguishes the tale of Melchisedech from those which precede it, according to Filomena, is subject-matter: theirs sacred, hers profane. But here the narrator draws too clear a distinction, for the earlier tales also speak to the human condition, while her own tale is by no means indifferent to the question of faith.'[39]

What really is at stake here is, however, in my opinion, the general function of the narrator's comments with respect to the tales they tell. More often than not these comments serve to justify the particular place occupied by the tale in the series, to establish a link with previous or subsequent stories, to stress the relationship with the chosen theme of the Day, or even with some other general topic especially dear to Boccaccio. They single out, therefore, those features of a tale that may further one or more of these specific purposes. The tale of Landolfo Rufolo is introduced by Lauretta as an example of the vagaries of Fortune (II.4.3–4). But this introduction fits only imperfectly with the story. An excessive love of riches and his later caution and prudence account, at least in part, for Landolfo's misadventures (II.4.5) and for the happy ending (II.4.30). In Panfilo's introduction (II.7.3–7), the tale of Alatiel is linked to Boccaccio's insistent denunciation of women's vanity. It should persuade women of the dangerous risks they run because of their beauty and of the sorrow it can cause them. But the extraordinarily beautiful Saracen princess does not seem overly distressed by the series of adventures that befall her, and even manages at the end, 'restituita al padre per pulcella' [having been returned to her father as a virgin (II.7.1)], to marry the king to whom she had originally been promised. The summary presentation of the Tancredi and ·Ghismonda tale, the first of the Fourth Day, as 'un pietoso accidente, anzi sventurato e degno delle nostre lacrime' [a piteous story of misadventure, worthy of our tears (IV.1.2)], is simply a reminder – and a particularly appropriate one, coming as it does at the start of the Day's storytelling – of the chosen theme.[40] In introducing the tale of Federico degli Alberighi, the narrator, Fiammetta, refers only to the resistance of Monna Giovanna to the amorous attentions of Federigo (V.9.3) so as to show the connection with the preceding tale, centred on the reluctance of the disdainful young lady wooed by Nastagio degli Onesti. The privileged position assigned to the Griselda tale – the last tale of the *Decameron*, closing a Day devoted to examples of magnanimity – along with Dioneo's right not to respect, and even to reverse, the imposed theme, results in the presentation of the tale as an example of the 'matta bestialità' (X.10.3), of the Marquis of Sanluzzo. These are but a few instances. My point is that the comments of the narrators are not mainly intended to provide an interpretation of the tales, but to contribute to the order and unity of the whole work. They cannot be taken *au pied de la lettre*, as a guide to our reading of the tales. Their purpose is structural rather than exegetic.

With this in mind, let us return to the narrators' comments on the first three tales. Panfilo's main concern is to justify the eminent position occupied by the Ciappelletto tale, the first of the First Day. His remarks, therefore, refer only to the epilogue, since this allows him to present the tale as an example of God's mercy and of the salutary effect of our faith in Him, and to inaugurate the storytelling of the *lieta brigata* in the name of God:

Convenevole cosa è, carissime donne, che ciascheduna cosa la quale l'uomo fa, dallo ammirabile e santo nome di Colui, il quale di tutte fu facitore, le dea principio. Per che, dovendo io al vostro novellare, sì come primo, dare cominciamento, intendo da una delle sue maravigliose cose incominciare, acciò che, quella udita, la nostra speranza in Lui, sì come in cosa impermutabile, si fermi e sempre sia da noi il suo nome lodato. (I.1.2)

[It is proper, dearest ladies, that everything done by man should begin with the sacred and admirable name of Him that was maker of all things. And therefore, since I am the first and must make a beginning of our story-telling, I propose to begin by telling you one of His marvellous works, so that, when we have heard it out, our hopes will rest in Him as in something immutable, and we shall forever praise His name.]

Neifile's introduction links the second tale to the first by stressing the constructive aspect of Abraham's paradoxical reasoning. The third tale, the tale of Melchisedech, according to Filomena, would simply show that wisdom brings great rewards, while folly may lead to great misery and should make the ladies of the company more wary when answering questions put to them. This preamble is clearly intended to build a bridge to the tales that follow by announcing the theme of clever and prompt replies,[41] a theme explicitly formulated later on by another narrator (Fiammetta), at the beginning of the fifth tale, as emerging from a trend already set by the previous tales: '... mi piace noi essere entrati a dimostrare con le novelle quanta sia la forza delle belle e pronte resposte ... ' [... I am pleased to see that we have, through our tales, begun to show how great is the power of clever and prompt replies ... (I.5.4)].[42]

Boccaccio's concern to move forward from Panfilo's solemn inauguration to the following tales of the Day shows up also, in a playful vein, in Dioneo's sly intimation of a connection between the tale he is about to tell, I.4, and the previous two:

Amorose donne, [...] avendo udito che per li buoni consigli di Giannoto di Civignì Abraam aver l'anima salvata e Melchisedech per lo suo senno avere le sue ricchezze dagli aguati del Saladino difese, *senza riprensione attender da voi* intendo di raccontar brievemente con che cautela un monaco il suo corpo di gravissima pena liberasse. (I.4.3, emphasis mine)

[Amorous ladies, [...] having heard how Abraham saved his soul through Giannoto di Civignì's good advice, and how Melchisedech defended his money from Saladin's wiles by his wisdom, I intend, *without expecting any disapproval*, to give you a brief account of the clever way in which a monk saved his body from very severe punishment.]

Needless to say, the monk's tale is not particularly edifying. Filomena's presentation of her tale, casting it as she does exclusively in terms of mental and verbal dexterity, provides the necessary transition to Dioneo's risqué tale. Thus for reasons of a structural order, Filomena – similarly to Panfilo and Neifile, but proceeding in the opposite direction – stresses only one aspect of her tale, and distances herself from the declared religious intent of the first two tales.

Filomena's words, therefore, cannot be taken as the basis for our understanding of the Melchisedech tale. Yet the slant of her introduction cannot but·confer some ambiguity on the ensemble, on what I would call the narrative syntagm.[43] More generally, the discrepancy between the tales and the comments of the storytellers destabilizes the religious triptych on the question of faith – a question omitted by the narrator of the third tale in her presentation and highlighted instead by the narrators of the other two, but each time on the basis of a selective reading of the three tales. This ambiguity is perhaps an essential part of Boccaccio's narrative strategy in giving shape to the elegant and complex structure of the *Decameron*. I would suggest that this ambiguity creates a particularly subtle kind of intellectual suspense. But it is only a suggestion.[44] What is certain is that this makes it especially difficult to answer the question, which inevitably comes to mind, as to Boccaccio's own opinion on the meaning of the parable and the diversity of religions. Filomena's call for caution on the part of her lady listeners could also be a hint to readers and interpreters not to jump to conclusions. There is no direct line from the parable to Boccaccio's personal stance. The parable is a tale within a tale, told by a fictitious storyteller. There are no specific reasons to identify Boccaccio with one or other of the characters, or even with the storyteller. Boccaccio is all of them taken together, but of course not in a biographical sense.

Whatever his personal religious convictions might have been, and quite apart from Filomena's restrictive interpretation, it remains true that Boccaccio's version of the parable is the most daring formulation of the tendential equivalence of the three biblical religions, and of human inability to argue convincingly for any single one of them. Out of the diversity of religions, faith, the very act of believing, emerges as the only true value. So it is no wonder that the Melchisedech tale fell victim to Counter-Reformation censorship.[45] If in the 1573 expurgated edition of the *Decameron* (the so-called Deputati edition) only the end of the parable is tampered with, in the 1582 Salviati edition the whole parable is omitted, with the result that the tale is altogether incomprehensible. Even worse is the rewriting of the tale by Luigi Groto, a minor Venetian writer, in his edition of the *Decameron* published posthumously in 1588. Here the parable is retained, but serves to resolve the predicament of a young man who finds himself confronted by three ladies he has been courting separately and in secret, when, his deceit being discovered, he must answer the question as to which of them is his true love. The lengthy narration of the *amoroso imbroglio* is of course the work of Groto, who fully expected to gain literary fame for his revision of the *Decameron*: 'I will give life and light to Boccaccio, and he will do likewise for me [...] I will rescue him from darkness and burial, and he in turn will rescue me from obscurity[46] [...] I promise by my work God will receive glory, the Church satisfaction, the Master of the Holy Palace contentment, that author life, Tuscany a new light, the republic of scholars enjoyment ...'[47]

The *Decameron* miraculously survived. The Melchisedech tale, together with the parable of the three rings, travelling down through the centuries like a message in a bottle entrusted to the waves of the sea, came into the hands of Lessing, who very likely read it in an Italian edition, though he also knew the old fifteenth-century German translation.[48] Lessing clearly perceived the far-reaching ideological implications of the parable and the relevance of the tale to his campaign against theological bigotry and religious intolerance, as he writes to his brother Karl in 1778: 'I would not at all appreciate having the actual content of my play [*Nathan der Weise*], that is about to appear, revealed prematurely; but if you and Moses [Mendelssohn] wish to know it, you have only to turn to the *Decameron* by Boccaccio, Giornata I, Nov. III. Melchisedech Giudeo. I believe I have been able to draw from it a most interesting episode, which will make good reading, and I will play a much worse trick on the theologians than with ten more fragments.'[49]

In his play, *Nathan der Weise*, Lessing has included, in fact, all the distinctive features of Boccaccio's tale and version of the parable:[50] the family tradition of passing the ring on from generation to generation (III.7.401–9); the right of whichever son inherited the ring to be held as the head of the family, as if he were the first-born ('in Kraft allein/ Des

Rings, das Haupt, der Fürst des Hauses werde,' III.7.410–11); the equal love bestowed by the father on his three equally obedient sons (III.7.413–36); the inconclusive comparison of the three rings and of the three religions (III.7.442–8); the intrinsic value of faith (e.g., III.7.499–504, 527–32); Saladin's revelation to the Jew of his original plan (III.7.556–65); the Jew's willingness to provide the money (III.7.550–7); the friendship and admiration of Saladin for the Jew (III.7.540–4), whose magnanimity is underscored by the change in name from Melchisedech to Nathan – Nathan being the name of the extraordinarily magnanimous protagonist of the third tale of the Tenth Day of the *Decameron*.[51] Lessing's is perhaps the most careful and perceptive interpretation of the Melchisedech tale. Of course he went further. Through the addition of a new episode he managed to lend the parable a meaning entirely in keeping with his enlightened humanitarian outlook. Thus, thanks to Lessing, Boccaccio unwittingly contributed to the drawing up of one of the most generous pleas for religious toleration, and ultimately for religious liberty.

NOTES

1 D'Ancona, 'Del *Novellino* e delle sue fonti,' in *Studi di critica e storia letteraria*, 2d p., 2d ed., revised and corrected (Bologna: Zanichelli, 1912), 48 and 129–30; Gaston Paris's 1884 lecture was subsequently published with the title 'La parabole des trois anneaux.'

2 (Turin: Rosenberg & Sellier, 1953.)

3 For the text of Etienne de Bourbon's *Tractatus de diversis materiis praedicabilibus*, see *Anecdotes historiques*, 281–2. For *Li Dis dou vrai aniel*, see the edition by A. Tobler (1884). For the *Gesta romanorum* see the edition by H. Oesterley (1872), chap. 89, 416–17. There are no modern editions of John of Bromyard's *Summa praedicantium*; I have used the 1518 edition, published in Nürenberg. Contrary to the general opinion, according to which the *Summa* belonged to the second half of the fourteenth century, L. Boyle ('date of *Summa praedicantium*,') has shown that it was very likely completed by the end of 1348.

4 Etienne de Bourbon, *Tractatus*, 282; *Li Dis dou vrai aniel*, 11.47–54, 222–8; *Gesta romanorum*, 416; John of Bromyard, *Summa praedicantium*, *Fides* 1.1.

5 Etienne de Bourbon, *Tractatus*, 281–2; see also *Li Dis dou vrai aniel*, 11.134–217. For John of Bromyard, *Summa praedicantium*, see *Fides* 1.1.

6 *Gesta romanorum*, 416.

7 For this reason I do not discuss the parable recorded in the fifteenth-century Hebrew chronicle *Schevet Jehuda*. Though regarded by Gaston Paris as reflecting 'la forme la plus ancienne et la plus authentique' (*La poésie du Moyen Age*, 138) of the parable (but see Penna, *La parabola dei tre anelli*, 10–17, for a quite different opinion), the *Schevet Jehuda* refers only to two religions and is different in many other respects.

8 See Penna, *La parabola dei tre anelli*, 86: 'Le differenze che la parabola presenta nei tre testi italiani, mi sembrano di scarso rilievo'; and Russo, *Letture critiche*, 86: 'In verità, le differenze tra la redazione del *Novellino*, e quella dell'*Avventuroso ciciliano*, e l'altra della novella del Boccaccio sono soltanto differenze d'arte, ma c'è coincidenza di particolari'; S. Battaglia, in his article 'Premesse per una valutazione del *Novellino*' (*Filologia romanza* 2 [1955]: 259–86), subsequently included in *La coscienza*, and then in *Giovanni Boccaccio e la riforma della narrativa*), tends to link the differences to the use of different literary techniques.

9 As we have seen, in the confessional versons – obviously with the exception of Etienne de Bourbon's – the authentic ring goes to the youngest son, i.e., the Christian son. The reason for the identification of Christianity with the youngest son, in the symbolism of the parable, is not immediately evident: 'Gaston Paris osserva che, veramente, il più giovane dovrebbe essere quello che rappresenta il popolo saraceno, ultimo a costituirsi nella storia: ma è facile che il poeta avesse in mente il racconto biblico di Beniamino, il figlio prediletto per le sue virtù – e, come ho detto, egli pensava all'effetto artistico, esortativo: per questo gli conveniva rappresentare, al suo uditorio cavalleresco, come il più debole quegli che aveva sofferto l'ingiustizia che bisognava vendicare' (Penna, *La parabola dei tre anelli*, 60). But the best explanation, in my opinion, is perhaps in the notion of the spiritual 'novelty' of Christianity, an explanation that could be derived implicitly from John of Bromyard's *Summa praedicantium*, Fides 1.4.

10 'Egli fece fare due altre anella simili a quello di colore, ma niente valevano.' I quote from the edition by G.F. Nott, 455–6.

11 For the *Avventuroso ciciliano*, I have adopted the translation given by A.C. Lee in *The Decameron: Its Sources and Analogues*, 10, with minor revisions.

12 The remark that 'E voi dovete sapere che per tutto lo universo i giudei sono odiati, né luogo, né signoria non hanno' [Jews are universally hated and have no homeland (Nott, 455)] does not exclude this interpretation, and in fact could even confirm it. Paris notes that in the *Avventuroso ciciliano* the true ring goes to the father's eldest and preferred son, but he attributes the precedence seemingly given to the Jewish religion simply to awkwardness on the part of the author: 'Le juif ici s'appelle Absalon. Dans son récit, le

père veut donner le vrai anneau à son fils ainé, mais, pressé par les sollicita-
tions des autres, il se résout à faire exécuter les deux faux. Ce trait, qui
indiquerait trop clairement l'avantage que le juif attribue à sa religion (car
le fils ainé c'est nécessairement le judaïsme), ne serait pas adroit, et il ne
doit pas être primitif; il est encore accentué plus loin: les désirs des deux
autres fils sont qualifiés de non dovuti, et le narrateur remarque avec com-
plaisance: "Ainsi celui que le père voulait fut en cela son héritier." À part
cet alourdissement peu heureux, le récit de Busone ressemble de fort près à
celui du Novellino, mais certaines observations de détail me font croire
qu'ils ont une source commune plutôt qu'ils ne sont copiés l'un sur l'autre'
(*Poésie du Moyen Age*, 150).

13 In the *Avventuroso ciciliano*, the ring itself constitutes the inheritance ('Quelli
che il padre volle fu di ciò [of the ring] sua rede'). S. Battaglia, 'Premesse
per una valutazione del *Novellino*,' 277, remarks: Per il terzo punto, la
parabola, il testo del *Novellino* nella sua esauriente brevità è impareggiabile.
Specialmente per aver taciuto che il vero anello faceva il vero erede: circos-
tanza che il Busone raccoglie dalla sua fonte, senza saperla inserire oppor-
tunamente ...'

14 For the English translation of the *Novellino* tale, I have consulted the paraphrase given by A.C. Lee, *The Decameron: Its Sources and Analogues*, 9. For
the *Novellino* I have used the edition by Segre and Marti, *Prosatori del Duecento. Trattati morali e allegorici novelle* (1976; rpt. of *La Prosa del Duecento*
1959), 124–5.

15 Cf. Paris, *Poésie du Moyen Age*, 150: '... il diffère de Busone, ainsi que des
Cento Novelle, en un point essentiel: il mêle à la question du vrai anneau
une discussion d'héritage.'

16 Ibid., 151: 'Notons que dans Boccace les trois fils sont présentés comme
également vertueux.'

17 For the Melchisedech tale I have followed, with minor revisions, the 1886
English translation by John Payne, with its intentionally archaic turn. I have
also used the G.H. McWilliam 1972 translation published by Penguin
books. I give here in its entirety the Italian text of Boccaccio's version of the
parable (I.3.1–16):

Se io non erro, io mi ricordo aver molte volte udito dire che un grande
uomo e ricco fu già, il quale, intra l'altre gioie più care che nel suo
tesoro avesse, era uno anello bellissimo e prezioso; al quale per lo suo
valore e per la sua bellezza volendo fare onore e in perpetuo lasciarlo
ne' suoi discendenti, ordinò che colui de' suoi figliuoli appo il quale, sì
come lasciatogli da lui, fosse questo anello trovato, che colui s'inten-

desse essere il suo erede e dovesse da tutti gli altri esser come maggiore onorato e reverito. E colui al quale da costui fu lasciato tenne simigliante ordine ne' suoi discendenti, e così fece come fatto avea il suo predecessore; e in brieve andò questo anello di mano in mano a molti successori, e ultimamente pervenne alle mani a uno il quale avea tre figliuoli belli e virtuosi e molto al padre loro obedienti, per la qual cosa tutti e tre parimente gli amava. E i giovani, li quali la consuetudine dello anello sapevano, sì come vaghi ciascuno d'essere il più onorato tra' suoi, ciascun per sé, come meglio sapeva, pregava il padre, il quale era già vecchio, che quando a morte venisse a lui quello anello lasciasse. Il valente uomo, che parimente tutti gli amava né sapeva esso medesimo eleggere a quale più tosto lasciar lo volesse, pensò, avendolo a ciascun promesso, di volergli tutti e tre sodisfare: e segretamente a un buon maestro ne fece fare due altri, li quali sì furono simiglianti al primo, che esso medesimo che fatti gli aveva fare appena conosceva qual si fosse il vero: e venendo a morte, segretamente diede il suo a ciascun de' figliuoli. Li quali, dopo la morte del padre, volendo ciascun la eredità e l'onore occupare e l'uno negandola all'altro, in testimonianza di dover ciò ragionevolmente fare ciascuno produsse fuori il suo anello: e trovatisi gli anelli sì simili l'uno all'altro, che qual fosse il vero non si sapeva cognoscere, sì rimase la quistione, qual fosse il vero erede del padre, in pendente; e ancor pende. E così vi dico, signor mio, delle tre leggi alli tre popoli date da Dio padre, delle quali la quistione proponeste: ciascun la sua eredità, la sua vera legge e i suoi comandamenti dirittamente si crede avere e fare, ma chi se l'abbia, come degli anelli, ancora ne pende la quistione. (*Decameron* I.3.11–16)

18 Branca and Degani, 'Studi sugli *exempla*,' 182; cf. Petronio's note to the passage in his edition of the *Decameron*, I, 147, n15: 'Esempli: dietro il senso moderno della parola, vi è forse anche quello di "racconto esemplare, moralità."'

19 Cf. Branca and Degani, 'Studi sugli *exempla*,' 186; see also Delcorno, 'Studi sugli *exempla*' 189–94.

20 See Degani, 'Studi sugli *exempla*,' 192–4, 195–7; and Delcorno, 'Studi sugli *exempla*,' 203, 208n42, and 210–11nn60, 69.

21 I have already mentioned Battaglia (see note 8 above); but see also Cottino-Jones, *Order from Chaos*, 29–31.

22 Battaglia remarks on the different ways of being sensitive to human reality implied in different rhetorical techniques ('Premesse per una valutazione del *Novellino*,' 276, 279).

23 *Il Novellino*, ed. C. Segre (1976), 124–5.
24 'E voi dovete sapere che per tutto lo universo i giudei sono odiati, né luogo, né signoria non hanno' (Nott, 455). See note 12 above. As has often been pointed out, the *Avventuroso* also adds explicit mention of the Christian religion in formulating the Sultan's question and his reasoning.
25 'Allora il Soldano, udendo costui cosie riscuotersi, non seppe che si dire di coglierli cagioni, sì lo lasciò andare' (Segre, *Novellino*, 125).
26 'Il Saladino udendo ciò, suo animo rivolse per contrario proponimento, e 'l Giudeo libera' (*Avventuroso ciciliano*, ed. G.F. Nott, 456).
27 Cf. Russo, *Letture critiche*, 86; and Battaglia, 'Per una valutazione del *Novellino*,' 278–9. I give here the Italian text of the framing tale (I.3.6–10, 17–18):

'Il Saladino, il valore del quale fu tanto, che non solamente di piccolo uomo il fé di Babillonia soldano ma ancora molte vittorie sopra li re saracini e cristiani gli fece avere, avendo in diverse guerre e in grandissime sue magnificenze speso tutto il suo tesoro e per alcuno accidente sopravenutogli bisognandogli una buona quantità di denari, né veggendo donde così prestamente come gli bisognavano avergli potesse, gli venne a memoria un ricco giudeo, il cui nome era Melchisedech, il quale prestava ad usura in Alessandria. E pensossi costui avere da poterlo servire, quando volesse, ma sì era avaro che di sua volontà non l'avrebbe mai fatto, e forza non gli voleva fare; per che, strignendolo il bisogno, rivoltosi tutto a dover trovar modo come il giudeo il servisse, s'avisò di fargli una forza da alcuna ragion colorata.

E fattolsi chiamare e familarmente ricevutolo, seco il fece sedere e appresso gli disse: "Valente uomo, io ho da più persone inteso che tu se' savissimo e nelle cose di Dio senti molto avanti; e per ciò io saprei volentieri da te quale delle tre leggi tu reputi la verace, o la giudaica o la saracina o la cristiana."

Il giudeo, il quale veramente era savio uomo, s'avisò troppo bene che il Saladino guardava di pigliarlo nelle parole per dovergli muovere alcuna quistione, e pensò non potere alcuna di queste tre più l'una che l'altre lodare, che il Saladino non avesse la sua intenzione; per che, come colui il qual pareva d'aver bisogno di risposta per la quale preso non potesse essere, aguzzato lo 'ngegno, gli venne prestamente avanti quello che dir dovesse; e disse: "Signor mio, la quistione che voi mi fate è bella, e a volervene dire ciò che io ne sento mi vi convien dire una novelletta, qual voi udirete ..."

[...] Il Saladino conobbe costui ottimamente esser saputo uscire del laccio il quale davanti a' piedi teso gli aveva, e per ciò dispose d'aprirgli il suo bisogno e vedere se servire il volesse; e così fece, aprendogli ciò che in animo avesse avuto di fare, se così discretamente, come fatto avea, non gli avesse risposto. Il giudeo liberamente d'ogni quantità che il Saladino il richiese il servì, e il Saladino poi interamente il sodisfece; e oltre a ciò gli donò grandissimi doni e sempre per suo amico l'ebbe e in grande e onorevole stato appresso di sé il mantenne.'

28 Translation mine. *Esposizioni sopra la comedia di Dante*, 231: 'E fu per setta dei seguaci di Maometto, quantunque, per quello che alcuni voglion dire, poco le sue leggi e i suoi comandamenti prezasse.'

29 See Paris, *Légende de Saladin*; Castro, 'Présence du Saladin'; and Battaglia's review of Castro's article in *Filologia romanza.*

30 For the rest of the Italian text see note 27 above.

31 Ibid.

32 The moral, though not social, equal. Cf. Baratto, *Realtà*, 205: 'La critica del Boccaccio è cioè una critica di ordine intellettuale, non sociale; investe i principi di autorità, non ancora il potere. Né egli può andar oltre: se questa attività critica, affidata allo scatto degli individui, divenisse coscienza collettività, essa metterebbe necessariamente in discussione l'assetto sociale. Il che, si è visto, è contrario al sostanziale conservatorismo del Boccaccio.' I agree with this view of Boccaccio's general attitude. But for this very reason I find it difficult to accept Baratto's analysis (ambiguous and uncertain, in my opinion) of the relationship between Saladin and Melchisedech at the end of the tale: 'Il reciproco riconoscimento annulla, nel momento in cui avviene, le distanze sociali, dissipa l'avidità momentanea dell'uno e l'avarizia dell'altro; e si conclude in un totale appagamento di sé, delle proprie qualità. Tale attimo, d'altra parte, restituisce al Saladino il suo piedistallo di superiorità sociale e morale: il potente non perde il proprio prestigio a riconoscere e ad apprezzare l'intelligenza di un inferiore; ed è pure una lezione della novella. Perciò, rotta la tensione dell'aneddoto, passato il momento eccezionale in cui i due si sono riconosciuti, la prospettiva usuale si ricompone: il Saladino e Melchisedech restano amici, ma l'uno e l'altro al proprio posto' (213). What is missing here (perhaps intentionally) is the distinction between the moral and the social order, a distinction parallel to the one between the intellectual and the social order mentioned by Baratto in the previous passage. On Boccaccio's concern not to disturb the social hierarchy, see also Greene, 'Forms of Accommodation'; and, with reference to the Melchisedech tale, Cottino-Jones, *Order from Chaos*, 43.

33 For the rest of the Italian text see note 27 above.

34 See Padoan, 'Mondo aristocratico,' in particular, 164–5; now in Boccaccio, *Le Muse.* See also Cottino-Jones, 'Saggio di lettura.'

35 G. Paris ('La parabole des trois anneaux,' 151), followed by M. Landau (*Die Quellen des Dekameron*, 1887–95), saw here a contradiction: 'Le juif s'appelle Melchisedech, et l'auteur nous le représente comme un usurier très avare, ce qui ne va guère avec le dénouement où il avance librement et libérale-ment à Saladin l'argent que celui-ci voulait lui soutirer par ruse.' M. Penna (*La parabola dei tre anelli*, 87–90) attempted an explanation based on the medieval notion of usury and avarice. But even if usury is simply money-lending with interest and avarice is lack of chivalrous largesse, the initial presentation of the Jew would still be in contrast with his liberality at the end. More convincingly, L. Russo (*Letture critiche del Decameron*, 89–90) resorted to the 'atmosphere of understanding, cordiality and mutual trust' at the end of the tale. What remains to be explained, more satisfactorily than Russo does, is the reason for this change in atmosphere.

36 I quote on the basis of the Italian translation: V. Šklovskij, *Lettura del Decameron*, 209.

37 According to G. Padoan ('Mondo aristocratico,' 166) the Melchisedech tale shows Boccaccio's little interest in a thoughtful discussion of religious mat-ters: 'La novella dimostra questo disinteresse del Boccaccio per ogni pon-derata discussione del fatto religioso [...] l'affermazione dell'uguaglianza delle tre grandi religioni lo lascia alquanto indifferente.'

38 See, for instance, Getto, *Vita di forme e forme di vita*, 36–7; also Padoan, 'Mondo aristocratico,' 166.

39 Marcus, 'Faith's Fiction,' 40. Marcus attempts to explain away the difficulty by distinguishing between the subject matter, common to all three tales, and the narrative mode – the manner of Filomena's narration – that would differentiate the third tale from the previous two. Filomena's tale, in fact, says Marcus, 'denies any continuity between divine and human utterance by making man's failure to discern final truth its salient theme' (44). For this reason it would break with the narrative genre of the edifying exempla, and 'provide a new point of departure for the *Decameron*, separating the ninety-seven tales which follow from the opening two stories of the collec-tion' (40). Unfortunately, as Marcus herself says, even the first two tales 'point to the discontinuity between the word of God and man – a rupture which distroys the justification for their chosen genre' (44).

40 The subject matter of the tale is, in fact, mentioned by Fiammetta, the storyteller, in the context of her discussion of the tragic theme chosen by Filostrato (IV.1.2).

41 The Melchisedech tale is particularly suitable for this purpose. In fact, in one respect – the one emphasized by Filomena – it points in the direction of the subsequent tales: in another – the subject matter of the parable – it harks back to the previous tales. This is why I cannot agree with Marcus's thesis

that 'Thematically and rhetorically the *Decameron* may be said to begin with the third tale of the first day' (Marcus, 'Faith's Fiction,' 40).

42 The admonishment addressed by Filomena to her female listeners is taken up and expanded upon by Pampinea, in her lengthy introduction to the last tale of the First Day, and once again at the beginning of VI.1, by Filomena, who repeats almost verbatim Pampinea's words. Women in particular should take the lesson to heart, since – as Pampinea and Filomena assert – it is more unseemly for a woman to make long speeches than for a man (I.10.4, VI.1.2). At any rate, as we all know, the instruction of women, together with their entertainment, is the declared purpose of the *Decameron* and is a recurring topos in the comments, more or less edifying, of the narrators (Proemio 14; I.5.4; I.10.4, 6–8, 20; II.9.3; III.3.4; III.6.3; V.8.3; VI.1.2–3; VII.1.3; IX.7.3, etc.). It is perhaps appropriate to recall, in this connection, Robert Hollander's study 'Utilità in Boccaccio's *Decameron*.'

43 In particular, the sentence 'il discendere oggimai agli avvenimenti e agli atti degli uomini non dovrà disdire' [it will not seem inappropriate to descend now to the deeds and adventures of men], which obviously refers to the calculated exchange between Melchisedech and Saladin, could be implicitly extended to cover man's inability to discern the true religion, and could thus cast a shadow of doubt on the supposedly decisive value of faith in God's eyes. If this is so, the sentence would correspond to Panfilo's reservation, expressed in I.1.6, as to his ability to understand, from a human perspective, the workings of God's mercy in granting the prayers of the faithful, even if addressed through such unsaintly mediators as Ciappelletto: 'Il che manifestamente potrà apparire nella novella la quale di raccontare intendo: manifestamente, dico, *non il giudicio di Dio ma quel degli uomini seguitando*' [Manifestly will this appear in the tale I am about to tell; I say *'manifestly' in accordance not with God's judgment, but with that of man* (emphasis mine)]. In fact, as Panfilo later explains (I.1.89–90), it remains hidden from us whether or not Ciappelletto repented on the point of death and was received into the Kingdom of God – which would lend a quite different meaning to God's mercy.

44 I would not like to push it any further than that. Marcus's view, that one of the main purposes of the whole *Decameron* is the training of the reader to appreciate the various levels of meaning in the text, is perhaps taking it too far. See her very interesting book, *An Allegory of Form*, e.g., 9–10.

45 See Chiecchi and Troisio, *Il Decameron sequestrato*; see also Mordenti, 'Le due censure.' For the Melchisedech tale in particular, see Chiecchi and Troisio, 121–31.

46 Groto, *Le lettere famigliari*, 108.

47 Ibid., 109.

48 In discussing a French translation of the *Decameron*, published in Cologne in 1712, Lessing – apropos of *Decameron* II.7 – refers to the Italian text and to the 1535 and 1561 editions of the old German translation (Lessing, *Werke*, V, 714–15), which he attributes to Heinrich Steinhöwel (*Werke*, V, 599). Lessing mistakenly thought that the first edition of the German translation had appeared in 1535 (V, 715n.: '"ie erste Ausgabe ist von 1535 in Folio,"' whereas it actually appeared in 1472 or 1473. Moreover, the author of the translation is in all likelihood not Heinrich Steinhöwel, but Heinrich Schlüsselfelder: see Hirdt, 'Boccaccio in Germania,' 33–5. A reprint of the nineteenth-century edition of this translation, annotated by A. von Keller, was published in 1968 (Amsterdam: Editions RODOPI). On the circulation of the *Decameron* in Germany, see Hirdt, 'Boccaccio in Germania.' On Lessing's travels in Italy, see Ritter Santini, *Da Vienna a Napoli*.

49 'Ich möchte zwar nicht gern, dass der eigentliche Inhalt meines anzuküdigenden Stücks allzufrüh bekannt würde; aber döch, wenn Ihr, Du oder Moses, ihn wissen wollt, so schlagt das *Decameron* des Boccaccio auf: Giornata I, Nov. III. Melchisedech Giudeo. Ich glaube, eine sehr interessante Episode dazu erfunden zu haben, dass sich alles sehr gut soll lesen lassen, und ich gewiss den Theologen einen ärgen Possen damit spielen will, als noch mit zehn Fragmenten.'

50 Lessing, *Nathan der Weise* III. vii (*Werke*, II, 275–82).

51 For the change in name from Melchisedech to Nathan, cf. H. Birus, 'Das Rätsel der Namen,' in the excellent collection, *Lessing's Nathan der Weise*, ed. K. Bohnen, 1984), 299. Nathan's explanation of why the faithful continue to believe in their religion even in the absence of any proof of its validity, provides a careful and convincing interpretation of *Decameron* I.3.16 – 'ciascun la sua eredità, la sua vera legge e i suoi comandamenti *dirittamente* si crede avere e fare': since it is impossible to establish which is the true religion everyone *rightly* perseveres in the religion of his forefathers (*Nathan der Weise* III.7.463–73 [emphasis mine]).

The Tale of the Monk and His Abbot (I.4)

RONALD MARTINEZ

The fourth tale of the First Day marks a shift in subject matter from the theological casuistry of Ciappelletto, Abraham the Jew, and Melchisedech, to the passions of the flesh.[1] Dioneo introduces his tale by reaffirming the purpose of storytelling as entertainment designed to produce pleasure and delight:

> 'Amorose donne, se io ho bene la 'ntenzione di tutte compresa, noi siamo qui per dovere a noi medesimi novellando piacere; e per ciò, solamente che contro a questo non si faccia, estimo a ciascuno dovere esser licito (e così ne disse la nostra reina, poco avanti, che fosse) quella novella dire che più crede che possa dilettare ...' (§3)

> [Amorous ladies, if I have rightly understood your intention, we are here with the duty of pleasing ourselves by telling stories. Therefore, provided we do nothing contrary to this, I think that it ought to be permitted to each – and our queen said as much just a little while ago – to tell whatever tale he believes can most afford delight ...]

Dioneo refers to Pampinea's institution of the storytelling a few pages earlier (*Introduzione*, §§109–14). Pampinea's reasoning there is that whereas games like chess make the losers unhappy, storytelling brings pleasure to all concerned. Her argument once approved, she proposes a day of narration in which each will be 'libero sia a ciascuno di quella materia ragionare che più gli sarà a grado' [free to speak of those subjects that are most agreeable to each (§114)]. In his reference to Pampinea's institution, Dioneo however slightly expands his franchise. Where Pampinea says that stories bring pleasure because they can be shared, Dioneo assumes that pleasure *is itself* the purpose of storytelling. And where Pampinea will allow the speakers to choose the subject most agreeable to each *on the First Day*, Dioneo assumes the license to include *all subject matter* that he thinks will delight – a form of *malizia* that becomes especially pointed when he uses 'piacere e diletto,' the phrase for the recreation of the *brigata*, to describe the amorous sports of the monk (§8).

Dioneo's licence harks back to his dialogue with Pampinea still earlier in the Introduzione (§§92–6), where the recreational purpose of the company is first defined:

'Donne, il vostro senno più che il nostro avvedimento ci ha qui guidati; io non so quello che de' vostri pensieri voi v'intendete di fare: li miei lasciai io dentro dalla porta della città allora che io con voi poco fa me ne uscì fuori: e per ciò o voi a sollazzare e a ridere e a cantare con meco insieme vi disponete (tanto, dico, quanto alla vostra dignità v'appartiene), o voi mi licenziate che io per li miei pensier mi ritorni e steami nella città tribolata.' (§§92–3).

[Ladies, it was your wisdom, rather than our perspicacity, that led us here. I do not know what you intend to do about your cares, but mine I left within the gate of the city when – not long ago – I passed through it in your company. Therefore either you dispose yourselves to enjoy yourselves and laugh and sing with me (as much, I mean, as is suitable to your dignity), or else you must allow me to return with my worries and remain in the beleaguered city.]

To which Pampinea answers:

'Dioneo, ottimamente parli: festevolmente viver si vuole, nè altra cagione dalle tristizie ci ha fatte fuggire. Ma per ciò che le cose che sono senza modo non possono lungamente durare, io, che cominciatrice fui de' ragionamenti da' quali questa così bella compagnia è stata fatta, pensando al continuar della nostra letizia, estimo che di necessità sia convenire esser tra noi alcuno principale ...' (§§94–5)

[Dioneo, you speak very well: it is in festivity that we must live, nor has any other reason made us flee from sorrow. But because those things that lack order cannot long endure, and since I began the discussions that have led to the formation of this elegant company in order to provide for the continuation of our enjoyment I find it necessary that we agree to have a leader ...]

After this exchange, and after her election as queen for the day, Pampinea determines the rule for the company: rotating leadership, division of labor, schedule of daily acitivites – including her suggestion that they not only play games, but tell stories. Dioneo's intervention in the constitutional convention of the *brigata* is the first sally of a strategy that bears fruit at the end of the First Day, when he obtains an exception to the order of narrators: from the Second Day on, he always takes the last place – 'for as long,' he says, 'as our company shall last' (I, Concl. §§12–13). Because Dioneo will therefore always speak after the queen or king for that day (who would otherwise speak last), he always has the last word. In fact, given the implications of the First Day's ranking, he is always in a sense the unofficial king. Dioneo's strategy thus establishes a tension between rule and license that runs through the whole collection.

The tension Dioneo establishes is provided for and contained from the beginning by the prudence of Pampinea, who imposes an order but also recognizes a need for that festive release that is a principal motive for escaping the stricken city. Order and measured festivity form the temper of the company, a temper established by Pampinea's imposition of a rule and Dioneo's regular dispensation from maintaining it. In this sage institutionalization of the classic tension between Apollonian restraint and Dionysan energy lies what has often been recognized as one of the defining characteristics of the whole book (Greene, 'Forms of Accommodation' 1968). As the exchange between Dioneo and Pampinea suggests, it is a tension finally based on the model of the healthy – that is, well-tempered – human body. The escape of the company from the city, and the activities established by Pampinea, are therapeutic measures aimed at preserving physical and mental health, as Glending Olson has demonstrated with parallels drawn from the *consilia* of contemporary medical treatises on the plague.[2] Thus beneath Dioneo's mischief can be discerned an intent that is part of Boccaccio's larger strategy for constructing a book that will have a salutary effect on its readers. In this context, Boccaccio's selection of the subject of the first story both as Dioneo's first offering and the first bawdy fabliau of the *Decameron* comes into focus. For the first tale is both about a Rule – the *Rule of St Benedict* governing monastic life – and about the breaking of that Rule by and for the sake of the body. Dioneo's demarcation of his own choice of subject and his implicit polemic with the other narrators is carefully mediated by the elegant linkage of his *favola* with the three parables just recited.[3] The clever remark about female burdens ('i monaci si debban far dalle femine priemere come da' digiuni e dalle vigilie' [monks should feel the weight of women as they do of fasts and vigils (§21)] that turns the tables for the monk places Dioneo's tale firmly in the framework of the First Day, which is characterized by witty remarks that catalyse reversals in the action.[4] Though Dioneo marks a shift, he does so by shrewdly drawing threads from the previous tales: he moves to the flesh, but in a monastery, so that the subject of religion, begun with the enigma of Ciappelletto's beatification, is maintained. The most important continuity, however, is articulated explicitly by Dioneo, and contains a seminal idea for the whole tale:

'... avendo udito che per li buoni consigli di Giannotto di Civignì Abraam aver l'anima salvata e Melchisedech per lo suo senno avere le sue richezze dagli aguati del Saladino difese, senza riprensione attender da voi intendo di raccontar brievemente con che cautela un monaco il suo corpo di gravissima pena liberasse.' (§3)

[... having heard that through the good advice of Giannotto di Civignì Abraham saved his soul and Melchisedech through his wit defended his riches from the plots of Saladin, I am going to tell you briefly, without fear of reproach, with what wariness a monk saved his body from a most severe punishment.]

The series good counsel, wit, and wariness represent just those arts of mind that readers consider typical of the Boccaccian hero.[5] But Dioneo is also outlining a traditional hierarchy of faculties and possessions. In the first book, *Ethics*, Aristotle reiterates the Platonic division of external goods, goods of the soul, and goods of the body.[6] Though his order differs, Dioneo's division is identical. The strategy of Dioneo's subversion is plain: not only does he invert the theological commonplace that would have the soul freed (*liberata*) from the prison of the flesh; he is claiming the right of the monk to use his wit to free his body, as others use their wits to rescue other possessions that define the person. This claim rests on the assumption that the freedom and pleasure of the body are good, and that the 'vigore e freschezza' [physical vigour] of the young monk is very good. The claim is particularly significant in the context of the tale because the monastic *Rule* expressly denies the monk power over his own body.[7] This is a key issue; it will be returned to later.

Dioneo's division of goods is linked in turn to the tripartite articulation of the soul, familiar to readers of Dante's *Vita nuova*, into animal, vital, and natural spirits.[8] In these terms the goods of the rational mind are salvation and beatitude; possessions are the goods presented to the appetition of the vital spirit; and freedom from pain and restraint is the good of the natural body. The example of the *Vita nuova* is especially relevant to Dioneo's tale because of Dante's conceit of personifying each spirit with a voice (the figure of *sermocinatio*, widely practised among the *stilnovisti*, especially Guido Cavalcanti). Thus in the *Vita nuova*, the natural soul, among whose functions is the nourishment of the body, foresees and laments the hardships – we could justly call them fasts and vigils – it will suffer as a consequence of the narrator's sight of Beatrice.[9] In Dioneo's tale, the natural and vital spirits of the monk, undaunted by the fasts and vigils of the monastic regimen, rises to dominate both monk and abbot in the course of the tale as if a voice of protest of the long-repressed flesh.[10] As we shall see, at a key moment in the tale the flesh literally calls out.

The physical and temporal setting of the *novella* prepares and frames the emphasis on the physical body and its appetites. The setting of the tale during the noonday hour, when the weariness of the flesh – *acedia* – impedes the action of the spirit, establishes an archetypal scene of fleshly temptation.[11] The monk sees the girl on an excursion outside the monastery walls, in the fields (*campi*) later also described as woods (*bosco*), and has no sooner seen her than he is seized by desire. The situation, action, and rapidity of the scene evoke several precise antecedents, including the rape of Proserpina in Ovid's *Metamorphoses* and the sight of Matelda as a *pastorela* in Dante's Eden.[12] For the moment it should be noted that the woods and fields and the presence of the girl herself invoke traditional figurations of the body: in that the body is made of matter (*silva* in the philosophical vocabulary of Boccaccio's day) like earth and trees; and in that the female is associated with the body, the man with reason.[13] Eden itself, the garden of prelapsarian innocence, is a figure of the body. The evocation of Eden and of the noon hour inevitably signals that the monk's lapse into the flesh reiterates the fall of man.[14]

The subsequent action also depends upon space and architecture to frame its allegorical implications.[15] The monk's noonday walk breaches the *Rule* he lives by and blurs the distinction between the cloister and the world; with his transfer of the girl within the monastery he enacts the entry of the female into the male body and her domination of the seat of reason and control. The crucial scene in which the monk witnesses the girl surmounting the abbot, the female riding and dominating the male, re-enacts one of the icons of erotic folly in the antifeminist literature of Boccaccio's age – Aristotle's submission to being ridden, like a horse, by his wife.[16]

If the younger man is seized by the fierce appetite of lust when stimulated by noonday heat, by the paradisal *locus amoenus* of the fields and woods, and by the beauty of the girl, the abbot, who is the official head of the community of monks, is taken within the heart of the monastery itself – by definition an enclosure – in the private *cella* of the monk. Again, the edifice of the monastery is an image of the body: the monk's cell portrays the secret inner chamber of the heart or the conscience. That the girl is brought first into the cloister and then into the *cella* reminds us that both monastery edifice and human body are open to the outside, the former through doors and fenestration, the latter through the perforations of the senses. As we shall see in a moment, the two perforations mentioned in the tale – the entrance (*uscio*) of the cell and the peephole (*pertugio*) and the two related senses, sight and hearing, play key roles in the action.

First the senses. Dioneo, in showing the seduction of the two religious, draws twice on the erotic convention of the degrees of love (*gradus amoris*) in sight, speech, and touch. The tale emphasizes with particular frequency the moment of sight: the monk sees the girl ('gli venne *veduta*') and no sooner sees her than succumbs ('ne prima *veduta* l'ebbe, ch'egli fu fieramente assalito da concupiscenza carnale' §5). The abbot, too, looks at the girl with vehemence ('postole *l'occhio adosso e veggendola* ...' §15), an idiom that makes the act of sight one of touch as well, and that echoes the monk's sight of the abbot earlier when he placed his eye on the peephole: '*pose* l'occhio e vide' (§8) and anticipates the final placement of the girl on top of the abbot ('sopra il suo petto *pose* ...' §18).[17] But if sight dominates, as it might be expected to in a tale of sexual lust, the emphasis on sound effects is more unusual and thus more striking: the amorous pair betray their presence to the abbot by their cries of pleasure, and the monk, who possesses not only a convenient peephole but also appears to have a keen sense of hearing, overhears the abbot scuffling his feet as he walks through the monastery. The abbot's *stropicio* (scuffling) outside the door balances the crying out, the *schiamazzio* (§7) coming from within. The auditory sense is, like the visual, treated as a sense of touch, for it is the sound of a woman within the cell that tempts the abbot to enter: 'tutto fu tentato di farsi aprire' (§7). *Tentare*, of course, means, literally, to touch. The abbot's pause to listen before the door of the monk's cell is the most revealing moment in the narrative, and focuses the drama of the body and its temptations that we have been following thus far.

The monk's pause before the threshold of the cell where he detects a woman, and his return and entrance therein, stage the moral debate in the abbot's soul. The monk's cell functions as the 'segretissima camera del cuore,' to use a phrase in Dante's *Vita Nuova* (31), so that in approaching the cell the abbot is also approaching the hidden thoughts of his own heart. The passage where the abbot listens to the voices coming from inside deserves citing in full:

> avvenne che l'abate, da dormir levatosi e pianamente passando davanti alla cella di costui, sentio lo schiamazzio che costoro insieme faceano; e per conoscere meglio le voci s'accostò chetamente all'uscio della cella ad ascoltare, e manifestamente conobbe che dentro quella era femina e tutto fu tentato di farsi aprire ...(§7)

> [it came about that the abbot, having arisen from sleep and passing quietly before the cell, heard the cries that the two of them were making; and in order to better hear the voices he leaned quietly against the door of the cell to listen, and knew clearly that inside was a female; he was strongly tempted to have himself let in ...]

The passage exemplifies an auditory seduction: the abbot, who both walks softly and approaches quietly (*pianamente, chetamente*) hears voices, listens more closely, hears a woman, and is tempted – touched – with the wish to enter. The first moment of his response is the impulse to enter and witness, or perhaps join, the activity wihin; there is no evidence in the text that his first thought is to discipline the monk: he simply wants to enter and see the female. It is crucial to the passage that what the abbot responds to are the *voices*: Boccaccio's text points the emphasis on *sentire* and *schiamazzio* by using the paragogic form of the past tense of *sentire* (*sentio*). This gives the phrase an onomatopoeic effect when joined to the iterative *schiamazzio*; for *schiamazzio* itself is of course derived from *chiamare*, to call. The voices of pleasure and play in the cell call to the abbot; they are a siren song. His fall is not yet complete, but it is well begun in the approaches of sight and sound to the portals of his senses, and in his initial motions of curiosity and excitement.

The temptation of the abbot takes place precisely at the door, the *uscio*, because the threshold signifies the entranceway to the heart and its secret desires. In Dante's *Commedia*, free will is the power that counsels ('la virtù che consiglia,' *Purgatorio* 18.62) and guards the threshold of consent ('de l'assenso de' tener la soglia' 18.63) from which it monitors and controls the spontaneous impulses of appetite that arise in human clay. Commenting on Virgilio's explanation of love and free will, Charles Singleton quotes a passage from the *Moralia* of Gregory the Great that speaks directly to the predicament of the abbot:[18]

> For we 'enter our chambers' (*cubicula*) when we go into the recesses (*secreta*) of our own hearts. And we 'shut the doors' (*ostia*) when we restrain forbidden lusts ... and so whereas our consent set open these doors of carnal concupiscence ('concupiscentia carnalis ostia') it forced us to the countless evils of our corrupt state.

The monk introduces the female into the enclosed space of the monastery. But for the abbot the woman locked in the monk's room is a figure of the desire that lurks in the cell or *cubiculum* of his heart and to which he succumbs when he opens the door and enters the monk's cell – unlocking voluntarily the threshold of assent and entering the secret place now possessed by the woman, by the body. The abbot's entrance is not, however, entirely his idea. It is carefully foreseen and prepared by the monk.

Dioneo's tale does not dwell on the decay of the religious orders (though that is implied), nor does it take aim at the evil of carnal concupiscence. The distribution in the text of the icons of the body – cell, prison, forest, wood, the female, the senses, physical weight, and the related spatial categories of open and closed, inner and outer – are devoted to showing how the monk, though a younger man, is more perceptive, shrewder, mentally more agile than his abbot, the man who should ex officio be his master, teacher, and father. To be sure, the tale depicts a triumph of the flesh, of carnal concupiscence that fiercely attacks and overwhelms both monk and abbot immediately as they gaze upon the girl. But the tale is also a rivalry between two men, and the monk's triumph over his abbot is part and parcel of his triumph over the fasts and vigils that have not diminished his physical vigour.

Thus the real scandal of the novella is that the roles of monk and abbot are reversed.[19] But not only that. It is because the monk is better informed than his teacher about the desires of the flesh that he proves to be the wiser man. Trapped in a difficult spot because of his runaway lust ('da troppa volontà trasportato' §7), the monk secures his freedom with a plan designed in view of a specific end – 'la quale al fine imaginato da lui dirittamente pervenne' (§10) – and that defeats the abbot's own scheme to investigate the matter of the girl in the cell and punish the monk. It is by being capable of imagining the goal of his plan in advance, and foreseeing the reactions of the abbot, that the monk can mentally circumscribe and defeat the abbot.[20] As Panfilo will say at the end of the Tenth Day:

> 'Il senno de' mortali non consiste solamente nell'avere a memoria le cose preterite o conoscere le presenti, ma per l'una e per l'altra di queste sapere antiveder le future è da' solenni uomini senno grandissimo riputato.'
>
> (X, *Conclusione*, §2)

> [The wisdom of mortals does not consist entirely in having past things present to memory or knowing things present; rather, to know how to foresee future conditions by virtue of knowing past and present is reputed by serious men to be the greatest wisdom.]

In the tale, the monk's victory is represented in the spatial terms whose relevance we have established. Though enjoying the tide of his pleasure, the monk is yet able to hear the abbot's scuffling outside the cell – the reach of his sensitivity is wide. The abbot, on the other hand, must approach and listen in order to identify the voices. The monk, too, immediately goes to the peephole to spy on the abbot, while the abbot's curiosity and confusion of motive prevents him from acting. In having overheard the abbot's approach, and knowing the location of the *pertugio*, the monk demonstrates his superior keenness of sense and knowledge of his physical surroundings. When the monk does look through the peephole, he sees the abbot listening at the door. Having already outlistened the abbot while at a disadvantage, the monk is now in a position where he can see and not be seen. This moment of vision signifies a superior position of understanding; as Boccaccio puts it, the monk 'ben *comprese* l'abate aver potuto conoscere quella giovane esser nella sua cella' [comprehends that the abbot had been able to discover that the girl was in his cell (§8)]. The monk's comprehension, or *containment* of the abbot's awareness puts the monk in the position of dominance. Later in the tale, the monk, unseen, again sees the abbot. This time, however, the abbot is entering the monk's cell, where he will confront the girl:

> essendo nel dormentoro occultato, come vide l'abate solo nella sua cella entrare, così tutto rassicurato estimò il suo avviso dovere avere effetto, e veggendolo serrar dentro, l'ebbe per certissimo. (§19)

> [hidden in the dormitory, as soon as he saw the abbot enter his cell alone, he realized to his relief that his scheme would prevail; and seeing the abbot lock himself in, he counted it as certain.]

The monk's visual advantage throughout the tale is an expression of his superior insight and self-knowledge. The word for his plan to escape his own danger and catch the abbot – 'il suo *avviso*' (§19) – is closely related to words for sight and seeing (*viso, vedere*) and implies the mental foresight (*antiveder, avvedere, avveduto*) that guarantees the monk's victory. In actually witnessing and hearing the abbot's acts with the girl 'n'andò a un pertugio per lo quale ciò che l'abate fece o disse e udì e vide' [he went to a small hole in the wall through which he heard and saw what the abbot did and said (§20)]. The monk merely confirms his foreknowledge, his *antiveder*, and gives him the ocular proof he needs to show the abbot that he knows. His plan for trapping the abbot has a breadth and penetration, an apprehension of the goal, that contrast sharply with the abbot's ambivalence of purpose at the monk's door. Indeed, after the initial vacillations at the *uscio*, all of the abbot's permutations of behaviour, including his casuistical reasoning before the spectacle of the girl's beauty, are virtually foreseen by the monk. They are previously comprehended. The monk knows and sees – 'l'ebbe per certissimo' (§19) – inductively what the abbot will do under the circumstances. And he knows because he has previously learned the truth of 'la forza della natura' [the invincible goad of the flesh]. In Dioneo's mischievous little tale, the monk becomes clever by heeding the voices of the flesh.

Dioneo's narrative is thus pointedly subversive of the motives and self-knowledge of the abbot, as Schilling and Almansi have argued.[21] That the abbot vacillates in intention, that he bends when tried by the fire of temptation, that he is less clever and *avveduto* than his monk (though still shown to be *accorto uomo*, §22, when he wisely realizes he has been beaten) constitutes a kind of turning-upside-down of the hierarchy meant to obtain in a monastic community, where the abbot has the status of both lord and father – indeed, as Branca notes, the abbot in I.4 resonates with other ecclesiastical authoritative figures of the First Day, such as the Abbot of Cluny (I.7.1) and Pope Boniface VIII (I.1.7).[22] The hierarchy in question was crystallized for Benedictine monks in the *Rule*, or *Order* of St Benedict, to which the monk refers in the final scene with the abbot.

As we have seen, the tale stages the violation of the rule in its premiss, by granting the monk the right to protect his own body from punishment, and this trend is continued in the opening scene of the tale, in which the monk is found wandering alone outside the monastery.[23] A rule – if not the *Rule* – is mentioned explicitly when the monk presents the key of his cell to his abbot and requests permission (*licenza*) to exit the monastery. The monk's key makes explicit the presence of a specific rule, one which anticipates the monk's reference to the *Regula* itself at the end of the tale. The surrender of the key to the abbot is moreover a significant moment in the action of the tale. Mention of the key focuses the importance of the action that takes place in and near the cell door, the *uscio*, which is the site both of temptation and of allegory. The *Rule* itself allegorizes the space of pleasure and sin: 'cavendum ergo ideo malum desiderium, quia mors secum *introitus* dilectationis posita est' [evil desires are to be feared, because death is placed at the entrance to pleasure (Benedict 1958:56)]. At the same time, the presentation of the key to the abbot begins the monk's conscious manipulation of the abbot, and, as has been noted (O Cuilleanáin, *Religion and the Clergy* 101) as the first moment in the complicity of abbot and monk that emerges fully at the conclusion of the tale. In exchange for the dubious licence to exit the monastery, the monk confers with his key licence for the abbot to open the door of his concupiscence. The key is thus a fulcrum both for allusion to the *Rule* and its violation as well as for the references to allegorized locations (woods, cell) where the flesh is tempted.

The monk's allusion to the *Rule* points in fact to the source of much of Boccaccio's detail and narrative logic in the novella, and deepens the implications of its subversive celebration of nature. In the final scene of the tale, the monk, responding to the abbot's sentence of confinement, speaks in his own defence:

Il monaco prontissimamente rispose: 'Messere, io non sono ancor tanto all'Ordine di San Benedetto stato, che io possa avere ogni particularità di quello apparata; e voi ancora non m'avavate mostrato che' monaci si debban far dalle femine premiere come da' digiuni e dalle vigilie; ma ora che mostrato me l'avete, vi prometto, si questa mi perdonate, di mai più in ciò non peccare, anzi farò sempre come io a voi ho veduto fare.' (§21)

[The monk promptly answered: 'My lord, I have not been yet long enough in the order of St Benedict that I could have learned every detail of it; and you had hitherto not shown me that monks should allow themselves to be hard-pressed by women as they are by fasts and vigils. But now that you have shown me, I promise that if you forgive me this slip, I will in this respect sin no more, but do as I have seen you do.]

The monk scores numerous hits. He points to the abbot's defeat by the flesh, signified by his submission to the girl like horse to its rider, and he lets the abbot know that he knows it.[24] He points to the abbot's hypocrisy with a glancing allusion to the woman taken in adultery – 'Iam amplius noli peccare' [Go, and sin no more (John 8:11)] – in which Christ shows up the hypocrisy of her accusers. He also hints, with *priemere*, a verb that Boccaccio uses elsewhere in the *Decameron* with reference to older men squeezed dry of vital juices, that the abbot's erotic efforts are less than productive.[25] Most important, despite his disclaimer, the monk invokes the letter of the *Rule* itself: the abbot is to teach the monks, especially in difficult cases, with his example:

So that when one takes the name of abbot he should rule his followers with a double teaching; to wit, he should show them, more by deeds than by words, all that is good and holy (id est omnia bona et sancta factis amplius quam verbis ostendat). To apt monks he may present the Lord's directions verbally, while to the simpler and the hard of heart he must show the divine teachings in his actions (duris corde vero et simplicioribus factis suis divina praecepta mostrare). And all that his teaching has shown his monks to be contrary to God's law he should avoid in his own acts (in suis factis indicet non agenda).

(Benedict, *Regula* 28; translation mine)

For if it were otherwise, the text continues, then God would be able to tax the abbot with the charge of hypocrisy – in the words of scripture, with having noted the mote in his brother's eye while ignoring the beam in his own ('qui in fratris tui oculo festucam videbas, in tuo trabem non vidisti' [Luke 6:42]).

The charge to the abbot that he serve as an example to his monks by what they see him do, is the converse of the principle, also explicit in the *Rule*, that God and the abbot see and know what the monks are doing all the time (Benedict *Regula*, 56, 58, 60). In the life of Benedict written by Gregory in the second book of his *Dialogues*, Benedict is presented as virtually omniscient. In one episode Gregory narrates how a group of monks who had obtained food and drink from a woman are confronted by Benedict when they return quite late to the monastery. They deny having dined out. Benedict rounds on them:

> 'Why do you lie in this way? Did you not enter the dwelling of a certain woman (talis feminae habitaculum non intrastis)? Did you not accept such and such food (nunquid hos atque illos cibos non accepistis)?' When the venerable father had told them of the woman's hospitality, of the kind of food they ate, and of the number of their tipples, recognizing all the things in which they had failed, they threw themselves trembling at his feet, and confessed that they had sinned. He at once forgave their sins, instructing that they should do no further such in the absence of one whose presence to them in spirit they ought to realize (ipse autem protinus culpam pepercit, perpendens quod in eius absentia ultra non facerent, quem prasentem sibi esse in spiritus scirent).
>
> (Benedict, *Regula* 28; translation mine)

The passage speaks to the abbot's quick forgiveness of the monk in Boccaccio's tale. But in Dioneo's tale it is the monk who both sees the lapse⁻ of his abbot and sees into his heart ('In the desires of the flesh we believe that God is watching us' [Benedict, *Regula* 56]). Again, however, it is the monk who knows in advance what the abott will do when tempted. It is commanded in the *Rule* that the monk is to confess the hidden things in his heart to his abbot: 'If the cause of sin were hidden in the soul, let (the monk) manifest it to the abbot or older counsellors, to one who knows how to heal his and other's wounds without revealing them' (Benedict, *Regula* 134). In the tale, something different occurs. The monk precipitates the abbot's revelation of his lust, not to a spiritual counsellor but to the girl, and this confession, witnessed by the monk, cements a secret pact between abbot and monk: 'Peccato celato è mezzo perdonato.' Thus the term *aprire* (to open) is linked in the tale to the opening of the monk's cell: 'farsi aprire ... aprir la cella ... quella aprì e entrò e l'uscio richiuse [to have opened ... to open the cell ... she opened and entered and closed the door (§§7, 13, 14)], whose implications we have noted, to the unveiling of the abbot's lust ('a *aprirle* il suo desiderio pervenne' [he revealed (opened up) his desire to her [§18)] and to the monk's cognizance of the abbot's fall *'vide apertissimamente'* [he saw very openly/clearly (§8)].

The text of the *Rule* also illuminates the monk's final witticism and his more than *double entendre* on the word *priemere* (press, squeeze). As the monk implies with his reference to fasts and vigils (echoing Dioneo's beginning of the tale), the abbot's inferior position is a form of humility. Now the goal of Benedict's monk, and therefore in a sense the principle of the *Rule*, is the practice of humility. It is presented in the *Rule* as a sequence of steps, after the model of Jacob's ladder – the figure that is perhaps parodied in Boccaccio's use of the *gradus amoris* for the seductions of abbot and monk. At the beginning of his chapters on this ladder of humility, Benedict lays down the principle with a citation from Luke 14.11: everyone who exalts himself shall be humbled, and who humbles himself shall be exalted (Benedict, *Regula* 50). The third step teaches the monk to submit to his superiors ('se subdat maiori'); the fourth step has the monk patiently and quietly putting up with everything inflicted on him, from fasts to vigils. In the fifth step, Benedict quotes Psalm 65: 'You have laid tribulations on our backs' ('posuisti tribulationes in dorso nostro'). The goal, reached in the twelfth step, is to be totally humble, as in the words of Psalm 37: 'I am bowed down, and totally humbled' ('incurvatus sum et humiliatus' [Benedict, *Regula, 67*)].

To refocus the passages cited above on Dioneo's tale: the abbot, placing his dignified corpulence under the girl, becomes the visible exemplar of that prostration, that bowing down of the self recommended in the *Rule*. But it is not before fasts and vigils that he has bowed down, but, as the monk observes, before, and under, the weight of a *femmina*. The monk's and Dioneo's twisting of the monastic goal is clear here: they have humbled the abbot's presumption that he can resist the temptations of nature.[26] It is much the same lesson that Filippo il vecchio learns from Filippo il giovane in the Introduction to the Fourth Day: 'e sentì incontanente più aver di forza la natura che il suo ingegno' [and he immediately realized that nature had more strength than his ingenuity (IV. Introduzione, §29)].

Dioneo's parodic subversion of the *Rule* begins a trend in his tenure as a narrator. Although only three of his tales directly concern the religious (III.10; VI.10), all include elements of parody, proverbial and earthy wisdom, inversion of roles, the exuberance of youth, sexual action, a carnival or festival attitude, and the subversion of traditional authority, secular or sacred, that we notice in his first offering.[27] Dioneo narrates tales in which the carnival spirit of inversion and misrule, the assertion of the 'lower bodily stratum' as Bahktin has it, a Dionysian release and festivity that undoes or puts into question the usually more decorous fictions of the female narrators.[28] Victoria Kirkham has recently reiterated the identification of Dioneo with luxury and concupiscence in the exposition of the virtues and vices that she discerns within the *cornice* of the *Decameron*.[29] But the confinement of Dioneo to a type merely of *luxuria* seems excessively programmatic. His name is itself a set of possibilities: both Dioneo, from Dione; a name for Venus, hence venereal. But by another etymology Dioneo is Dionysian. In the *Comedia delle ninfe* (26, 82–4) Dioneo is the son of Bacchus and Ceres. To associate Dioneo with the proverbial results of bread and wine and with the god of intoxication is perhaps scarcely an improvement from the point of view of a moralizing reading of Boccaccio's text. Even in the early *Comedia delle ninfe*, however, Dioneo is joined with temperance (Adiona) in a dialectical union. Dioneo's multiple associations widen and enrichen the meanings Dioneo and his tales assume in the economy of the mature *Decameron*.

In his insistence on reversal, on pleasure, on laughter, Dioneo is the *Decameron*'s genius of play.[30] At the same time, his important roles in the whole collection, and the resemblance of his theme of natural Eros to the tale of Filippo il vecchio and il giovane, told by the narrator, suggest his resemblance to Boccaccio himself as *magister ludi*.[31]

It is precisely by virtue of his insistence on laughter and delight that Dioneo escapes the moral net, for the jab or bite in his parodic tales lies in the fact that they are less pornographic than funny. The sophisticated ironic laughter provoked by Dioneo is cerebral, a function of the reason, rather than prurient. The corrosiveness of laughter is as destructive to prurience as to prudery.[32] Like speech, laughter is proper to humankind, and thus inseparable from the *proprium* of reason. Dioneo, like a mysterious Orphic Renaissance Dionysus, functions ironically as a voice of reason, and never more than in the tale that he chooses to begin his tale-telling, where the insistence on the monk's youth and vigor attacks, in a manner thoroughly Aristotelian, the excesses of corporeal discipline in the monastic life.[33]

Dioneo's subversion of the theological hegemony over signification is cunning: like the monk, he well knows the psychological traps, the inner workings of the hypocritical and repressed mind.[34] As Baratto finely observes, Dioneo's (and Boccaccio's) phrasing for the moment when the monk is carried off by lechery points to the problematic contradiction in opposing morality and nature: 'fieramente assalito fu dalla concupiscenza carnale ...' [he was fiercely assailed by carnal concupiscence ... (§5)].[35] The use of the official terminology of disapprobation for the simple inevitability of nature is evidence of Dioneo's control and subversion of moralizing discourse. The gesture is repeated at the end of the tale, when the reader is told to confidently expect that the girl would return frequently to the monastery ('si dee credere' §22), presenting the newly acquired knowledge of the 'stimoli [cocenti] della carne' [burning stimuli of the flesh (§15)] as articles of faith, *quod credas*.[36] This shrewd irony is the rhetorical complement to the parodic structure of the plot and the allegorically charged physical setting of the *favola*. Dioneo's irony does not castigate the attractions and illusions of the flesh, but rather illuminates the hypocrisies of the spirit. Parody and irony are used to prise open and exploit for comic debunking the template of allegorical equivalences constructed in the text, so that the edifice of allegorical details – *uscio, pertugio, cella* – becomes a device for exposing the unavowed lust of the abbot, the father and pillar of the community.

But Dioneo's work is far from merely destructive. As the opening rounds of sparring with Pampinea suggest, it is part of a deliberate verbal therapeutic, a polemical and festive excess that self-consciously (and thus ironically) places itself against the dominant force of decorum, but is also reciprocally accepted and included by it.[37] With his initial challenge to Pampinea in the Introduction, and with the shift of subject he marks with his initial offering, Dioneo tempers the seriousness of the *brigata*'s mood; with his departure from the rule of narrative order in the second day, he tempers and complicates the principle of rule itself. It is worth recalling here Pampinea's invocation, early in the novella, of the reason why narrative is superior to gaming: it has no losers. By placing the altercation of flesh and spirit, and of earnest and game, at the level of discourse rather than action, the *brigata* establishes a society in which there can be no *divieto di consorzio* (*Purgatorio* 15.87), no prohibition of community. The opposition of ethical rules in ordinary life – monastic restriction, sexual license – are transcended in a higher law of discursive tolerance. In a transferred sense the *brigata*, like the Christians of the apostolic age, are freed from the old prohibitions because of a new law that acts within them, a law decreeing the innocence of discourse. For it is clear that the routines initiated by Pampinea mimic monastic rule: the narrators lead a communal existence requiring voluntary submission to a principal figure, they adopt fixed hours for meals and diversions, observe Friday for ablutions, and keep the Sabbath. Theirs is not the *opus Dei*, nor the office of psalms and prayers, but the oral narration of tales.[38] And as the cloister, the vestibule of heaven, exists in tension with, but for the sake of, the dangerous secular world, the narrative community of the *brigata* exists in tension with, and finally for the sake of, the human city beleaguered by the plague.[39]

NOTES

1 Almansi, *Writer As Liar*, 63, notes that the first tale is a novella, the next two parables, and the fourth the first fable or *favola* narrated, according to the division Boccaccio gives in Proemio §13.
2 Olson, *Literature As Recreation*, 177–83. See also 55–64 for discussion of literature as a means for attaining *gaudium temperatum*; and 205–11 for the *Decameron* as a book designed to create well-being. On the relation of therapies against the plague to therapies against the follies of love, see Mazzotta, *World at Play*, 28–35.
3 For Almansi, *Writer As Liar*, 64, Dioneo's linkage of his story to the previous tale, is 'an artificial and tenuous link.' Despite such lapses, Almansi's reading is useful in outlining the narrative ingenuity of the tale, and his conclusion that the tale's *combinatoire* succeeds in conveying 'a deft moral statement' is certainly right as far as it goes.
4 Padoan, *Il Boccaccio, le muse*, 33–5.
5 Branca, *Boccaccio medievale*, 135–7, 149–50, 153–64.
6 Saint Thomas Aquinas, *In X libros Ethicorum*, 25–6. Aquinas's gloss reads: 'Primo quidem dividendo bona humana in tria. Quorum quaedam sunt exteriora, sicut divitiae, honores et amici et alia huiusmodi; quaedam vero interiora; et haec rursus dividuntur in duo genera. Quia quaedam eorum pertinent ad corpora, sicut robur corporis, pulchritudo et sanitas. Quaedam vero pertinent ad animam, sicut scientia et virtus et alia hujusmodi ...' For the influence of Aristotle's *Ethics* on Boccaccio's views of play and human felicity, see Mazzotta, *World at Play*, 258–69.
7 Saint Benedict, *Regula*, 158, referring to the admission into the monastery: 'quippe qui ex illo die nec proprii corporis potestatem se habiturum scit' [for from that day he will have not even the power over his own body]. See also 110. Bernard Schilling, 'The Fat Abbot,' 21–7, brings up the *Rule* as a background for exposing the Abbot's hypocrisy.

8 See Dante Alighieri, *Opere minori*, 31–2, and ed. De Robertis's notes. Victoria
   Kirkham, in her important article on the narrators and their relation to the
   virtues and the appetites ('Allegorically Tempered *Decameron*), identifies
   Dioneo with the part of the soul that rules over the concupiscent appetite.
9 Dante Alighieri, *Opere minori*, 32. 'In quello punto lo spirito naturale, lo
   quale dimora in quella parte ove si ministra lo nutrimento nostro, cominciò
   a piangere, e piangendo disse queste parole: "Heu miser, quia frequenter
   impeditus ero deinceps"' [At that moment the natural spirit, which
   dwelleth there where our nourishment is administered, began to weep, and
   in weeping said these words: 'Heu miser, quia frequenter impeditus ero
   deinceps' (Woe is me! for that often I shall be disturbed from this time
   forth!). Trans. Dante Gabriel Rossetti, *The New Life of Dante Alighieri*, 32].
10 'un monaco giovane, il vigore del quale nè la freschezza nè i digiuni nè le
   vigilie potevano macerare' (§4). In Plato's myth of creation in the *Timaeus*, the
   framers of the human body place the natural spirit in the liver, far from the
   rational head, so that its noisy activities in feeding, etc., will not be heard in
   the higher regions (Plato, *Plato's Cosmology*, 286). Although the portion of
   Plato's dialogue containing this passage was not directly available to Boccaccio, the tradition of the three parts of the soul and the rationale of their sepa-
   ration was of course widely known and understood; see Aquinas, *Ethicorum
   ad Nicomachum*, 42–4, in *Aristotelis librum De anima commentarium*, 73.
11 For *acedia* and the noonday devil in monastic life and in medieval literature,
   see Agamben, *Stanze*, 5–14.
12 Dante of course refers to Proserpina as well; see *Purgatorio* 28.49–51. The
   parallel with *Purgatorio* 28 is noted by O Cuilleanáin, in *Religion and the
   Clergy*, 101.
13 Peter Lombard (Petri Lombardi), *Patrologia Latina* 198, col.342, is pithy:
   'mulier typus carnis, Adam rationis.'
14 Of course, not all traditions record that Adam fell at, or just after, noon; this
   was Dante's view, however, in *Paradiso* 26.141–2.
15 Kleinhenz, 'Stylistic Gravity,' 296, observes that there are nine terms for
   enclosures in the language of the novella; and O Cuilleanáin, *Religion and
   the Clergy*, 101, points out Boccaccio's skill in using the spatial opportunities
   of the monastery setting; Schilling, 'The Fat Abbot,' 27, notes that Benedict's *Rule* stresses that the monastery is self-contained.
16 See Henri d'Andeli, *Le lai d'Aristote*, verses 410–74 for this episode. One of
   the important early anthologies of Italian vernacular lyric poetry, the Banco
   Rari 217 or Laurenziano Rediano manuscript, uses as an illustration for one
   of Guittone d'Arezzo's *canzoni* an illustration of the figure of Amor mount-
   ing a lover in probable allusion to the *Lai d'Aristote*; see Moleta, 'Illumi-

nated *Canzoniere,*' 1–36. In his edition, Anthony Cassell discusses the
conventional misogyny of Boccaccio's *Corbaccio* (1975) and refers to
many of these topics. For a reading of this scene in the story that emphasizes the inversion of hierarchies, see O Cuilleanáin, *Religion and the Clergy,*
101.

17 The discussion of all the senses as extended dimensions of touch was common; see Aquinas, *In Aristotelis librum De anima,* 21, '... tactus est fundamentum omnium aliorum sensum: manifestum est enim, quod organum tactus
diffunditur per totum corpus, et quodlibet instrumentum cuiuscumque
sensus est etiam instrumentum tactus ...' Kleinhenz, 'Stylistic Gravity,' 293,
observes that the parts of the tale in which erotic attachment occurs (§§ 4–5,
14–15) employ the *cursus velox* to suggest the violent rapidity of lust.

18 Dante Alighieri, *Purgatorio 2: Commentary* by Charles Singleton, 434. See
Saint Gregory, *Patrologia Latina* 75, *Moralia,* pars prima, IV, xxvi, 47.

19 O Cuilleanáin, *Religion and the Clergy,* 101.

20 For a similar observation, see Baratto, *Realtà,* 232–3. Several of the manuscript illustrations of *Decameron* I.4 underline the importance of the monk's
visual comprehension of the abbot's activity. In the miniature by the Maître
de la Cité des Dames, on f. 20r of the Pal. Lat. 1989-A MS. in the Vatican
library published by Branca (Giovanni Boccaccio, *Boccaccio visualizzato,* 206,
and reproduced in color by Branca in Boccaccio, *Decameron: con le illustrazioni dell'autore e di grandi artisti,* 87), the two scenes of espial are juxtaposed, with that of the monk overseeing the abbot's submission to the
girl on the right: but where the abbot is shown in profile as he observes,
the monk is shown from behind, so that the reader's point of view is
made complicitous with that of the monk. (A similar image in MS. 5070
of the Bibliothèque de l'Arsenal in Paris, by Guillebert de Metz, slightly
attenuates the contrast by placing the monk in three-quarters profile; see
Decameron: 15th Century Manuscript, ed. E. Pognon, 15.) A similar relationship is suggested using different means in an unidentified, probably
Franco-Flemish image reproduced by Padoan in *L'Avventura,* 5. The miniature displays a visual space divided into four panels by colonnettes. In the
first two panels from left to right, the abbot, standing at a small square window, watches the monk disport himself in his cell; in the second two panels,
it is the monk who stands at a narrow opening in the door observing the
abbot surmounted by his partner. When the monk is viewed by the abbot,
we see his face peering in the small window, as if we, the readers, were in
the room with the monk; but when the monk gazes on the abbot, we are at
the monk's shoulder as he gazes through the *pertugio* at the abbot; here too
the reader shares in the monk's visual 'comprehension' of the abbott. The

xylograph from the De Gregori incunabulum (Venice, 1492), reproduced by Branca (Boccaccio *Decameron: con le illustrazioni*, 86), includes three scenes in one frame: the monk and the girl outside, in transgressive 'pastoral' space; then, on the left side of the cutaway building, the abbot listening at the monk's door while facing the reader; and, on the right, the monk in profile gazing on the abbot with the girl sitting on top of him: thus the monk is always in some respect external to the spaces inhabited by the abbot, ergo comprehensive of him. In Codex Ital. 63, f. 20v, in the Bibliothèque Nationale (anon. Florentine artist, 1427), published by Branca (*Boccaccio medievale*, pl. 25; also in colour in Boccaccio, *Decameron: con le illustrazioni*, 86) the monk's comprehension of the abbot is complete, as the monk is shown peering throught the *pertugio* or crack in the door at the abbot undergoing his compression; the two figures on the bed are entirely enclosed in the chamber, while the monk stands outside it in literally marginal space that is unruled and unbounded. This illustration also suggests, in the monk's bent-over posture as he gazes on his spiritual father, his incipient fulfilment of the order of the rule to submit to burdens that will be wittily affirmed at the end of the tale.

21 See, for this analysis, Schilling, 'The Fat Abbot,' 23–6; Almansi, *Writer as Liar*, 72, refers to the abbot as a type of *heautonapatoumenos*, a self-deceiver.

22 Branca, *Boccaccio medievale*, 94.

23 See Benedict, *Regula*: 'ut non sit necessitas monachis vagandi foris, quia omnino non expedit animabus eorum' [so that it be not necessary for the monks to wander outside, which is not at all good for their souls]. As Branca's note points out (Branca, *Decameron*, 1976, 1021) the monastery can be identified as Benedictine by the habit worn in Boccaccio's autograph illustration in the Hamilton 90 manuscript. There were two Benedictine foundations in the area of Lunigiana where Boccaccio sets his tale: the monastery of Montelungo, near Pontremoli, and the small Camaldolese priory of Santa Croce del Corvo, in the mountains above Lerici, notorious as the place where, according to Boccaccio (*Trattatello in laude di Dante*, 193), Dante met Frate Ilario and showed him a copy of the *Inferno*. Both the solitude of the location: 'in luogo assai solitario era' (§5) and the fact that the Priory declined and was abandoned by the 1360s, as is incipiently the case of the monastery in the novella: 'già di santità e di monaci più copioso che oggi non è' (§4) suggest that, as Branca claims, Santa Croce del Corvo is the place where the tale is set. See now also Branca, 'Due redazioni del *Decameron*,' 35–6. For possible implications of the association of the Priory with Dante, see Branca's notes 6, 7, 10, and 16.

24 Compare the self-reproaches of Calandrino, who thinks himself pregnant,

at having allowed his wife Tessa to straddle him (IX. 3. 21). Holloway ('Supposition and Supersession,' 49), in an effective critique of Tzvetan Todorov's (1969) obtuse and mechanical reading of the tale, points out the important witticism in the monk's word for the 'slip' or 'error' he will eschew in future ('mai più in ciò non peccare'): a witticism that reduces the concept of sin to that of imprudent choice of sexual position.

25 See *Decameron* II.10.40; IX.5.64.

26 The implication of the *Rule* in the abbot's 'humiliation' is pointed out by Schilling, 'The Fat Abbot,' 41. For an elaborate stylistic joke involving both the use of the solemn *cursus planus* for a superficially dignified effect, and the designation of the abbot's weight or *gravezza* [gravity], a term used amphibologically, see Kleinhenz, 'Stylistic Gravity,' 295.

27 Dioneo's tale for the bawdy third day (III.10), narrating the sexual athletics of an anchorite and his disciple, is closely related in theme and tone to our tale. For discussion of Dioneo's relation to popular bawdry and his complex dialectical relationship with Fiammetta in the *cornice*, see Smarr, *Boccaccio and Fiammetta*, 174–92. Emma Grimaldi has discussions of Dioneo in her full-length semiotic analysis of his narrative function, but her study breaks little new ground (see Grimaldi, *Il privilegio di Dioneo*, 21–6, 317–49).

28 This dimension of Dioneo's role has been brought out by Smarr, *Boccaccio and Fiammetta*, 189–90, and Mazzotta, *World at Play*, 232–4.

29 Kirkham, 'Allegorically Tempered *Decameron*,' 3.

30 Mazzotta, *World at Play*, 41, recalls Alanus de Insulis' genealogy in which Iocus – sport or play – is the bastard sprung from Venus and Antigenius.

31 Smarr, *Boccaccio and Fiammetta*, 189, notes that Dioneo tells the one tale set in Boccaccio's native town of Certaldo, but she downplays any special relation between Boccaccio and Dioneo. Branca, in 'Note' (*Decameron* 1976), 997, records that Boccaccio refers to himself in a letter to Petrarch (*Epistole* 2) as one befouled by Venus ('a Dyona spurcissimum dyoneum'). Since Boccaccio derives defects for himself from all the planets, the identification would not be significant except that it is the only one that coincides with a Decameronian narrator.

32 On the distancing effect of laughter, see Mazzotta, *World at Play*, 265–7. As Mazzotta points out (119), Dioneo's parody works in part because the veil required for moral allegory is structurally indistinguishable from the veil required for pornography; but it should be added that Dioneo's bawdy tales are also parodies of obscenity as much as of allegory. Smarr, *Boccaccio and Fiammetta*, 190–1, also stresses the distancing of Dioneo's words and tales from reality.

33 See Thomas Aquinas, *In X libros Ethicorum ad Nicomachum*, 48–9, for

Aristotle's fundamental point that both moral qualities and physical health are corrupted by excesses of any form.

34 See Smarr, *Boccaccio and Fiammetta*, 179–82 and 189–90, for remarks on Dioneo's self-control and self-conscious positions of antithesis with respect to the rest of the *brigata*.

35 Baratto, *Realtà*, 231.

36 Note Dioneo's repetition of this construction at VII.10.7, where it is used to describe what ought *not* to be believed.

37 As Mazzotta notes, Dioneo is himself preoccupied with order during the day that he rules, and his exception to the rule of tale-telling constitutes – a new rule. See Mazzotta, *World at Play*, 233.

38 For a view of Boccaccio's collection as determining an imaginative or literary space, see Mazzotta, *World at Play*, 266–9.

39 The theme of the brigata's narrative in opposition to the disintegration of the plague has been richly developed in recent criticism. See Mazzotta, *World at Play*, 40–6.

The Tale of the Marchioness of Monferrato (I.5)

DANTE DELLA TERZA

Pampinea, the queen of the day, asks Fiammetta to entertain her congenial audience, and Fiammetta, accepting the invitation, tells her story.
Her immediate predecessor has been Dioneo, the daring, thought-pro-
voking, slightly mischievous storyteller, who, beginning on the next
day, will be asked to seal the narrative itinerary with a story, the tenth,
predictably salacious, often brilliant, and intensely awaited by his
eager companions. The interrelationship between the tales of Dioneo
and Fiammetta can be seen to form a chiasmus. Dioneo's challenge of
the First Day is answered by Fiammetta: his is the story of a young
monk accused of sexual dalliance by an equally licentious, voyeuristic
abbot who is his rival for the attentions of a young girl; Fiammetta
responds with the chaste and dignified account of the marchioness of
Monferrato. When Fiammetta is queen in the Fifth Day, she recounts
the splendid and memorable episode of Federigo degli Alberighi and
is followed by Dioneo, who, true to his character, turns to marital infi-
delities and accommodations with the story of Pietro da Vinciolo.
Fiammetta's and Dioneo's tales are juxtaposed in each of the above-
mentioned cases, and, although in neither could one truthfully argue
that one novella represents a correction of the other, there are ways in
which impressions created in the audience by one tale carry over into
the following one, and these should not be overlooked.

At the opening of novella I.5 there persists the memory of the story
Dioneo just told in the positive response to it exhibited by the audience. The consensus and appreciation of the assembled group are
expressed in their controlled laughter and whispered pleasantries, a
sort of homage on their part to the authority of Fiammetta's predecessor as they prepare to hear the new speaker. It is, in a sense, like the

river evoked by Giambattista Vico's powerful imagination, which carries along some of the sweet taste of its waters well into the ocean that receives it.

The audience response to Dioneo's story, which has defied a code of narrative *bienséance* with its verbal permissiveness and daring allusions, is at first one of uneasiness. The young ladies blush appropriately (with 'onesto rossore' [an honest blush]). This is followed immediately by an almost open consensus, as the lady listeners come to terms with the enticing qualities of Dioneo's pleasurable innuendoes and accept the story wholeheartedly. The two moments presented in sequence, however, should not be understood to be sequential. Indeed, Boccaccio's syntagmatic approach to the reaction of the ladies is most interesting in its modernity. The opening of the novella with a past participle, *raccontata* [told] ('La novella da Dioneo *raccontata*,' §2, emphasis mine),[1] seems to imply that the audience's reaction of reticence was an afterthought, a conclusive event taking place when the story has already been told. The emphasis given to the act of listening – '[del]le donne ascoltanti' [of the listening women (§2)] – indicates, however, that the perception of 'prima' [before] (i.e., the telling of Dioneo's story) and 'dopo' [after] (i.e., after the audience's reactions) is deceptive, a pseudo-temporal representation of actions that were instead simultaneous, boldly interpenetrating one another. The gerund forms which follow the second temporal adverb, 'poi' [then] signal the description of a participatory emotion in its making: 'e *poi* quella, l'un l'altra guardando appena del ridere potendosi astenere, soghignando ascoltarono' [and *then*, looking at one another hardly able to keep from laughing, they smiled and listened to it (§2)]. The ladies are not trapped by lewd sexual innuendos which their education compels them to refuse; rather they are at once amused and slightly shocked, but their amusement quickly assumes the winning role since they scold Dioneo with friendly benevolence.[2]

When Fiammetta's turn to tell her story is formally announced, she does not show any particular willingness to react again to Dioneo's personal style, to his predilection for certain plots and developments. Her narrative purview turns rather to the common message conveyed by the clever responses that conclude the stories of all of her four predecessors; her inclination is, however, not to stress the beauty and the timeliness of the clever retorts per se, but rather their impressive power to transform human behaviour, their impact: 'mi piace noi essere entrati a dimostrare con le novelle quanta sia la *forza* delle belle e pronte risposte' [it pleases me that we have set out to demonstrate in our novellas the *power* of clever and prompt repartees (§4)]. She will align her own story with the established trend, coherent despite the narrative freedom of the First Day.

Fiammetta follows with an observation that directly concerns the event she is about to recount. While men, she says, are well advised to choose to love a lady of higher station, ladies should never transgress the boundaries of their social status by falling in love with a man of superior rank. This is certainly an allusion to a rule of social behavior codified by Andreas Capellanus in his *De Amore*, which is here quoted rather freely by Fiammetta.[3] In order to grasp the meaning of the message that Fiammetta brings to the attention of her audience, one should examine its formulation in Capellanus's text. In the *De Amore* a lady who is courted by a knight of greater nobility than she makes the following statement:

> mulier ait: etsi dictis rationibus ad vestrum forte me possetis amorem coartare, alia me ratio ab hac necessitate defendit, quia, etsi omnia nostris succederent amplexibus prospera, si illud vulgi deveniret ad aures, omnes aperte mea fama reprehensione confunderent, quasi ultra modum propriae naturae metas excesserim.

> [The lady says: let us suppose that you succeed and are able to win my love by the strength of your persuasiveness and compel me to comply with your desire, there is still good reason for me to resist your pleasurable suit. Even if we were happy in our acquired intimacy my reputation would be ruined by those who are always ready to accuse me of having gone beyond the proper limits imposed upon me by my birth.]

Fiammetta's declaration only in part follows the rules outlined by Capellanus. It is, for instance, quite obvious that Capellanus's dedication of his elaborate rules for the behavior of lovers to a noble young man named Gualterius, undoubtedly directs its appeal to a male suitor, encouraging him to learn the art of persuasion in order to overcome a lady's resistance, regardless of her rank. On the other hand, given the closeness of Boccaccio's formulation to that of Capellanus, it is possible to affirm that the principle stated by Fiammetta, according to which men can be allowed to fall in love with a lady of superior rank while women should be content within their own, will be seriously challenged only later, when bourgeois society will feel authorized to level, at men in particular, accusations of social climbing through marriage.[4] By choosing a story in which the protagonist is a woman, Fiammetta, without promoting any special social revolution, demonstrates an acute interest in winning from her female audience a form of consensus for what the marchioness says or does. Precisely what the marchioness says or does is offered as an example to be followed by Fiammetta's female audience. The Pampineas, the Neifiles, the Elissas, Filomenas and other ladies are able to appreciate fully the remarks of Capellanus's lady, a *plebeia*, and those of the marchioness regarding rank and women's options; this, despite the nobility of their blood (to which Boccaccio alludes in the introduction to the *Decameron*) and perhaps also because of it. The passage quoted from the *De Amore's* 'Loquitur nobilior plebeiae' is not meant to establish an equivalence between Andrea's reluctant *plebeia* – whom we would today call a bourgeoise – and the noble marchioness. This would be an error. However, it shows that the clever discourse with which the lady from Monferrato deflects the inappropriate advances of the king of France, is, paradoxically, in line with the self-effacing approach to love of Capellanus's *plebeia*.

The message of the marchioness's mimetic gesture is egalitarian. It makes the claim that there is something common to all women, that they share a characteristic that can be reduced to the following syllogism: all hens are equally palatable and interchangeable; women are comparable to hens; therefore, all women are equally palatable and interchangeable. There is nothing in me, the marchioness seems to imply, that you will not find in any other woman you might approach. The question to be asked is, however, the following: If the noble lady's speech, which devalues her highly boasted charm, is analogous to the *plebeia's* expression of concern precisely for the effect her amorous choices may have on public opinion, what could prompt her to undermine her well-deserved reputation as a woman of great beauty? What would make her adopt the strategy of retreat into self-effacing modesty?

The king of France gives her no choice. He adopts, and subsequently betrays, the chivalric convention to which Fiammetta refers at the beginning of her story. She explains that the action is set in motion by the irresistible attraction the king feels toward a distant lady, 'senza averla mai vista' [whom he has never seen (§7)]. It is the *amor de lonh* (distant love, lit., love from afar) so dramatically emphasized by Jauffre Rudel in his provençal *canzos*, '*No sap chantar qui so no di*':

Nuls hom no's meravill de mi
s'ieu am so que ja no' m veira
que 'l cor joi d'autr'amor non ha
mas de cela qu'ieu anc no vi.
Ben sai c'anc de lei no m jauzi
ni ja de mi no s jauzira
ni per son amie no m tenra
ni coven no 'm fera de si'.

[No one should be surprised / if I am in love with a lady who will never
see me. / My heart feels love / only for the lady I have not seen. / I am well
aware that I never enjoyed her company / neither will she enjoy mine. /
She will never consider me her lover / and will never allow me to see her
in private.][5]

Rudel's attitude posits a kind of transcendence of love: love is an
attraction towards the absolute, which is pursued through a spiritual
act of contemplation and renunciation. A French critic, Michel Henri
Bailet, in his study of the *Decameron*, cites another case, that of Gerbino
and the daughter of the king of Tunis (IV.4), both equally in love and
eager to bridge the geographic space separating them, to 'come close
enough to hear and see one another only to be in the next instant separated forever.'[6] The topos of Rudel's poetry (see also his poem 'Lon-
quan li jorn son lonc en may')[7] is disregarded by Gerbino, whose
passionate love longs for fulfilment, and this is perhaps the reason
which the story ends tragically.

In his first act the king of France follows appropriately the convention of *amor de lonh*. No sooner has a gallant and trustworthy knight of
his court praised the distant marchioness as 'bellissima e valorosa'
[most beautiful and worthy] than the king opens his heart to love: 'le
quali parole per sì fatta maniera nell'animo del re di Francia entrarono
che, senza averla mai veduta, di subito ferventemente la cominciò ad
amare' [These words made such a deep impression on the king's mind
that, without ever having seen the marchioness, he became at once fer-
vently enamored of her (§7)]. The ways and byways followed by the
king in his pursuit of the lady, however, represent in themselves a
transgression of the ideal motivation of the dreamlike attitude of *amor
de lonh*. He pretends that Monferrato is a necessary stop, unavoidable
for a Crusader like himself, who is on his way to the Holy Land. While
he is in Monferrato the lady will be the pleasurable object of his atten-

tions, but she will be soon forgotten, since he must leave for Genoa, the seaport from which he will sail to the land of the third Crusade, the destination to which duty leads him.

As regards the lady for whom the king longs, she appears divided between two allegiances. She has, on the one hand, a ceremonial duty to fulfil for which she must joyfully ('lietamente') receive the powerful king and entertain him out of the respect a member of the nobility owes to one of his rank. On the other hand, she must consider the dangers to her personal dignity and honesty that emerge from the situation that confronts her: 'e appresso entrò in pensiero che questo volesse dire, che uno così fatto re, non essendovi il marito di lei, la venisse a visitare' [she then came to wonder about the meaning of a kingly visit while her husband was far away (§9)].

In a sense both protagonists envision a twofold scenario which differs according to their different aims. The king has in mind a private, intimate encounter with the lady, and to this end sends most of his entourage directly to the seaport of Genoa, inviting only a carefully selected group of his closest associates to accompany him to Monferrato. The marchioness, given short notice of the visit by an emissary of the king, summons up the few remaining gentlemen who have not followed her husband to the Holy Land 'que' buoni uomini che rimasi vi erano' [the few gentlemen who had not left Monferrato (§10)] to advise her as she prepares her court for the solemn event of the king's visit. At the same time she proceeds to formulate, behind the kitchen door, a strategy of self-defence. The pomp and circumstance with which the king is welcomed and the quiet reserve behind which the marchioness builds the wall of her self-defence are important narrative strategies through which Boccaccio, more or less openly, makes the following points: (1) a king must be received in a manner befitting him; and (2) only when the rules of rank and *bienséance* are observed by the king's host is it possible for her to rebuke his illicit passion openly ('baldanzosamente'). In the lady's clever, albeit self-deprecating remark, women are compared to hens, with all due respect for the difference, of course, in 'ramage' and 'plumage.' A king who is incapable of distinguishing the attributes that make any woman substantially equal to any other human being of her own sex, shows little wit; but a king who must be reminded of it acts well below the dignity of his rank. In his pursuit of lady hens he is himself no more and no better than the rooster jokingly evoked in the question he puts to his beautiful interlocutor. Does the king of France have no other business to attend to? No other purpose in life?

But to return to the encounter of the two protagonists during the lavish dinner, there the marchioness appears to the king far more attractive than the knight's description had conveyed. The knight had mentioned only her great beauty and valor. Now another adjective as well, 'costumata' [gracious, of impeccable manners], is used to describe her. It broadens the spectrum, and the more complete portrait of the lady's beauty only increases the king's passion (Boccaccio, in the caption with which he prefaces the novella, defines this passion, with technical precision, as a 'folle amore').

We have considered the episode involving the king's surprise at being served only hens, though elegantly prepared and in countless dishes, and the lady's response to his query. We should not fail to note that the king's question is inspired by an *esprit gaulois*, since it is precisely the implied irony that furnishes the key to the lady's answer: 'Dama,' he says, 'Nascono in questo paese solamente galline senza gallo alcuno?' [Madam, are only hens born in these parts and not a single cock? §14)]. The noble lady considers the king's provocation a kind of blessing, since it offers her the opportunity to remind him of the responsibility of his position and of the mistaken assumption which has led him to undertake a misguided journey (in fact, a journey within a journey), and to pursue a devious goal while the Holy Land is at stake. By telling the story of the hens in the way she does, the marchioness paradoxically and ironically shows that in order to defend her virtue, a good greater by far than beauty, she must understate her beauty, hiding it in a cloud of indifference, and depict a world where, in spite of strictly formal differences, everyone looks like everyone else. The king learns his lesson and extinguishes the fire of a passion which does him no honor. The assertiveness of the lady, described by Boccaccio as 'baldanzosa' [daring], and the sudden departure of the king, are, as Michel Henri Bailet has put it, 'the result of a double rejection, both equally justified, of a superficial and transitory feeling.'[8] With his departure the king is, in a sense, saved from his caprice, but his salvation is left *in sordina*, so as to give full emphasis to the triumphal performance of the noble lady of Monferrato.

In order to arrive at the general meaning of the novella within the context of the *Decameron*, let us turn to some interpretations that have been suggested by its critics. The very useful bibliography which accompanies each novella in the notes to Vittore Branca's edition of the *Decameron* shows some stories to have been the target of constant critical attention, while others have been considered less significant or merely perfunctory. Some are considered more, some less central to an understanding of Boccaccio's involvement in the universe of his characters. For this novella, Branca mentions Bailet, whose few pages on it have been mentioned earlier; he cites two essays by C. Rovida (written between 1842 and 1852); a chapter of Licurgo Cappelletti's *Studi sul Decameron* (1880), dedicated entirely but hurriedly to the Arabic source of the story, an essay by André Pézard, 'Figures françaises dans le contes de Boccaccio,' (1948), and Giorgio Cavallini's treatment of the novella in his *Brevi studi stilistici e letterari* (1968).[9] One should add Olimpio Musso's 'Una leggenda monferrina nel Boccaccio (*Decameron* I.5'), and the consideration given to the novella in studies of the *Decameron* First Day by Marga Cottino-Jones (cited by Branca but apropos of the Introduction to the *Decameron*), Angelo Marchese, and Cok Van der Voort.[10] Not much really, if one takes into account the fact that only scanty remarks in the more general studies are dedicated to the tale of the marchioness. Van der Voort explores with useful precision and good sense ground which had been covered by previous critics. Branca, in his *Boccaccio medievale*, comparing the parallel structures of the First Day and the Sixth, finds the wit that seals the novellas of the First Day stories to be predominantly sarcastic and negative, while that of the Sixth Day stories is characterized by a productive assertiveness.[11]

The critical approach that seeks to transcend the barrier of the day to connect a novella with the spirit of the entire *Decameron* could serve us well here. We should consider if it is possible to characterize Fiammetta qua storyteller, taking into account the vertical line of the novellas Boccaccio attributes to her in his selective wisdom. They are the following:

Day I	novella 5 (marchioness of Monferrato and the king of France)
Day II	novella 5 (Andreuccio da Perugia)
Day III	novella 6 (Ricciardo Minutolo and Catella)
Day IV	novella 1 (Tancredi and Ghismonda)
Day V	novella 9 (Federigo degli Alberighi)
Day VI	novella 6 (Michele Scalza and the ugliness of the Baronci)
Day VII	novella 5 (jealous merchant from Rimini)
Day VIII	novella 8 (Sienese friends Spinelloccio and Zeppa)
Day IX	novella 5 (Calandrino and Niccolosa)
Day X	novella 6 (Charles of Anjou and the daughters of Neri degli Uberti).

The number five appears to predominate in the stories involving Fiammetta, and she is queen of Day Five.

If cities and regions involved in Fiammetta's narrative topography are many (Monferrato, Perugia, Naples, Naples again, Salerno, Florence, Florence again, Rimini, Siena, Florence, Castellammare di Stabia), many too are the attitudes her novellas present. Fiammetta is a mimetic narrator, who, while she can uphold the point of view of the great marchioness who denies her favours to the king of France, she can also present sympathetically the emotions of the Neapolitan seducer (III.6), who was right and did well to trick the naive Catella. In VII.5 she defends the deceit of the woman from Rimini, justifying her betrayal of a blindly jealous husband. *Chaque chose à sa place*. What is not allowed in the genteel milieu of Italian feudal society becomes legitimate in the phantasmagoric atmosphere of the Gulf of Naples. The king of France, Philippe le Borgne, must act like a king, as must Charles of Anjou when faced with his royal responsibilities, while Ricciardo Minutolo must follow his youthful whim and his own instincts in pursuing the favour of his beloved. 'In chiesa co' santi, in taverna coi ghiottoni [the church is for the pious, the tavern for the drunks].[12]

Besides endearing herself to the reader for telling the stories of Andreuccio da Perugia, Tancredi and Ghismonda, and Federigo degli Alberighi, among the most beautiful in the *Decameron*, Fiammetta is also the vehicle for the expression of some of Boccaccio's narrative concerns. It is she who tells us how to read Andreuccio's tale by stressing in her account the relationship between space (the operative ground of Andreuccio's movements in Naples) and time (the twenty-four hours within which the adventure takes place) – a suggestion which has been intelligently exploited by Giovanni Getto.[13] She offers us pertinent explanations of the implicit morality of each novella she tells, and it may be that remarks she makes elsewhere in the *Decameron* can help us understand some of the issues related to the story of the marchioness.

Critics of the novella have spared no effort in trying to identify the sources of the marchioness's response to the king of France. Domenico Comparetti, appropriately cited in Branca's notes, in 1865 pointed to *Il libro dei sette savi*, and his hypothesis was broadly developed and analysed in the 1880s by Stanislao Prato, Licurgo Cappelletti, Marcus Landau, and Gustav Gröber.[14] Yet something in a letter written on 21 January 1587 by Aldo Manuzio the Younger to Pietro Pisone Soazza deserves our serious consideration. Manuzio quotes a passage from the third book of Paolo Emilio Santorio's *Historiae Regni Neapolitani* (c.

1580) in which we find a response like the marchioness's regarding women and hens.[15] In Santorio's account Manfredi's step-sister, Siligaita, whom he is trying to seduce, remarks:

> Coena quam, frater, gustasti ex gallinarum carnibus universa fuit confecta; diversos et haud multum inter se dispares tulit sapores; re tamen ipsa, ex una omnes materia stetere: sic in Venere voluptates variae quidem quod ad cogitationem animorumque libidinem ceterum ex uno fonte potantur.[16]

> [The dinner you have just enjoyed, my brother, is all prepared with hen's meat. Very different are the flavors involved, basically, however, all derive from the same substance. The same happens with Venus's pleasures. They differ in the covetous imagination of those who thirst for them but who when they drink realize that they all derive from the same source.]

Neither Giovanni Villani in Book VI of his *Cronica*, where he discusses Manfredi, nor Fra Jacopo D'Acqui in his *Cronica imaginis mundi*, make any mention of Siligaita's story. It could therefore be argued that what we have is a later legend. Words spoken by Fiammetta in the sixth story of the Tenth Day support the hypothesis that the story of Siligaita and Manfredi is our source. When King Charles of Anjou plans to abduct the adolescent daughters of Neri degli Uberti, he is severely scolded by his friend and adviser Guy of Montfort: 'Ora evvi così tosto dalla memoria caduto le violenze fatte alle donne da Manfredi avervi l'entrata aperta in questo regno?' [Can you have so soon forgotten that it was Manfredi's abuse of (his subjects') women that opened the gates of his realm to you? (X.6.30)]. Since there is a strong similarity between King Philippe's dishonest passion and that of Charles of Anjou, and both stories are told by Fiammetta, the reference to Manfredi's violence against women in X.6 strongly suggests that the episode found by Manuzio in Santorio's history is the one that inspired the sentence uttered by the marchioness of Monferrato in Novella I.5.[17]

Fiammetta, in another story she tells, that of Calandrino and Niccolosa (IX.5), makes a comment that can help us resolve the debate concerning the historical verisimilitude of the episode of the marchioness. We know from the research of Olimpio Musso (in the article cited above) that Corrado degli Alemarici, the presumed husband of the marchioness, was a widower when he joined the Crusades and was not even a marquis, since his father, William the Elder, himself a Crusader, lived until late 1191. His wife, the highly respected Julia of Austria, was seventy years of age when Philippe le Borgne was only twenty-five. But Fiammetta tells us how to read the truth of Boccaccio's tales:

> Se io dalla verità mi fossi scostare voluta o volessi avrei ben saputo e saprei sotto altri nomi comporla e raccontarla; ma perciò che il partirsi dalla verità delle cose state nel novellare è gran diminuire di diletto negli intendenti, in propria forma dalla ragione sopra detta aiutata, la vi dirò. IX.5.5[18]

[I could easily have told it in some other way, using fictitious names, had I wished to do so, but since in departing from the truth of what actually happened, the storyteller greatly diminishes the pleasure of his listeners, I shall turn for support to my opening remarks and tell it in its proper form.]

For Boccaccio, the author, historical credibility is indispensable to the enjoyment of a story. The task of the author is to dismantle the diffidence of the reader, to reassure him that nothing has been faked. Only in this way is the reader prepared to enter the land of make-believe, where history – *was ist eigentlich gewesen* – and invention together contribute to poetic and narrative truth.

NOTES

This paper has been published in Italian in Dante Della Terza, *Tradizione ed esegesi. Semantica dell'innovazione da Agostino a DeSanctis* (Padua: Liviana, 1988), 29–42.

1 The emphasis here and in the following discussion of the text is mine.
2 As we know, the incipit of I.5 is repeated word for word in VI.8. There Filostrato has just told the daring story of Madonna Filippa from Prato, who, having been surprised by her husband Rinaldo de' Pugliesi in bed with her lover, Lazzarino, succeeds in justifying her behavior in an open court. The repetition of a given sentence only indicates Boccaccio's acquired habit of reducing to a rhetorical pattern of communicative normalcy what at the beginning had been a narrative and 'poetic' intuition: the repeated sentence becomes a reliable stylistic tool which can transmit the atmosphere of one novella to one that follows.

3 'Loquitur nobilior plebeiae' in *Andreas Capellanus, De Amore*, 56–63.

4 The same principle expressed by Fiammetta is found in an early sixteenth-century theatrical text, Cardinal Bibbiena's *Calandria* (cited by Branca). There are, in truth, other cases in Boccaccio's *Decameron* which seem to argue for greater freedom of aspirations on a woman's part: one would obviously begin with *Decameron* X.7, where a young bourgeoise émigrée, Lisa, the daughter of Bernardo Puccini, dares to fall in love with King Peter of Aragon and Sicily. But the event is of such an exceptional nature that the king himself grants her the right to be in love with him. This right *octroyé* is enforced by a ritual through which the king and the queen adopt her and choose a proper husband for her. The stated equality, on the other hand, in Castiglione's *Cortegiano*, between the court lady (*dama di palazzo*) and the male courtier, should be considered more an issue of her personality than of her rights.

5 Rudel, *Songs*, 1978.

6 's'approchent l'un de l'autre jusqu'à la portée de la voix et du regard pour être définitivement séparés l'instant d'après,' Bailet, *L'homme de verre*, 132.

7 'ma' no sai quoras la veyrai/ car trop son nostras terras lonh' [but I don't know when I will see her/ since our lands are so distant]. See also Rudel, *Songs*. The notion of *amor de lonh* in Boccaccio's minor works has been studied by Giuseppe Chiecchi in 'Narrativa, Amor de lonh,' (75–95).

8 Rudel, *Songs*, 166: 'le résultat d'un double refus également motivé envers un sentiment superficiel et passager.' For Bailet, see note 6 above.

9 Rovida, 'La novella V' and 'marchesana di Monferrato'; Cappelletti, *Studi sul Decamerone*; Pézard, 'Figures françaises'; and Cavallini, *Brevi studi*.

10 Musso, 'leggenda monferrina,' Cottino-Jones, 'Saggio di lettura,' 111–38, and see her *Order from Chaos*, 44–5; Marchese, 'Strutture narrative,' 237–86; and Van der Voort, 'Convergenze e divaricazioni.'

11 Branca, *Boccaccio medievale* [1956], 101–4.

12 If, instead of attempting to reconstruct the attitudes exhibited by a single narrator like Fiammetta or any of her companions, we turn our critical attention to Boccaccio's authorial omniscience, we will see that for him, in the enlightened and highly civilized atmosphere of Florence, only a fool like Calandrino could believe in the magic virtues of the heliotrope (VIII.3), but it becomes plausible in 'remote' Friuli for messer Ansaldo to ask a magician to create a beautiful May garden in the month of January for Madonna Dianora (X.5), or for messer Torello to fly on a magic carpet from a land of dream and make-believe to Pavia in the space of a single night (X.9).

13 Getto, *Vita di forme*, 78–94.

14 Comparetti, *Intorno al libro.* See also Prato, 'L'orma del leone'; Cappelletti, *Studi sul Decamerone*; Landau, *Die Quellen des Dekameron*; and Gröber, *Über die Quellen.*

15 Paolo Emilio Santorio (Caserta 1560–Urbino 1635), Bishop of Cosenza, then of Urbino, wrote the *Historiae regni neapolitani* around 1580. Manfredi, the natural son of Emperor Frederic II, after the death of his father, was for a while ruler of Naples and Sicily; Aldo Manuzio the Younger takes Manfredi's attempt to seduce his step-sister and her allusion to hens from Book III of the *Historiae* (A. Manuzio, *Lettere*, Rome 1572), 87.

16 Luigi Russo stresses the episode of Siligaita in *Novelle scelte del 'Decameron,'* 63n84.

17 Santorio and Boccaccio may both have learned the legend from separate sources. The allusion to Guido di Monforte in X.6 shows how well versed Boccaccio was in the history of Naples at the time of Manfredi.

18 Interesting remarks about the rhetoric of truthfulness included in Fiammetta's statement are to be found in Stewart's *Retorica*, 15–16. Stewart cites appropriately Cicero's *De Inventione* I, XXI, 29, where the relationship between truth and pleasurable *narratio* is explored.

The Tale of the Inquisitor (I.6)

JANET LEVARIE SMARR

It seems a bit odd to undertake to write at length about a three-page tale, especially a tale so apparently simple that very few people have discussed it at all apart from noting that it is one of the First Day's examples of vice.[1] But nothing by Boccaccio is ever as simple as it seems. The vice which this tale exemplifies and mocks has been variously described as hypocrisy or avarice; both are certainly involved. Boccaccio's own summary states succinctly: 'Confonde un valente uomo con un bel detto la malvagia ipocresia de' religiosi' [A worthy man confounds with a witty saying the malicious hypocrisy of the clergy (§1)]. But Emilia's opening line redefines the sin and changes the emphases in her slightly different summation: 'Né io altressi tacerò un morso dato da un valente uomo secolare a uno avaro religioso con un motto non meno da ridere che da commendare' [Nor will I refrain from speaking of a biting remark made by a worthy layman to an avaricious clergyman with a witticism as laughable as it is praiseworthy (§3)].

The story, very briefly, concerns a rich man who boasts to his friend that he has a wine so good that Christ would drink it. The Florentine inquisitor, more to milk than to emend the rich man, extorts large sums from him to avert a dangerous trial for blasphemy and orders the man to appear before him each day after Mass. Sitting at lunch with a number of other people, the inquisitor asks his victim about the contents of the Mass. One day the man replies that a statement during the service had made him feel sorry for the inquisitor and his fellow friars. The line from the evangelist (Matt. 19:29) was: 'Voi riceverete per ognuono cento e possederete la vita eterna' [You will receive a hundred for one and will possess eternal life (§12)]. Indicating the inquisitor's pseudo-charitable contribution of leftover broth to the poor, the man says he fears that the inquisitor will drown when he gets back a hundred for one in heaven. The laughter of those present prevents the inquisitor from acting out his anger, and he tells the victim he need not return.

Let us begin with the historical basis of this tale and then turn to its more literary qualities. It is the only tale of the First Day to be set in Florence. Girolamo Biscaro, in a long study appearing bit by bit in *Studi medievali* from 1929 to 1933, investigated the inquisitors of Florence in the early fourteenth century and found that Boccaccio's tale may have pointed to real events.[2] The Florentine inquisitors, who were Franciscans with their office at Santa Croce – the church at which our 'valente uomo' is required to attend Mass – had a well-established tradition of spending liberal sums on food and drink, as well as on cloth and clothing. The members at his lunch table might include lawyers and judges who were consulted on specific cases, visiting and local clergymen, notaries, armed bodyguards, and public officials. It was in the early 1320s that one inquisitor first hired a notary to handle the expenditure and intake of money, since as a Franciscan the inquisitor himself was forbidden to handle the stuff. Two inquisitors, however, far outdid the rest in abusing their office.

One inquisitor, Frate Mino da S. Quirico, who served from 1332 to 1333, imposed enormous fines for 'verba hereticalia' that had been said light-heartedly, spending the money from fines on fancy meats, excellent wines, and fruits of the best quality. When he went to Monticelli, he had a habit of lodging with the sisters of St Claire rather than in the male monastery, and he paid them for his lodgings, which included elegant dinners. Scandalous reports inevitably ensued. But the worst was that he routinely extorted large sums of money by threatening legal procedures against innocent persons and then granting them a judgment of innocence in exchange for what were termed gifts or the payment of legal expenses. Fra Mino also imposed disastrous penalties, which he then altered for a hefty price. He would hire false witnesses in order to bring charges against citizens wealthy enough to arouse his interest. Once an innocent victim had been condemned, those who had spoken on his behalf could then be accused of false witnessing, thus multiplying the profits of the case. Adding insult to injury, he would ask the victim to put the coins into a bag himself so that the Franciscan could keep his hands clean from touching money. Boccaccio refers mockingly (§9) to the 'grascia' [grease] with which the inquisitor had his hands rubbed to cure his avarice, and to the use of 'certi mezzani' [certain go-betweens] who brought this grease to the 'frati minori, che denari non osan toccare' [minor friars, who do not dare touch money]. As with crooks today, Fra Mino was finally caught and fired because his financial records did not reflect his expenditures in a credible manner. Biscaro suggests that this was the inquisitor of Boccaccio's tale.

He offers one other possibility, however, one favored by Luigi Russo: a Fra Pietro dall'Aquila, who became inquisitor in 1345.[3] Fra Pietro had worked some deals with Mino while the latter was in office, and was similarly described by witnesses as 'uomo di guadagno e per denaro molti cittadini aveva condannato per eretici quasi per nonnulla' [a man out for profit and who for money had condemned many citizens as heretics for the slightest causes]. In less than two years he had used his office to set aside for himself an enormous sum of wealth: roughly 7000 florins. The narrator, Emilia, does set the events of her tale 'non è ancora gran tempo, nella nostra città' [not long ago, in our city (§4)], but the 1330s and 1340s might qualify equally well. Branca, in his notes on the tale, accepts Biscaro's thesis that Boccaccio may have had either or even both these men in mind as he wrote this tale.[4] The fourteenth-century reader would be able to see the greedy inquisitor as a type or exemplum while at the same time having the fun of supplying possibile specific identities. Thus the tale can combine an apparent historical veracity with a careful vagueness that leaves the story open to multiple applications.

Baratto discusses the story as an example of 'narrazione commentata,' in which the narrator takes sides and comes to the aid of the underdog by way of an ironic or [caricatural style] 'stile caricaturale.'[5] Examples of that subtle kind of narratorial comment include the superlatives in describing how the inquisitor 'impetuosissimamente corse a formargli un processo gravissimo addosso' [ran most impetuously to bring a very serious case against him (§6)], and the antithetical phrases such as 'era non meno buono investigatore di chi piena aveva la borsa che di chi di scemo nella fede sentisse' [he was no less good an investigator of who had a plentiful purse than of who was lacking in faith (§4)]. These antitheses are more than a matter of sly style.

From the start of the narration, the text sets up a number of opposed terms and also a number of references both to the gospel of Matthew and to Dante. We have already seen in Emilia's opening summary the opposition between 'secolare' [layman] and 'religioso' [clergy], and in Boccaccio's summary the opposition between 'valente' [worthy] and 'malvagia ipocresia' [malicious hypocrisy]. Both words are involved in this last phrase, for the evil of 'malvagia' opposes the good of 'valente' but also the emptiness or falsity of 'ipocresia' opposes in a monetary sense the solid value of 'valente.' That monetary image will remain fundamental to the tale. Indeed, Emilia's second sentence balances the inquisitor's two concerns: 'era non meno buono investigatore di chi piena aveva la borsa che di chi scemo nella fede sentisse' [he was no less good an investigator of who had a plentiful purse than of who was lacking in faith (§4)]. Victoria Kirkham, suggesting that we identify the narrator, Emilia, with the virtue of faith, has pointed out that the balancing of coins and faith has a precedent in *Paradiso* 24.83–7,[6] where St Peter, examining Dante's faith, says:

> ... 'Assai bene e trascorsa
> d'esta moneta gia la lega e 'l peso;
> ma dimmi se tu l'hai ne la tua borsa.'
> Ond'io: 'Sì ho, sì lucida e sì tonda,
> che nel suo conio nulla mi s'inforsa.'

> ['very well have you discussed the alloy and weight of this money; but tell me whether you have it in your purse.' Whereupon I replied: 'Yes I have, so shiny and so round that nothing makes me doubt its coinage.']

Here we have not only a source for Emilia's balanced phrases, through the question of whether Dante has a full purse of faith, but also the theme of valid versus false coin which Alan Shoaf has so eloquently discussed in his book, *Dante, Chaucer, and the Currency of the Word* (1983), and which I have suggested is implicit in the contrast between 'valente' and 'ipocresia.' As his title manifests, the empty or redeemable value of money signifies also the emptiness or value of language, and the interpretation of phrases is an important theme in Boccaccio's tale, as we shall see. Emilia's sentence includes another pair of terms, 'piena' [full] and 'scemo' [lacking], which will have bearing not only on purses and faith but also on the issue of gluttony and feeding the hungry poor. Thus we have already within the first two sentences a network of connected themes which need to be explored.

Let us start with the pair, *money* and *faith*. The terms are paired repeatedly. The inquisitor acts, we are told, not for 'alleviamento di miscredenza ... ma empimento di fiorini' [the lessening of misbelief ... but the increasing of florins (§6)] and St. John Chrysostomos becomes, in a literal translation, 'San Giovanni Boccadoro,' adored by the inquisitor.[7] Having heard that the unnamed victim of this tale is a man of

large property holdings and a well-stuffed purse, the equally unnamed
inquisitor 'cum gladiis et fustibus impetuosissimamente corse a formargli un processo gravissimo addosso' [with swords and staves most
impetuously brought a very serious case against him (§6)]. The phrase
'cum gladiis et fustibus,' Branca informs us, had become a general
expression, but its source is the gospel of Matthew 26:47. This reference
to Matthew gains in potential importance because the witty saying
which climaxes the tale is also from that gospel. Looking up the original context of the phrase, which has retained its Latinity in Boccaccio's
discourse, we find that it pertains to the crowd which came to arrest
Christ in the same chapter where Judas, for a bag of coins, betrays his
master: 'And while he spake, lo, Judas, one of the twelve, came, and
with him a great multitude with swords and staves, from the chief of
priests and elders of the people.' This little phrase, then, implies that
the inquisitor is like Judas or that chief of priests, in stark contrast to
the rich man who, we are told, had spoken lightly 'non già per difetto
di fede' [not really from lack of faith (§5)]. Indeed the rich man
becomes analogous to Christ as victim of a trumped up arrest and trial,
and as victim of a man who, though he ought to be a follower of Christ,
is more interested in money. The inquisitor, in abusing his office for
monetary gain, is, like Judas, selling Christ anew. It is thus fitting that
the penalty imposed on his victim, after the threat of burning has been
transformed by a bribe, is 'una croce.' This means not a crucifixion, of
course, but a cross sewn on one's clothes, and with his typical concern
for appearances the inquisitor specifies its colors. Nonetheless, the
identification is reinforced by the final word of the tale as the narrators
laugh and approve of 'il nuovo avviso del crociato' (I.7.2) [the novel
remark of the man with the cross].

The selling of Christ is related to the sin of simony, and it is not surprising to find in Dante's *Inferno* 19 another piece of Boccaccio's story.
The same St Peter who examines Dante on faith in *Paradiso* 24 is
evoked in Dante's excoriation of the simonist popes. The individual
with whom Dante is speaking describes his hole in the rock as a 'borsa'
[purse] (72) into which he has been stuffed because he stuffed his purse
on earth. Earlier in the canto, Dante had compared the same hole to a
baptismal font (16–18). Thus again the image of money is set against
the image of faith. Dante, in disgust, says to this pope (112–14):

Fatto v'avete dio d'oro e d'argento;
e che altro è da voi a l'idolatre,
se non ch'elli uno, e voi ne orate cento?

[You have made for yourself a god of gold and silver; and what difference
is there between you and an idolator except that he prays to one god and
you to a hundred?]

Here is another echo of the hundred-for-one phrase from Matthew
19:29: 'And everyone that hath left houses, or brethren, or sisters, or
father, or mother, or children, or lands, for my name's sake, shall
receive a hundredfold and shall inherit eternal life.' The context of this
line is the story of a rich young man who asks Christ how he may be
saved and is perturbed to hear that he must give all he has to the poor
in order to win treasure in heaven. It is to Peter that Christ says the line
just quoted here. Dante's simonist, having inverted this command by
amassing money rather than giving it away, has now received a hundredfold what he did give; that is, by giving away God, he has found
himself with a hundred gods, the gold coins he adores. So too the leftover soup, the only thing the inquisitor is willing to give away, is what
will inundate him in the end, according to the witticism. It is humourously fitting that a wealthy man, presumably a merchant, should be
struck by and apply this calculation of what is basically a return on
investments.

Clearly, in investment terms, it would be better to give away money
than soup. Also contributing to the Dantean theme of faith as coin is
the reference at the end of *Purgatorio* 30 to Dante's tears of repentance
as a 'scotto,' or payment. Obviously the inquisitor's job should be to
exact this kind of payment from people for the good of their souls,
rather than to extort money.

Now we note that Dante's coins have, in Boccaccio's tale, turned
into soup. Indeed, images of food and drink play an important role
here as in the surrounding tales.[8] The preceeding story, as you recall,
tells how the Marchesana of Monferrato dissuades the King from trying to seduce her by serving him nothing but chicken and constructing a witticism about all chicken being the same no matter how it is
dressed. Tale I.7, the one following in this volume, recounts how Bergamino 'bites' the avarice of Cangrande della Scala by narrating how
Primasso ate his own three breads while waiting to observe the
rumoured hospitality of the abbot of Cligni. In three tales in a row,
then, the climactic 'motto' involves food. Just as tales four and five
deal with the lust of monks and then of a ruler, so tales 6 and 7 deal
with the avarice of a friar and then of a ruler.[9] The chicken of the first
of these tales is served up as a sign and not just as a meal. It clearly
represents women's flesh – the king asks whether there are only hens

and no rooster around – and thus also the sin of lust for the flesh. Is there any relation between the foods in tale six and the theme of avarice? If we read Boccaccio's line about the soup as a transformation of Dante's line about the simonists' gold, a connection does seem to be offered. Gold is what both simonists (Dante's and Boccaccio's) want to gain; leftover soup is the only sign of charity which the inquisitor is willing to make, and it is a false sign. Perhaps as well we should balance the leftover soup against the very good wine of the rich man who has no 'difetto di fede' [lack of faith]. The lighthearted sacrilege that even Christ would enjoy this wine possibly associates it with the communion wine which Christ offers us to drink. That wine is the true sign of God's charity towards us, while the inquisitor's broth is a caricature of charity.

The mealtime, with its gathering of people at table, is frequently a setting for Boccaccio's moments of public revelation. This particular tableful, however, offers us a further connection to Dante's *Paradiso* 24. The 'buono uomo' [good man] of our tale explains his ironic worry for the inquisitor thus: 'Poi che io usai qui, ho io ogni dì veduto dar qui di fuori a molta povera gente quando una e quando due grandissime caldaie di broda, la quale a' frati di questo convento e a voi si toglie, sì come soperchia, davanti; ...' [Since I have been coming here, I have seen every day given out from here to many poor folk sometimes one and sometimes two enormous cauldrons of broth, which is taken away as leftovers from you and the friars of this convent; ...] *Paradiso* 24 opens with Beatrice's prayer on behalf of Dante as follows:

'O sodalizio eletto a la gran cena
del benedetto Agnello, il qual vi ciba
sì, che la vostra voglia è sempre piena,
se per grazia di Dio questi preliba
di quel che cade de la vostra mensa,
prima che morte tempo li prescriba,
ponete mente a l'affezione immensa
e roratelo alquanto: voi bevete
sempre del fonte onde vien quel ch'ei pensa.'

[O company elected to the great meal of the blessed Lamb, who feeds you in such a way that your desire is always satisfied, if by the grace of God this man foretastes some of what falls from your table before death sets the time for him, give heed to his immense desire and bedew him somewhat: you drink forever from the fountain from which springs what he is thinking.]

The group of souls summoned to examine Dante's faith are compared to a group at dinner, and Dante is to be the poor hungry recipient of what falls from their table. By the last two lines of the prayer, the image is one of drink as well as food. The group at table has an endless supply of something to drink, and is asked to pass a bit down to Dante, 'roratelo.' Perhaps the image of drink raining down as dew directly onto Dante suggested to Boccaccio the flood of soup awaiting the friars.

In any case, sacramental and spiritual meanings are signified through physical images by Dante, reinforcing the possibility that Boccaccio's wine and soup represent something like true charity and hypocritical charity. The merchant boasting to his 'brigata' about his wine presumably wanted them to drink it so that they could confirm how good it is. The friars offer only what they themselves do not want. The mealtime of the inquisitor and his associates is an occasion that, while pretending to manifest his charity, manifests his greed. The gluttony involved historically in these dinners might well have been common knowledge in Boccaccio's day; and although the story does not specifically describe the meal, the quantity of soup left over suggests that there is much more than enough to eat. In any case, the mere presence of the victim of this friar's greed at the meal where the friar makes a show of charity brings home the hypocrisy involved. Indeed, Boccaccio explicitly links the broth to the theme of false show by referring to the inquisitor's 'brodaiuola ipocresia' [brothy hypocrisy (§20)]. One might compare this meal as the occasion of hypocritical charity to the meals in X.4 or V.9, which are the scenes of truly generous acts.

We might also recall that the simonists, as well as other frauds and illegitimate moneymakers, are in the *malebolge*, that is the part of hell most like the stomach. There the transformation of spiritual offices into cash is presented as the action of a perverse stomach in transforming the spiritually nourishing into the spiritually worthless. So too Boccaccio associates the inquisitor's simony with his false show of nourishing the poor and with his own physical self-nourishing at the expense of his soul. Apparently the inquisitor is eating a good lunch while the merchant is attending the required Mass. The parallel suggests that we consider which of the two is better nourished. The merchant's wine, insofar as it can be associated with Christ's communion wine, suggests – although of course without the merchant's slightest awareness – that physical food can be a sign of that which gives us spiritual life. The inquisitor, while handing out broth for the bodies of the poor, neglects their spiritual nourishment by his focus on materialism.

The issue of understanding things physically or spiritually is raised by the two acts of wilful misinterpretation that begin and end the tale. The merchant's claim 'se avere un vino si buono che ne berebbe Cristo' [that he had a wine so good that Christ would drink it (§5)] is taken inappropriately literally by the inquisitor: 'Dunque hai tu fatto Cristo bevitore e vago de' vini solenni, come se Egli fosse Cinciglione o alcuno altro di voi bevitori, ebriachi e tavernieri ...' [Then have you made Christ a drinker and lover of fine wines, as if He were Cinciglione or some other one of you drinkers, drunkards, and bartenders (§8)]. This wilfull literalness goes along with his treatment of the merchant, who we are told did not lack faith, 'quasi costui fosse stato Epicuro negante la eternita dell'anime' [as if this man were Epicurus denying the immortality of the soul (§9)]. The parallel between 'come se Egli fosse Cinciglione' [as if He were Cinciglione] and 'quasi costui fosse stato Epicuro' [as if this man were Epicurus] underlines the absurdity of the inquisitor's exaggeration. His greed, especially as it barters the duties of spiritual edification for mere money, more surely denies the immortality of the soul than the merchant's casual use of the name of Christ. It is the inquisitor's own literalness, however, which denies the spirit of the words. The satisfactoriness of the witticism as revenge comes from its equally intentionally inappropriate literality. Getting back a hundredfold what one has given becomes literally and physically taken to mean drowning in soup. Yet the merchant's words cut because everyone involved in the scene understands what they really mean in terms of the inquisitor's spiritual state, and that the 'malvagio stato che voi di là nell'altra vita dovrete avere' [evil state which you will have to have over there in the other life (§15)] will not be because of the soup but because of the greed which this one act of charity tries to mask. When we recall that Dante (in *Inferno* 20.3) names hell the realm of the 'sommersi' [submerged], we can see clearly that the inquisitor's drowning implies damnation. Indeed, in *Inferno* 8.52–3, Dante even says about one of the sinners in the Styx: 'molto sarei vago/ di vederlo attuffare in questa broda' [I would be very eager to see him immersed in this soup]. The verb 'confonde,' in Boccaccio's rubric, which by the fourteenth century meant to damn as well as to humiliate, confute, silence, or defeat, bears in its root the meaning of pouring liquid (the past participle 'confusus' refers to the mixing of liquids). Thus the merchant's act of confounding the inquisitor may also relate to the pouring of soup as an image of damnation. The merchant's 'compassione,' however, is a much more appropriate Christian response to a living sinner than the inquisitor's 'gladiis et fustibus.'

Both instances of interpretation within the tale reinforce Boccaccio's position in the defence and conclusion to the whole *Decameron*: that readers must be responsible for what they make of the language they hear or read. His own stories can be taken as bad counsel if 'e torte e tirate fieno a averlo' [they are twisted and stretched into having it (Conclusion §14)]. This discussion in the Conclusion even echoes a piece of our tale: Boccaccio's tales 'e nuocere e giovar possono, sì come possono tutte l'altre cose, avendo riguardo all'ascoltatore. Chi non sa ch'è il vino ottima cosa a' viventi, secondo Cinciglione e Scolaio e assai altri, e a colui che ha la febbre è nocivo? direm noi, per ciò che nuoce a' febricitanti, che sia malvagio?' [can both harm and help, as can all other things, depending on the hearer. Who does not know that wine is an excellent thing for the living, according to Cinciglione and Scolaio and many others, and yet is harmful to one who has a fever? Shall we say that because it harms the fevered it is bad? (Concl. §§8,9)] Cinciglione, named by the inquisitor in his twisted interpretation of our merchant's words, returns here to vindicate both the goodness of wine and the goodness of language, including Boccaccio's stories, when the interpreter makes spiritually proper use of them. The link reinforces our inference that the wine in our story, through its association with Christ and the distortion of meaning by the inquisitor, implied the possibility of spiritual nourishment and of a passing beyond the physical or literal to a spiritual understanding.

As this tale is told on *mercoledì* [Wednesday], or Mercury's day, the theme of interpretation, especially interpretation of a divine message in Scripture, is appropriate. The sixth tale on the other *mercoledì*, the tale of Giotto in the rain, similarly concerns – as I have argued elsewhere[10] – the relation of appearances to reality and of literal to spiritual interpretation. Both stories argue against a superficially literal reading of appearances on behalf of a further investigation into underlying truths.

Not only does Cinciglione find his way into Boccaccio's conclusion, but Boccaccio himself finds his way into our tale at hand. Almost an entire page of our three-page tale is spent in describing the 'grascia di san Giovanni Boccadoro' ([grease of Saint John Goldenmouth (§9ff)] as a most effective medicine for the avarice of clergy and friars, 'avvegna che Galieno non ne parli in alcuna parte delle sue medicine' [although Galieno does not mention it anywhere in his writings on medicine (§10)]. The saint's name is actually first given as 'Giovanni Barbadoro,' a reference, Branca suggests, to the beards of the friars; but it is then transmuted into 'Giovanni Boccadoro,' which is a closer translation of 'Chrysostomos.' Now, in the one tale of the day set in Florence, the name Giovanni Bocca surely evokes in us at least a passing thought of our author. His tale is also meant to be effective medicine for the avarice of churchmen.[11] Moreover, although the golden mouth is used in context to refer to the gold coins which the friars love, relating them perhaps to their love of spending the money on eating well, the original Saint Chrysostomos was so named because of his eloquence at preaching. Thus again Shoaf's association of coins with words proves applicable. Both are signs, and for both the issue is how we use them. The tale uses language to attack the control over language – over both what one may say and what one's words mean – asserted by the Inquisition.[12] Boccaccio's self-identification with the healing eloquence of a truly good ecclesiastic counters the attack against him, in the conclusion, of those who say 'che io abbia mala lingua e velenosa, per ciò che in alcun luogo scrivo il ver de' frati' [that I have a wicked and poisonous tongue because in some places I write the truth about friars (Concl. §25)]. He is telling us that he is not a Boccaccio but a Boccadoro, who speaks not malicious poison but nourishing truth.

NOTES

1 Even Cormac O Cuilleanáin, *Religion and the Clergy,* has remarkably little to say about it. Marga Cottino-Jones, 'Saggio di lettura,' 128–9, describing the tendency of the tales of Day One to produce a final harmony, indicates I.6 along with I.10 as cases where the wrongdoer is not transformed and improved, and therefore cases where the conflict between main characters remains imperfectly resolved.
2 Girolamo Biscaro, 'Inquisitori ed eretici a Firenze (1319–1334), *Studi medievali* n.s. 2 (1929): 347–75; 3 (1930): 266–87; 6 (1933): 161–207. This last portion is the most directly relevant.
3 Russo, *Letture Critiche,* 118. However, he also notes, p.119, the inquisitor's similarity to Falsembiante in the *Fiore,* who declares his method of frightening people with a threat of heresy trials in order to come to a financially rewarding agreement with them.

4 *Decameron*, ed. Vittore Branca, in vol. 4 of Giovanni Boccaccio, *Tutte le opere*, 1027.

5 Baratto, *Realtà*, 80 and 405–7, discusses the use of superlatives and antitheses in a rhetoric of caricature with which the narrator, clearly taking sides with the victim, continually comments on the events and characters.

6 Kirkham, 'Allegorically Tempered *Decameron*,' 1–23; also reprinted in her *Sign of Reason*, 131–72.

7 Branca's notes, 1028, point out this parodistic translation.

8 Capozzi, 'Food and Food Images,' 1–13, gives a good general introduction to this topic, though without specific reference to our tale.

9 Russo, *Letture critiche*, 115–17, comments that a group of tales on the first day share in the antihierarchical undermining of authorities: thus a usurer bests the Saladin, a monk his abbot, a marchesa her king, and a merchant the authority of the Inquisition. Russo therefore reads the tale as part of a broader attack against established powers rather than as specifically anti-clerical. Giuseppe Chiecchi 'Dolcemente Dissimulando,' xxvii, xxxii–iii, 27–8, and in a number of documents throughout his book (see p. 244 for the full list of references), observes that this was – not surprisingly – one of the tales which was simply eliminated altogether from the censored version of the *Decameron*, there being no imaginable way to modify it into anything acceptable to the Inquisition.

10 Smarr, *Boccaccio and Fiammetta*, 193–6.

11 Russo, *Letture critiche*, 119, suggests that Boccaccio is not interested in the satirical message as a social corrective but only as an amusing topos for his artistic elaboration. 'In Boccaccio, la satira è stata ammazzata come satira, nel suo scopo vendicativo o correttivo dei costumi, ed essa è diventata mero contenuto, uno spasso della fantasia dell'artista.' I find this distinction hard to make; but the argument is part of a larger critical debate about whether Boccaccio is emphasizing aesthetic values apart from moral and social values, or whether the latter remain important. In any case, Russo's suggestion seems to me to run counter to his own earlier comment on the tale's anti-authoritarianism.

12 Cazale-Berard, 'La strategia,' 23, cites I.6 as the prime example of the manipulation of language 'a dir i mali del mondo: un mondo dove signoreggiano gruppi o istituzioni fattisi abusivamente detentori della parola, e tra questi i più subdoli, gli "ipocriti religiosi."'

The Tale of Bergamino (I.7)

MICHELANGELO PICONE

The seventh story of the *Decameron*'s First Day features a man of the court, Bergamino, who in order to counteract the negative effects of a sudden change in his relationship with his lord, Can Grande della Scala, resorts to telling a story about Primas, the glorious forefather of the modern *fabulatores*. In Bergamino's tale, Primas, finding himself in difficult circumstances not unlike those of the storyteller, succeeds in having his worth as a man of letters recognized and rewarded by the Abbot of Cluny.

From this brief preliminary summary it is at once clear that the story of Bergamino and Can Grande reproduces in miniature the global structure of the book in which it appears. In other words, it repeats, in a *mise en abîme*, the central problematic of the *Decameron* as presented in the frame tale. Indeed, Bergamino is nothing other than the textual *imago* of the storyteller on duty, Filostrato, who in turn is one of the ten textual projections into which the book's single *auctor* splits himself. In like fashion Bergamino's situation reflects that state of historical disturbance which in the macrotext is figured by the plague. Finally, in both macrotext and microtext there emerges a single possibility of salvation, represented by the art of the word, the narrated story. The point of departure for both macrotext and microtext – the book and the novella – is thus the tale, with its mechanisms of production and reception. The thesis that the hundred tales want to prove, and the theme that our story intends to address, are therefore identical: both concern the process of artistic composition itself. In sum, we could say that *de se fabula narratur.*

This evident 'doubling' of the frame tale of Boccaccio's ten storytellers, which spills out of its confines in order to invade the space of the hundred tales, and the consequent reinforcement of the commentary function assigned to the frame tale, characterize not only the seventh tale but spread like tentacles over the entire First Day. This phenomenon confers special status on the day: it is one of the support columns (together with the last day and the book's central day, the sixth) of that classicized temple of medieval brief narrative that is the *Decameron*. Indeed, it is precisely this doubling that lends unity and homogeneity to the whole day, a day that in turn is destined to validate, not only theoretically but also practically, the literary code according to which the book is composed. The First Day is therefore meta-narrative par excellence. Beyond the story *within* the story, present in the third and seventh tales, we find above all, and with great rhetorical emphasis, the story *of* the story.

We must look to such formal unity, rather than to any affinities of content that critics have variously formulated, when seeking to analyse a specific novella of Day One. Our approach must consider each tale not as an independent text but as one that receives from its context – the day and the collection – the norms pertinent to its literary codification and its critical decodification.[1] When seen from a similar perspective, the seventh story, more than just an extravagant tale included in a narrative pot-pourri of short story types not catalogued in the other days, will appear as an 'archi-story': a tale occupying a diegetic range that is hierarchically superior to the others. Moreover, it comes in a day that, like the frame tale, represents the novellistic 'archi-genre,' the theoretical and practical reflection on the art of storytelling.

Therefore it seems opportune, before offering a direct reading of the novella, to make a few preliminary and general observations about the structure of the First Day of the *Decameron*. In attempting to clarify the day's distinctive traits, I shall make use of a fairly simple hermeneutic grid, inspired by logical-grammatical categories and by the semantic structure of the sentence. I shall begin by analysing the subject of the narrative (split into s/he who acts and s/he who suffers the consequences) and its social and cultural attributes. I shall then examine the predicate (the action carried out by the subject, from which the tale receives its superficial meaning) and its spatial-temporal details and qualifications. Finally, I shall attempt to explain the narrative's deepest cultural and artistic meaning, projecting it upon the background of both the literary tradition (the models involved, the 'sources') and the rhetorical technique (the new stylistic treatment to which old narrative models are subject).[2]

In its choice of agents, the First Day of the *Decameron* offers a vast cross-section of medieval society, following a model already established by the *Novellino*.[3] At the top of the social pyramid we find great historical characters: kings, noblemen, knights, all representatives of the order of the *bellatores*. Among the kings, the figure most emblematic of courtly values is surely that of Saladin (I.3), followed by King Phillip of France (I.5), the chivalric protagonist (together with Richard the Lionhearted) of the Third Crusade. In contrast to these figures we have the degenerate king of Cyprus, Guido di Lusignano (I.9). On a level just below this are feudal lords like Can Grande della Scala (I.7), gentlemen like Ermino de' Grimaldi (I.8), and great prelates like the Abbot of Cluny (I.7). The parallel world of the 'ladies of old,' the grandes dames, includes the marchioness of Monferrato (I.5) and the 'noble lady of Gascony' (I.9).

At the extreme opposite end of the social spectrum appear characters belonging to the order of the *laboratores*, within which a position of absolute emphasis and prestige is reserved for the merchants and bankers, who are raised to a level of near parity with the exponents of the upper classes. Significant in this regard are the cases of Melchisedech, who compares favorably with the great Saladin (I.3), or of Abraham the Jew, who exhibits a subtle and sophisticated mode of reasoning (I.2). Among the generalized bourgeois class are both the wealthy citizen who is the object of the religious hypocrite's inquisition (I.6), and madonna Malgherida dei Ghisolieri, maestro Alberto's object of desire (I.10). The low clergy receive conspicuous representation as well, from Ciappelletto's friar confessor (I.1) to the two monks of Lunigiana (I.4) and the Florentine inquisitor (I.6).

The group that receives the author's greatest attention, and that serves as a fulcrum between the upper class as custodian of political and religious institutions and the lower class as custodian of economic institutions, is certainly that of the *oratores*. Here we have, on the one hand, exponents of the mechanical *artes*, such as notaries (Ciappelletto, I.1) and doctors (maestro Alberto, I.10); and on the other, scholars of the liberal *artes*, goliardic men of letters like Primas (I.7), or men of the court like Bergamino (I.7) and Guiglielmo Borsiere (I.8). To this latter category is entrusted the capital task of setting forth the book's cultural genealogy, reflecting in the work the very image of its author, the man of letters who lives proudly on and for his intellectual labour.

This summary description of the agents of the Day One tales readily shows how the rigid barriers that traditionally distinguish the various social levels are progressively weakening. Not only is there some mobility between one level and another, but the new social order foreseen by Boccaccio finds its balance precisely in the median category of the *oratores*. In other words, this class is founded on the new intellectuals, who, endowed with the ornate and effective word, make use of it in order to affect historical reality decisively. They not only transform reality but overturn it, making it more consonant with that image of the earthly Paradise that so embellishes the book's narrative frame.

Beyond the moral silence symbolized by the plague, then, the culture of the word offers itself as the only one capable of overcoming social distinctions, as humanity's only remaining possibility for salvation. In opposition to the great historical equalizer that is Death there comes the other essential force of cultural homogenization, the Word. From the *Decameron*'s very first pages Boccaccio leaves no doubt that his protagonists are those holding the power of the word, against whom the keepers of other powers – political, religious, and economic – will struggle in vain. In reality, the antagonists of the Day One stories, who for the most part belong to the upper classes and therefore represent a condition of hereditary privilege, are irremediably defeated and/or completely seduced by the verbal art displayed by the protagonists, representatives of the new intellectual aristocracy, to the formation and affirmation of which Boccaccio makes a decisive contribution.[4] With respect to the exemplum and the hagiographic tale, the *Decameron* novella thus presents a radical inversion. Its heroes are no longer people of preconstituted and uncontestable authority, but men and women who assert themselves in history exclusively by virtue of their ability to fix the reality of the moment in an appropriate linguistic formulation, to crystallize the factum in the dictum, the event in the *motto*, or clever remark.

The protagonist/antagonist opposition quickly emerges in the rubric, where the hero is the grammatical subject and the first element of the sentence.[5] In this representation of the characters, the thematic content of their actions is announced at once, and it too is synthetically emphasized in the rubric. In effect, all the actions taken by the characters concern verbal communication: we always witness speech acts transmitted by the protagonist to his or her antagonist. Thus in the course of this First Day in the cultural reconstruction of the world, we move from acts related to divinity and faith, like the evil-doer's antiphrastic confession in the first novella and the *a contrario* conversion of the Jew in the second, to acts exclusive to the human sphere. First, there are those pertaining to a situation of factual contrast, like the story that eliminates a great danger in the third novella, or the 'healthy malice' devised by the monk in the fourth. Then there are those concerning a primarily verbal defensive situation: the facetious remark of the noblewoman who annuls a royal privilege (I.5); the comic response of the bourgeois man who unmasks religious hypocrisy (I.6); the story told about the man of the court in order to castigate his lord's sudden forgetfulness (I.7); the witticism that attacks the gentleman's congenital avarice (I.8); the remark that flogs the king's habitual baseness (I.9); and finally the witty response that refutes the topical association of love with youth (I.10).

As is evident, the day's narrative progression tends towards the unconditional affirmation of the *homo loquens*, exalting an ideal of *humanitas* that can be achieved through full possession and total control of the art of rhetoric. If, indeed, one theme runs through this apparently themeless day, we can locate it precisely in the presence of the liberating and exalting word. The protagonist can modify the chain of events, overcome the obstacles erected by the antagonist, only through the illusionistic transformation of historical reality carried out by means of the clever word, the witticism.

The clever reproach succeeds, in sum, by highlighting a reality that differs from the sensory one, a reality more brilliant and attractive than actual experience. Symptomatic in this regard is the carnivalesque distortion of factual truth achieved in Ciappelletto's confession. The mystificatory *inventio* of 'San Ciappelletto' is an extreme metaphor for the objective most pursued in the book: artistic truth. Such an illusory reality, evoked magically by the word, annuls the negative effects of the contingency of human events, infusing them with a glimmer of eternity. If we then pass from the microtextual to the macrotextual level, we understand how the *Decameron* novella, perfect realization of the art of the word, aspires to curb the catastrophic effects of the plague on the decayed and corrupt city while it reveals the true city of man that it intends to restore in the distance.

These thematic choices appear therefore to be motivated by a profound meta-narrative need: to develop a theoretical discourse about the meaning of literature. The selection of places and times for the stories seems to be perfectly congruent with such an intention. One fact that critics have not yet sufficiently noted and explained, for example, is that the curtain of the *Decameron* rises on Paris. This vector, pointed immediately in the first two stories at Paris and at France, cannot be considered accidental. Rather, it may be taken to reflect the right of primogeniture that the literature in *langue d'oïl* exercises with regard to all the other Romance literatures in the field of brief narrative. Moreover, Ciappelletto is a Tuscan transplanted to Paris (interestingly, this projects an inverted image of the mythic one that the *auctor* wants to leave of himself), and Abraham the Jew goes from Paris to Rome in order to receive there – albeit in a completely unpredictable way – the revelation that will transform his life. These movements may allude to a passage, a real *translatio studii*, of the art of the tale from its land of origin, France, to its new home, Italy. We should therefore no longer be surprised that Boccaccio locates the day's central story, the sixth, in Florence, thus making that city the gravitational centre of these cultural translocations, the *locus* where the renewal of the art of the tale is about to occur. This same criterion explains the choice of the other places: first and foremost the Orient (I.3 and I.9), the Eden of the story inserted in a frame. There appear as well the three most prestigious feudal courts of north-central Italy, places of refuge for the troubadoric diaspora and ports of entry for the narrative *matière* in *langue d'oïl*: Lunigiana (I.4), Monferrato (I.5), and Verona (I.7). Finally, there are Genoa (I.8), a city bordering on France and the embarkation point towards the East, and Bologna (I.10), the new Italian *patria studiorum* capable of competing with the old Parisian seat.

Analogous requirements seem to govern the structuring of the temporal dimension as well, with the same fundamental needs of meta-narrative projection of the recounted events at work. With the exception of stories four and six, whose penury of historical information may be attributed to their greater proximity to the models, respectively, of the *fabliau* and the homiletic tale, all the other stories furnish ample historical documentation along with the names of the characters. However, such information fulfils exclusively literary requirements. The artistic construction of a tale must be articulated through semiotic processes characterized by a high level of allusiveness, both literary (consider the continuous involvement of the great cultural code represented by Dante's *Commedia*) and linguistic (consider the use of the technique of *interpretatio nominis*). More precisely, we can point out at least three temporal typologies in this day. First of all, some stories (I.3, I.5, I.9, plus the novella inserted into I.7) take place in a mythic past, between the end of the twelfth century and the beginning of the thirteenth. This legendary time saw the triumph of that great courtly civilization of 'ladies and knights of old' that is nostalgically recalled throughout the *Decameron*, during which period there arose the great myths of love and adventure that Boccaccio now intends to transcribe, albeit in a modernized and more bourgeois version.

Other tales (I.1, I.7, I.8, and almost certainly also I.4)[6] lie in a past that one may call historical, between the end of the thirteenth and the beginning of the fourteenth centuries. This is the epoch dominated by the gigantic figure of Dante, tutelary deity of the entire *Decameron*, the *auctor* to whom Boccaccio continually compares himself but from whom he also intends to distinguish himself. The other tales (I.2, I.6, I.10) take place in the near past, in a time closer to that of the ten story-tellers. In contrast to the absolute exemplarity of the two other temporal dimensions, this third one is largely ambivalent. On the one hand it is negative, since it appears to be marked by total moral decay: its symbol is the plague. On the other hand, however, that era is positive too, since it contains the seeds of regeneration, the desire to restore the perfection typical of the earlier heroic epochs; the symbol of such palingenetic tension is the *lieta brigata* [happy band] itself.

In my observations up until now I have often referred to the literary models that informed the composition of the *Decameron*. I shall now attempt to offer a synthetic outline of the 'sources' of the First Day, making use of research that has already been undertaken in this field. The sequence of the ten stories appears to reflect a precise need to represent the great genres of medieval narrative, coupled with the need for hierarchical and even historiographic ordering of the narrative materials themselves. In fact, it is significant that the first story parodically rewrites the oldest and most prestigious genre of the medieval *narratio brevis*, the *vitae sanctorum*, while the next two tales relate to that other capital Middle Latin experience, the exemplum. Similarly, the fourth novella imitates the *langue d'oïl* narrative genre with which vernacular literature had reached one of its most innovative heights: the *fabliau*. The fifth novella recalls the very archetype of the book of stories inserted in a frame: the *Book of Sindbad*, surely known to Boccaccio in Johannes de Alta Silva's Latin translation entitled *Dolopathos* (a title based on Greek, as is the *Decameron*).

To these remote models for the first five stories there correspond other models, closer both historically and geographically, that shape the next five. The *Novellino* appears as a direct source in the ninth story but also as one of the prototypes for the seventh (as well as the third). Present too is the genre of the narrative gloss on the *Commedia*, with which Boccaccio will experiment in the late *Esposizioni*, implicit here in the composition of the eighth novella. Finally, there is that stylistically most perfect model of narrative prose, the spiritual and cultural Bildungsroman of the most admired Italian *auctor*, Dante, if one reads the tenth novella (as I do) as representing the ironic reversal of the young Dante's elitist amorous *quête* in the *Vita nuova*, which becomes the democratic erotic adventure of the elderly maestro Alberto.

The best and most careful critics have already demonstrated, amply and exhaustively, how Boccaccio rewrites these models in the *Decameron*, following an extensive process of irony and parody.[7] However, one should also note that this day contains some theoretical statements concerning the articulation of the narrative message, along with discussions of the personality of the sender of such a message. Pampinea's long preamble to the tenth novella (I.10.3–8), not coincidentally repeated almost to the letter in the meta-novella of madonna Oretta (VI.1), offers a complete technical treatment of the uses of the witty remark, thereby articulating a genuine poetics *in nuce* of the novella genre. Furthermore, Lauretta's harsh tirade, contained in the eighth novella (I.8.7–10) and directed against those degenerate men of modern courts, constitutes a defence of the ethical-aesthetic conception of literature that governs Boccaccio's work. Moreover, it argues that the man of letters must assume a more active role in his daily life experience, thus conceptualizing an ideal figure of the man of the court that positions him between Dante's Marco Lombardo and the Renaissance courtier.

Having detailed the context and the characteristic traits of the First Day, I shall now move to a reading of the seventh novella. The tale's theme involves the condition and function of the man of letters, here personified by Bergamino. In other words, the story seeks to describe the life and work of the *fabulator* while simultaneously answering a series of questions about his civil and social status, among them: Who is he? How does he live? What are his aspirations? What are his duties? What are his difficulties? Who are his allies and his adversaries? At the same time, the novella is concerned with the other pole of communication, the public, here reduced to a single but exceptional representative: Can Grande della Scala. In addition to examining the effect that an optimal deciphering of the message may exercise on human and social relations, the main focus of interest goes to the decodification of the message sent by the *fabulator*. Finally, the novella develops an in-depth reflection on the message itself. Not only does it pass judgment on the rhetorical technique used to formulate the message, it also offers an exceptional practical example in the inserted story of Primas.

Such an unfolding of linguistic, rhetorical, and literary competence leads to the clearing of an impasse that has suddenly arisen between the sender and the receiver of the message, an impasse caused by the missing production/reception of the message itself. It is in fact the refined proof of narrative ability offered by Bergamino (through the paradigmatic exemplum of Primas) that repairs the momentarily broken relations between the man of letters and his lord, just as the novella of Bergamino, told by Filostrato, allows the storyteller (and the *lieta brigata*) to outflank the mortal danger of the plague; and just as the frame-tale involving Filostrato (and of the *brigata*), written by Boccaccio, brings *salus* to ladies afflicted by amorous melancholy. We thus face an infinite duplication of narrative discourse, the application of a game of literary mirrors that modern criticism (from Gide on) has referred to as *mise en abîme*.[8] Bergamino's practical demonstration of oratorical and rhetorical abilities and the theoretical musing about the methods and limits of the *ars narrandi* arise from a single motivating factor. They wish to recount the story *of* the story before the story *in* the story, to sketch on the one hand the profile of an ideal author and reader, and to elaborate an implicit poetics of narrative *inventio* and *elocutio* on the other. The tale opens with the exaltation of the character of 'messer Cane della Scala,' a figure belonging to the history of great men, but even more to high literature.[9] The Can Grande/Bergamino pair alludes in fact to another couple, mimicking a far more decisive and dramatic relationship in the history of Italian letters, the one between Can Grande and Dante Alighieri.[10] Not by chance Boccaccio's *descriptio* of this character is finely embroidered with echoes of Dante's *Commedia*:

'Sì come chiarissima fama quasi per tutto il mondo suona, messer Can della Scala, al quale in assai cose fu favorevole la fortuna, fu uno de' più notabili e de' più magnifichi signori che dallo imperadore Federigo secondo in qua si sapesse in Italia' (I.7.5)

[As his brilliant fame throughout almost all the world attests, messer Can della Scala, whom fortune favoured in a great many ways, was one of the most noteworthy and magnificent lords known in Italy from the time of the emperor Frederick II until the present day.]

In this tale Boccaccio represents as fulfilled the *ante eventum* prophecy that Dante had hazarded about the glorious future of his patron, Can Grande:

'notabil fien l'opere sue /... / parran faville de la sua virtute /.../ Le sue
magnificenze conosciute / saranno ancora ... /... e disse cose / incredibili
a quei che fien presente' (*Paradiso* 17.78–93)

[notable shall his achievements be/ ... / some sparkles of his virtue shall
appear / ... / so recognized shall his magnificence become hereafter / ... /
... and things said he / incredible to those who shall be present (Trans.
Longfellow)]

Boccaccio in fact intends to offer a concrete example of the lord of
Verona's 'magnificence,' as already announced in the Dantean text,
and thus to sustain through a novella the *Commedia*'s epic praise. In
other words, Boccaccio wants to give us a tangible sign of those good
deeds that the famous Florentine exile, prototype of the man of letters,
enjoyed thanks to the 'cortesia del gran Lombardo' [courtesy of the
great Lombard, *Paradiso* 17.71)]; he aspires to offer the detailed scenario
of an 'incredible' act or gesture by Can Grande.[11]

The background against which Can Grande carries out his act of
courtesy is the topical one of the court, represented at the height of
its worldly splendor, in the moment when it gives life to the complex
ceremonial of the 'festa' or festival:

Il quale, avendo disposto di fare una notabile e maravigliosa festa in
Verona, e a quella molta gente e di varie parti fosse venuta e massimamente
uomini di corte d'ogni maniera, subito, qual che la cagion fosse, da ciò si
ritrasse, e in parte provedette coloro che venuti v'erano e licenziolli. (§6)

[Having decided to hold a noteworthy and wonderful festival in Verona,
many people having arrived from a variety of places, mostly men of the
court of every type, he suddenly, for some reason, cancelled it, and he
provided in part for those who had come and sent them off.]

The festival is in reality the most propitious occasion for the man of the
court to show off, to unfurl his artistic repertoire and prove his oratorical abilities.[12] At its conclusion the lord who has organized the festival
will compensate the performer in proportion to his merits and his
fame, and according to the amount of pleasure the lord has received. In
this particular case, however, for reasons that are not given, Can
Grande cancels the festival at the last minute. This nevertheless does
not stop him, as a magnanimous and liberal lord, from rewarding 'in

part' all the performers who have shown up, giving them permission, *licenza*, to leave the court.

This sudden change in the program of the festivities leads to the much more profound alteration of personal relations between Can Grande and Bergamino:

'Solo uno, chiamato Bergamino, oltre al credere di chi non l'udì presto parlatore e ornato, senza essere d'alcuna cosa proveduto o licenzia datagli, si rimase, sperando che non senza sua futura utilità ciò dovesse essere stato fatto. Ma nel pensiero di messer Cane era caduto ogni cosa che gli si donasse vie peggio esser perduta che se nel fuoco fosse stata gittata: né di ciò gli dicea o facea dire alcuna cosa.' (§7)

[Only one man remained, named Bergamino, a quick and ornate speaker beyond the belief of those who had not heard him, and who, having not gotten anything and having received no permission to leave, hoped that staying would be to his future profit. But messer Cane had gotten the idea that everything he had given away was lost in an even worse way than if it had been tossed in a fire; nor did he say anything about this or have anything said to him (Bergamino).]

Bergamino, whose fame as 'presto parlatore e ornato' [a quick and ornate speaker] a refined and valued fabulist, precedes his arrival at the Scaliger court, does not in fact receive the same treatment that Can Grande accords the others. Convinced as he is of his own worth, however, Bergamino does not lose heart. Rather, he believes that the 'permission' not granted, the absence of largesse, and the lack of gifts come not from forgetfulness or even lack of esteem, but from a calculated postponement on the lord's part. He thinks that his performance, the show of 'cosa che a suo mestier pertenesse' [something pertaining to his craft (§7)], has only been put off. He therefore waits, from one moment to the next, for Can Grande to ask him to give a solitary and exclusive demonstration of his capacities. Not only does he expect adequate compensation, 'futura utilità' [future profit (§7)], he also clearly understands his own personal value and position (by now official) as an intellectual. This value and position translate into prominent social status: he arrives at court 'co' suoi cavalli e co' suoi fanti' [with his horses and his servants (§8)].

Can Grande, on the other hand, in a manner totally incongruous with his customary behavior, forgets to pay Bergamino; in fact, he seems to erase him from his mind. Such exceptional behavior on the lord's part, and the resulting situation of non-recognition in which the subject finds himself (at stake here, as has been said, is not an occasional gift but the very reputation of the man of the court), plunge Bergamino into a psychological condition of profound sadness and moral disheartenment: 'incominciò a prender malinconia' [he began to show melancholy (§8)]. Note the substantial proximity of the condition of the non-recognized intellectual with that of the unrequited lover, already described in the Proem (§11): in both cases, 'melancholy' is the state of those whose passion finds no outlet.

To break this historical and psychological impasse (and we know this too from the Proem), man needs to make recourse to 'new conversations,' to a dialogical attitude, with the novella being the paradigmatic form of reasoning and dialogue. That is precisely what happens here. Can Grande, in fact, in the course of another ritual event of courtly life, a *desinare*, or dinner, with the intention of being entertained more at Bergamino's expense ('per istraziarlo' [to torture him]) than by his company ('che per diletto pigliar d'alcun detto' [than to take pleasure in any speech of his]), asks Bergamino to explain his black mood: 'Bergamino, che hai tu? tu stai così malinconoso! Dinne alcuna cosa' [Bergamino, what is it? You're so sad! Tell us something (§10)]. Can Grande does not therefore demand arbitrarily and authoritatively that Bergamino exercise his craft as *fabulator*, as we often see done to Azzolino (Ezzellino da Romano) in the *Novellino*, here held as a model.[13] It is instead Bergamino who seizes the opportunity, with great speed and intelligence, to show off by means of a gratuitous and very refined example of his narrative repertory, thus challenging his lord's courtly virtues. The ability to understand the historical situation, and to seize the propitious moment in order to turn it to one's favor, are gifts that Boccaccio recognizes in the new intellectual class that the *Decameron* consistently exalts.

Bergamino's answer to Can Grande is unplanned ('senza punto pensare quasi molto tempo pensato avesse' [without thinking at all, almost as if he had thought about it for a long time]) and instantaneous ('subitamente' [at once] §11), and it far surpasses the 'Dinne alcuna cosa' [Tell us something] requested by the lord. In effect, the response is articulated in a 'novella' (as specified by the rubric), a perfect artistic organism in which the man of the court may successfully represent the deep sense of his psychological condition, the spiritual etymon of his *malinconia*, thereby setting the stage for its extirpation. In this way, Bergamino's words to Can Grande become a sort of *razo* of his state of mind, a rationalization that permits him to transcend, on an artistic level, the precariousness of his existence.

Bergamino's novella projects its content upon the scenario of a distant time and space, that is, on an exemplary event which happened to the very prototype of the man of the court, Hugh d'Orléans, known by the nom de guerre of Primas or Primate, the most authoritative exponent of the oft-represented squad of *clerici vagantes* called *goliardi* [goliards].[14] The event takes place in a legendary Paris during the mythical epoch (towards the middle of the twelfth century) that saw the great values of courtly civilization flourish, values that are now (in Bergamino's historical epoch) in a phase of slow decay. The recounted story thus assumes, in comparison with the lived story, the same relation as that between a laboratory experiment and phenomenal reality. All the elements that make up the experiment are in fact perfect, and the procedural conditions are optimal, so the result obtained cannot help but prove valid and satisfying for the experimenter. We may therefore conclude that the novella of Bergamino/Can Grande is the exemplum of Primas/Cluny abbot, subjected however to the variable of historical space and time.

The exemplum of Primas consists of two principal moments. During the first (negative) moment the abbot 'does not recognize' Primas (§§11–22); in the second (positive) moment we instead witness the abbot's full 'recognition' of Primas (§§23–6). Such events in the exemplary story reflect, respectively, the 'earlier' and the 'later' times of the containing story, first the situation in which Bergamino finds himself before making recourse to the 'quick and ornate word' (i.e., the novella of Primas), and then the one in which he hopes to find himself after demonstrating his artistic abilities.

After an invocation to a privileged addressee ('Signor mio' [My lord] §11]), the inserted story begins at once with the *descriptio* of the agents (§§11–12). But while in the containing novella the presentation of Can Grande precedes that of Bergamino, here instead we witness an inversion. The first to be described is the protagonist and not the antagonist (the same order of presentation appears in the rubric, as I have already observed). It is easy to see an almost literal reflection of the *descriptio* of Bergamino in that of Primas: 'un gran valente uomo in gramatica e ... oltre a ogni altro grande e presto versificatore' [a very able man in language and ... more than anything, a great and quick versifier (§11)]. Can Grande is likewise reflected in the presentation of the abbot: 'il più

ricco prelato di sue entrate che abbia la Chiesa di Dio dal Papa in fuori'
[the richest prelate in earnings that the Church of God has, from the
Pope on down (§12)]. Bergamino's novella also offers a similar characterization of the deeds of the two men, which make Primas 'tanto rag-
guardevole e sì famoso' [so respected and famous (§11)], and which are
instead 'maravigliose e magnifiche' [wonderful and magnificent (§12)]
for the abbot. These reflected images in the optative (so to speak) portion of the tale, while identical to the real ones in the historical part, are
however retouched. Bergamino emphasizes and specifies the Abbot's
'great courtesy': 'in tener sempre corte e non esser mai alcuno, che
andasse là ove egli fosse, negato né mangiar né bere' [in always
holding court and never denying either food or drink to anyone who
might go where he was (§12)]. He likewise accentuates Primas's great
fame: 'ancora che per vista in ogni parte conosciuto non fosse, per
nome e per fama quasi niuno era che non sapesse chi fosse Primasso'
[although he was not known everywhere by sight, there was hardly
anyone who did not know who Primas was, by name and by fame
(§11)]. The reflected image therefore perfects the real one – after all, literature is always a magic mirror! While Primas need but mention his
name in order to be recognized, Bergamino must give an exceptional
and unexpected artistic performance.

The shadow of the containing novella is also projected upon the
inserted story with regard to narrative action. Primas goes from Paris
to the Cluny abbey, about 'six miles' away, in order personally to
observe 'la magnificenza di questo abate' [the magnificence of this
abbot (§12)], and he carries with him as a viaticum three loaves of
bread to eat in case 'la via ... per isciagura gli venisse smarrita' [by bad
luck he should lose his way (§14)]. Bergamino likewise comes to Can
Grande's court, summoned there by the liberality of the Scaliger monarch and carrying 'tre belle e ricche robe' [three beautiful and rich
robes (§9)], which he thinks about wearing 'per comparire orrevole alla
festa' [in order to make an honorable appearance at the festival (§9)]. In
reality, however, they are the things that allow him to survive when the
road to a normal relationship with Can Grande is lost. Primas's misadventure at the abbey is analogous to Bergamino's, though the seriousness of the forgetfulness differs from case to case. In the latter, we are
dealing with spiritual forgetfulness: in a single stroke Can Grande
has cancelled any memory of Bergamino's merits, even of his presence at court. But in the former it is only a question of physical non-
recognition, so the forgetfulness is less serious.

In Bergamino's novella Primas arrives at the abbot's court at the dinner hour, admiring the sumptuous preparations and the ritual of the gastronomical festival: 'veduta la gran moltitudine delle tavole messe e il grande apparecchio della cucina' [once he had seen the great number of tables set and the great machinery of the kitchen (§15)], the steward 'comandò che l'acqua si desse alle mani' [ordered that water be brought for hand-washing (§16)]. Primas is then 'messo a sedere appunto di rimpetto all'uscio della camera donde l'abate dovea uscire per venire nella sala a mangiare' [seated just opposite the doorway of the room the abbot had to leave in order to enter the dining hall (§16)]. It is at the moment when the great prelate and the great man of letters meet that the incident occurs: the abbot, who has not met Primas before, does not recognize him, indeed notes that he is 'assai male ... in arnese' [very badly dressed (§18)],' no doubt because of the long trip, and identifies him as a 'ribaldo' [ruffian], the incarnation of a run-down, profit-seeking jester:[15]

> L'abate fece aprir la camera per venir nella sala: e venendo si guardò inanzi e per ventura il primo uomo che agli occhi gli corse fu Primasso, il quale assai male era in arnese e cui egli per veduta non conoscea: e come veduto l'ebbe, incontanente gli corse nell'animo un pensiero cattivo e mai più non statovi, e disse seco: 'Vedi a cui io do mangiare il mio!' (§18)

> [The abbot had the door opened in order to enter the hall, and while coming in he looked ahead, and by chance the first man he saw was Primas, who was very badly dressed and whose face he did not recognize. And when he had seen him, a bad thought, one he had never had before, rushed into his mind, and he said to himself: 'Look whom I give my food to!']

The justified non-recognition of Primas is followed by the unmotivated and unusual reaction – 'un pensiero cattivo e mai più non statovi' [a bad thought, one he had never had before] – that the abbot himself will qualify later as avarice, the negation of the fundamental *virtus* of courtly civilization, of *largueza*, or liberality. The abbot therefore behaves in a manner that does not correspond to his fame as a 'great' and munificent lord.

But let us analyse the abbot's moves in detail:

a) Above all he tries indirectly to learn the name of the undesirable guest that he finds sitting as his table ('domandò se alcuno conoscesse quel ribaldo' [he asked ... if anyone knew that ruffian (§19)]) but this attempt leads nowhere.

b) He then chooses the path of retreat, refusing to appear in the refectory in order to open formally the ceremony of the banquet; the chivalric custom of awaiting the arrival of the lord in the hall before preparing the meals is recalled in §17. In so doing he hopes that the 'ruffian' might willingly abandon the field. But this attempt fails as well, since Primas, worried about the delay – but only at a physiological level, as opposed to Bergamino's *malinconia*, begins slowly to eat, one after another, the three loaves that he had brought with him (§21).

c) At this point the abbot should intervene personally to discharge his guest, but not even this solution seems possible for him (§22).

It is precisely the constancy of the *clericus vagans*, his *mezura* or his demonstration of perfect internal control and total domination of the external situation, that clears the impasse, creating in the abbot a gnawing doubt and preparing the ground for the second moment in the narrative action, the passage from the non-recognition of the 'ruffian' to the recognition of the intellectual. Seeing that the unknown guest not only makes no move to leave, but continues to eat his third loaf, the abbot now begins to think:

'Deh questa che novità è oggi che nella anima m'è venuta, che avarizia, chente sdegno, e per cui? Io ho dato mangiare il mio, già è molt'anni, a chiunque mangiar n'ha voluto, senza guardare se gentile uomo è o villano, o povero o ricco, o mercatante o barattiere stato sia, e a infiniti ribaldi con l'occhio me l'ho veduto straziare, né mai nell'animo m'entrò questo pensiero che per costui mi c'è entrato. Fermamente avarizia non mi dee avere assalito per uomo di piccolo affare: qualche gran fatto dee esser costui che ribaldo mi pare, poscia che così mi s'è rintuzzato l'animo d'onorarlo.' (§§23–4)

[Hmm, what is this new thing that comes to my mind today, what avarice, what disdain, and for whom? For many years now, I have shared my food with whoever has wanted to eat it, without noting whether he is a nobleman or a bumpkin, poor or rich, merchant or barattor, and I have seen it ruined by an infinite number of ruffians. But never has the thought entered my mind that I just had about this man. Surely avarice does not assail me for a man of such small account: that man who appears to be a

ruffian must be someone very important, since I have been so obtuse
about honouring him.]

This magnificent soliloquy, during which the abbot acknowledges his
own capital sin, avarice, committed against the courtly ideal, introduces in his mind the suspicion that the reason why he has stepped
back from his lordly and chivalric habits cannot be attributed to a person 'of such small account' (as Primas appears physically to be), but to
'someone very important.' In other words, the abbot suspects that
beneath the clothes of the 'ruffian' there lies an exceptional personality.
Such a violent reaction as the one provoked by the mysterious guest
must have an exceptional motivation. For this reason, the abbot now
feels the need to ask his guest, finally addressing him directly and
establishing a dialogue, to identify himself:

> E così detto, volle saper chi fosse; e trovato che era Primasso, quivi venuto
> a vedere della sua magnificenza quello che n'aveva udito, il quale avendo
> l'abate per fama molto tempo davante per valente uom conosciuto, si ver-
> gognò, e vago di far l'amenda in molte maniere s'ingegnò d'onorarlo. E
> appresso mangiare, secondo che alla sufficienza di Primasso si conveniva,
> il fe' nobilmente vestire, e donatigli denari e pallafreno, nel suo albitrio
> rimise l'andare e lo stare. (§§25–6)

> [Thus said, he wanted to know who he was; and having learned that he
> was Primas, come to see what he had heard of his greatness, and whom
> the abbot had for a long time known by word of mouth to be a man of
> worth, he was ashamed and, wishing to make amends, sought to honour
> him in many ways. And after eating, according to what was appropriate
> for Primas, he had him nobly dressed, and having given him money and a
> steed, gave him the choice of whether to leave or to stay.]

The simple mention of the name of Primas, the indication of an
admired and oft-mentioned *auctoritas*, is enough to provoke a total
metamorphosis in the abbot's mind and behaviour, a transformation
from avarice to liberality, and a passage from scorn for the *ribaldo* to
onore for the high poet.

The catalysing effect that the name has in the exemplum of Primas is
identical to the one that the exemplum itself produces in the novella of
Bergamino. In fact, the force capable of overturning the sense of Bergamino's lived story from negative to positive flows directly from the

story told about Primas. It is a story in which Bergamino has reflected himself, his deeds, and the addressee of his deeds, Can Grande. Can Grande affirms as much at the end of Bergamino's admirable show of artistry:

> Bergamino, assai acconciamente hai mostrati i danni tuoi, la tua virtù e la mia avarizia e quel che da me disideri: e veramente mai più che ora per te da avarizia assalito non fui, ma io la caccerò con quel bastone che tu medesimo hai divisato. (§27)

> [Bergamino, you have ornately shown the damage you have suffered, your virtue and my avarice and what you want from me. And truly I have never been assaulted by avarice as I was just now for you, but I shall chase it away with that club that you yourself have devised.]

The true mirror of life is therefore the word embodied in literature. It is a mirror in which we find reflected the image of the *auctor* himself. Primas thus becomes the first name in a lengthy cultural genealogy ending with Boccaccio.

NOTES

A version of a portion of this essay was published in Italian in *Feconde vennero le carte: Studi in onore di Ottavio Besomi*, vol. 1, ed. Tatiana Crivelli (Bellinzona: Edizioni Casagrande, 1997), 107–22. This essay was translated by Michael Sherberg.

1 See Edoardo Sanguineti, 'Gli "schemata" del *Decameron.*'
2 For the bibliography relative to this day, see Vittore Branca's notes to his edition of the *Decameron*. The most recent analysis of the day is that offered by Baldissone, 'Il piacere,' 9–23; see also my essay, 'Lettura macrotestuale della prima giornata del *Decameron,*' in *Feconde venner le carte.*
3 For a more detailed analysis see my article, 'L'invenzione della novella italiana, esp. 132–7.
4 For a recent treatment of this problematic see the careful study by Franco Gaeta, 'Dal comune.'
5 The ninth novella is an exception, where the inversion antagonist/protagonist ('Il re di Cipri, da una donna di Guascogna trafitto, di cattivo valoroso diviene' [The King of Cyprus, stung by a woman from Gascony, from a bad

person becomes a valorous one (I.9.1)]) is perhaps due to the author's desire to emphasize the regenerative capacity of the word. But see, on the general *quaestio* of the rubrics, D'Andrea, 'Le rubriche del *Decameron*.'

6 As the only temporal indicator contained therein seems to specify: 'Fu in Lunigiana ... un monastero già di santità e di monaci piú copioso che oggi non è' [There was in Lunigiana ... a monastery at one time more full of sanctity and monks than it is today (I.4.4)]. In any event, the shadow of the famous letter by Frate Ilario is projected on this novella, as shown by Branca ('Boccaccio visualizzato,' 275–6).

7 Vittore Branca's contributions are fundamental in this regard; one need but recall his seminal chapter, 'Ironizzazione letteraria come rinnovamento di tradizioni,' in *Boccaccio medievale*. But see as well Luciano Rossi, 'Ironia e parodia,' and, for Dante's presence, R. Hollander, *Boccaccio's Dante*.

8 See Lucien Dällenbach, *Le récit speculaire:* 109–10, which addresses our novella.

9 For the slender bibliography relative to this novella, see the notes to Branca's edition of the *Decameron*. The studies by Russo, *Letture critiche del Decameron*, 112–26, and Baratto, *Realtà*, 214–17, have been useful to me.

10 The allusion is fully revealed by Boccaccio's friend Petrarch, who in the *Rerum memorandum libri* II.83, applies precisely to the pair Can Grande/Dante the anecdote that Boccaccio, too loyal to the Dantean myth, here refers instead to Can Grande/Bergamino.

11 For the Dantean echoes present in this story consult the careful notes in Branca's edition; see also Russo, *Letture critiche*, 114–15.

12 On the medieval *festa* see the collective volume *Spettacoli conviviali dall'antichità classica alle corti italiane del '400*, which contains an exhaustive bibliography.

13 See for example novella 31. However, the stories that are closer to our own are number 21 (for the theme of ingratitude) and 44 (which puts Marco Lombardo in a situation similar to that of Bergamino).

14 The bibliography on Hugh d'Orléans and his goliards is vast; see the small edition of the *Carmina burana*, ed. P. Rossi. Acute observations on intertextual echoes of Primas present in our novella are found in Russo, *Letture critiche*, 117–20.

15 The involvement of the Dantean cantos on barratry is fundamental here (the technical vocabulary comes from them: besides *ribaldo* there appears the same word, *barattiere*, I.7.23). For an analysis of barratry in poetry, see my article, 'Giulleria e poesia.'

The Tale of Guiglielmo Borsiere (I.8)

VICTORIA KIRKHAM

Lauretta's anecdote for the *brigata*'s first day out, a little parable about the courtier Guiglielmo Borsiere and how he made Ermino Grimaldi mend his miserly ways, has caught much less attention than its companions: black Cepperello's besaintment; Abraham's revelation of rottenness in the heart of Christian Rome; the tale of three-rings recollected by Melchisedech; abbatical obesity made weightless for a gardener's willing daughter; Dr Alberto of Bologna, white of head but not in the tail. Except for the powerful magnetic field of fun and evil centred on Ser Cepperello, the motley sequence of tales in Day One, like Day Nine, could not be as substantial a target for critical reflection as the other eight days, internally unified by sweeping themes of human life and love. But in spite of its open topic, Boccaccio planned Day One just as tightly as all that follows. Subjects stray at surface only, the *Decameron*'s first decade of narrative entertainments bond to form a family.

Decameron I.8 twins by motif with the tale before it. In I.7 Can Grande, the 'great Lombard' legendary for his hospitality,[1] was to give a splendid feast in Verona, but unexpectedly changed his mind and paid off all the 'men of court' who had been invited, save Bergamino, 'unbelievably quick and graceful as a speaker.' Bergamino and Guiglielmo Borsiere, perfect gentlemen with a particular gift for language, each shame an antagonist into loosing his purse strings. Broad parallels between their stories play out in alternatives of symmetrical opposition, a frequent Boccaccian tactic that is most obvious in the larger pattern of *giornate* coupled (stories with rewards fortuitous, then meritorious on Days Two-Three; romance tragic, then happy on Four-Five; husbands, then both men and women, tricked on Seven-Eight).

Can Grande, a princely ruler habitually lavish in giving, is stricken with a sudden turn of 'avarice' from which an apposite story prompts his recovery. Ermino Grimaldi, whose impulses towards generosity could hardly have been feebler (only 'a sparklet of politeness'), is a mercantile noble whose correction Guiglielmo Borsiere accomplishes with just one lapidary sentence on what is lacking in his house: 'Fateci dipignere la Cortesia' [Have Courtesy painted there].

The seventh and eighth tales are not the only ones on the First Day of the *Decameron* to make an issue of money. Ser Cepperello (I.1) dies after spinning a brilliant comic lie in the home of Lombard lenders; Abraham the Jew and Giannotto (I.2) are both merchants; Saladino (I.3), his treasury emptied by wars and munificence, hopes to trick money from the rich Jew Melchisedech; a hypocritical inquisitor (I.6), who idolizes 'Saint John Goldenbeard,' gets his palms greased with fat from 'Saint John Goldenmouth.' Examples of usury, prodigality, and greed precede the two cases of avarice cured in tales seven and eight. This gamut of possibilities for using (and misusing) wealth aptly falls on the first Wednesday in the *Decameron*'s two-week calendar, since 'mercoledì' [Wednesday] takes its name from Mercury, the god of commerce. To that Olympian belong as well eloquence and sweetness of speech.[2] It will return openly one week later, on the second Wednesday, Day Six. When it is Mercury's day, the main topic is language, especially quick, witty retorts.[3] At I.8, what power lies in the word, as Borsiere had ability to utter it, comes sharply to fore with Ermino Avarizia's sudden, total reform: 'And from that day forward, so great was the power (*virtù*) of the word spoken by Guiglielmo, he was the most liberal and the most gracious gentleman ... in Genoa in those times.' Borsiere and Grimaldi, in spite of their differences – a courtier prized for his speech, a businessman driven by greed – are kin in the astrological family of Mercury, whose members populate *Decameron* Day One.

At about 800 words, *Decameron* I.8 is one of the shortest tales in the *Decameron*. Except for Branca's commentary and some scarce passing references, it has slipped through scholarly trawls.[4] Branca suggests that the story makes capital, so to speak, of the Genoese reputation for stinginess, Genoa being the 'Scotland' of Italy. He provides documentation for the historical background and rightly points our attention to important related literary texts: Dante's *Inferno* 16, where Guiglielmo Borsiere lately of Florence is named as a newcomer to the circle of sodomy; also the commentary tradition on that canto, notably Boccaccio's own *Esposizioni sopra la Comedìa*.

Lauretta does not give the story she tells a precise historical setting. Emphasis in her evocation of time anterior falls not so much on when, exactly, the event took place, as its distance in the past, a long time back from her present: 'Fu adunque in Genova, buon tempo è passato ...' [There was then in Genoa, a good while ago ... (§4)]. This 'good while ago' marks more than half a century because Guiglielmo Borsiere was dead by early 1300. When Dante passed through Hell during April of that year, he could say that Guiglielmo had just recently been received there. Guiglielmo and messer Ermino must have met in Genoa towards the end of the thirteenth century. No documents attest to an Ermino Grimaldi then active, but the first name does later occur in that family. Risen to prosperity and influence through maritime commerce, in 1333 the Grimaldi's living members numbered 110, a phenomenal clan, and they remained among magnates of Italy throughout the Renaissance. Today a branch of descendants still rules the Principality of Monaco.[5]

Proper names consistent with documented reality and action historically plausible – Borsiere, an old-fashioned Florentine gentleman; Grimaldi, the *nouveau riche* merchant from Genoa – lend this story an appearance of truth. Other narratological signs, though, undermine its realism, trumpeting fiction most transparent. I have already mentioned the story's opening formula, close to the classic 'Fu adunque in Genova, buon tempo è passato ...' [Once upon a time in Genoa ... (§4)]. Rhetorical and linguistic modes typical of the fairy tale are also prominent in what immediately follows. Superlatives characterize Grimaldi, hyperbole that puts him on a fantastic plane. This Ermino, unknown to history, was not just the most prosperous man in town, he was richest in the land: 'di grandissime possessioni e di denari di gran lunga trapassava la ricchezza d'ogni altro ricchissimo cittadino che allora si sapesse *in Italia*' [with the greatest possessions and money he far and away surpassed the riches of every other richest citizen then known *in Italy*, emphasis mine (§4)]. Whereas we would then expect a direct correlation between his money and his meanness, the latter far outweighs the former, in terms of exponential exaggeration dear to the stock of storybook invention. The dimensions of Ermino's avarice require measurement not just on a local or national scale, but with reference to the whole world: 'E sì come egli di ricchezza ogni altro avanzava che *italico* fosse, così d'avarizia e di miseria ogni altro misero e avaro che al *mondo* fosse soperchiava oltre misura' [And just as he outdid everyone else who was *Italian* in riches, so he overreached beyond measure every miser and avaricious man *in the world* (§5; emphasis mine)].

If Boccaccio's Ser Ciappelletto was 'the worst man perhaps who ever was born,' his messer Ermino was emphatically the most niggardly. It is what people said at the time, what everyone knew, just as everyone had forgotten his real name and knew him by the nickname Herman, the Miser. Like the folk tale as a literary form, he and his reputation are communal property. Consequently, Ermino Grimaldi is less an inhabitant of a great Ligurian municipality than an archetype of greed. Genoa and the Grimaldi function in the novella not so much to locate the action geographically as to define its ethical locus.

If we were to label this story with one of the four terms Boccaccio uses in the Proem to the *Decameron* ('novella,' 'fable,' 'parable,' 'history'), the best descriptor, I think, would be 'parable,' a brief tale that teaches a lesson in living. In this sense, *Decameron* I.8 approximates a favorite didactic form of the Middle Ages, the exemplum. Whereas realistic narrative describes what has been and is, the exemplum 'capitalizes on a pre-existing fact, conditioned by aprioristic and traditional intentionality. That fact or episode, that theme or narrative fragment, is a constant given with a long ancestry that precedes the experience at the same time as it aims to exemplify and objectify it.'[6]

Boccaccio's categories in this exemplary novella are Avarice and Courtesy. The paradigm depends in good part on a tradition whose medieval fortune began about A.D. 400, when Prudentius authored the *Psychomachia*, a rousing battle of vices and virtues who clash on the field as militant female personifications. Pride falls headlong from her high horse as she tauntingly charges Humility; Patience watches, meek and passive, while Wrath commits suicide; Sobriety undoes Luxury; Avaritia, pretending to be Frugality, bags gold that Luxuria has scattered, but is caught and strangled by Operatio (Good Works or Beneficence).[7] Guiglielmo Borsiere's encounter with Ermino Grimaldi encapsulates another such singular combat. Transformed by the centuries and tamed by Italian civility, their confrontation re-enacts the perennial enmity between avarice and its opposite, here conceived as courtesy.

By Boccaccio's time, personification of the virtues with opposing vices was a familiar subject in religious art. One iconographic type, whose earliest examples are on capitals and porches of northern Romanesque churches, represents the virtue standing and trampling her enemy. So Patientia stomps Ira; Castitas crushes Luxuria, and Largitas triumphs over a flattened-down Avaritia.[8] Another form, which first appears at Notre Dame di Paris, Amiens, and Chartres, gives the virtues and contrary vices equal coverage in full figural cycles. Their numbers and names would vary as the tradition evolved, depending on what authority's list had been chosen for illustration. At Notre Dame there are twelve virtues and twelve vices: Faith and Idolatry, Hope and Despair, Charity and Avarice, Chastity and Luxury, and so on.[9] Giotto, who adopted the visual concept for the Arena Chapel at Padua early in the fourteenth century, would choose to fresco seven each, the sum that became standard, but in his scheme 'Avaritia' has no place. Charity, opponent to Avarice in French Gothic cathedral sculpture, is set by the Italian artist against Envy.[10]

By what precedent does Boccaccio pit against Avarice the virtue of Courtesy personified – once as a man in her well-bred advocate, once as a woman in the talismanic picture to be painted on Ermino's wall? Avarice was almost always among the vices, but its opposite could have several identities: in Prudentius's *Psychomachia* Avarice was defeated by Operatio; in Romanesque art, by Largesse; in Gothic Ile-de-France, by Charity. Further, nowhere in these systems does Courtesy appear. Who, then, is the lady with whom Ermino needs to make acquaintance? Her credentials for personification as a virtue come, we shall see, from a *contaminatio* of ancient and medieval sources, fusions characteristic of Boccaccio's pervasive, vigorous eclecticism.

We have already seen how Boccaccio uses a geographic crescendo to express moral *outrance* in the description of Ermino's miserliness, from Genoa, to Italy, to the 'whole world.' Like the place names, so the verbs in his syntax rise in intensity as a series, marked by their rhyming forms: '*trapassava* la ricchezza ... ogni altro *avanzava* ... *soperchiava* oltre misura' [he *surpassed* the riches ... he *outdid* everyone else ... he *overreached* beyond measure (§§4,5)]. The adverbial closure, 'oltre misura,' caps the construction with a phrase that tropes the meaning of the whole, literally, 'beyond measure'; by implication, beyond all bounds of decency, decorum, and belief. Lexical duplication reinforces the picture of excess Boccaccio creates in describing his Scrooge: he had '*grandissime possessioni* e ... *denari*'; '*trapassava* la *ricchezza* d'ogni altro *ricchissimo*'; 'd'*avarizia* e di *miseria* ogni altro *misero* e *avaro* [...] *soperchiava*'; 'Guiglielmo [...] avendo udite molte cose della *miseria* e della *avarizia* di messere Ermino' [the greatest *possessions* and *money*; he outdid the *riches* of every other *richest* man; he overreached every *miser* and *avaricious* man in *avarice* and *miserliness* (§§ 4, 5)]. As a result, the personage disappears behind a persona; a miserly man metamorphoses into the abstraction of his vice. Deprived by that vice of humanity, messer Ermino de' Grimaldi loses his identity. Genoese popular memory has reduced him to an anonymous type, Ermino Avarizia. Reductive, iterative vocabulary with the grammatical structures of tall-tale magnification, signifiers of excess beyond all limits, mythicize Ermino into a Miser of All Times.

By contrast, the equally studied lexicon attached to Guiglielmo progressively sharpens his identity, moving him from the broad species 'courtier' into ever clearer focus as a rare individual. The language linked to Guiglielmo is not in a rhetoric of genre. Rather, its origins are specific to Dante's *Commedia*, where, on the desert of sodomy, talk turns to courtesy. Ser Brunetto, at the end of *Inferno* 15, had run off to rejoin his troop. At the start of Canto 16, as Dante continues across the third ring of the seventh circle, approaching the Malebolge Abyss, three more souls break rank and hurry towards him. They are Guido Guerra, Tegghiaio Aldobrandi, and Iacopo Rusticucci. To them, says Virgil, courtesy is in order: 'A costor si vuole esser *cortese.*' Speaking for the three, Iacopo confirms his concern for courtesy with an anxious inquiry about current mores in Florence:

> '*cortesia e valor* di' se dimora
> ne la nostra città sì come suole,
> o se del tutto se n'è gita fora;
>   ché Guiglielmo Borsiere, il qual si duole
> con noi per poco e va là coi compagni,
> assai ne cruccia con le sua parole.'
>   'La gente nuova e i sùbiti guadagni
> orgoglio e dismisura han generata,
> Fiorenza, in te, sì che tu già ten piagni.' (ll. 67–75)

[tell us if *courtesy and valour* abide in our city as once they did, or if they are quite gone from it, for Guiglielmo Borsiere, who has been but short while in pain with us and goes yonder with our company, greatly afflicts us with his words.

The new people and the sudden gains have engendered pride and excess in you, O Florence, so that already you weep for it!]

Punished among the damned to whom courtesy is due, Rusticucci reveals how the newcomer Guiglielmo Borsiere is angering his fellows with reports, surely false, that 'courtesy and valour,' accustomed to dwell in Florence, have utterly departed the city. The sodomist, though, hears his worst fears confirmed as Dante's own outrage explodes against the 'new folk and their fast money.'

Franco Fido has noticed how Boccaccio's tale repeats the key words in Iacopo's question, 'cortesia e valor,' tying them to Guiglielmo Borsiere, but in reverse order.[11] Within small narrative space we are reminded no less than three times of Guiglielmo's courtesy and worth – or better, worth and courtliness: first, when Lauretta refers to him in her introduction as 'un valente uomo di corte' [a worthy man of court (§3)]; second, when she recounts his arrival in Genoa, and extends the epithet to embrace his manners and fair speech: 'Avvenne che in questi tempi ... arrivò a Genova un valente uomo di corte e costumato e ben parlante, il qual fu chiamato Guiglielmo Borsiere' [It came to pass that in those times ... there arrived in Genoa a worthy man of court, polite, well-spoken, who was called Guiglielmo Borsiere (§7)]; and third, just before he actually meets Ermino, who 'had already heard that this Guiglielmo Borsiere was a worthy man' ('valente uomo'). The pattern of repetitions carries us from an unspecified general situation ('how a worthy man of court ... attacked the greed of a very rich merchant'), to the precise names of the people and city involved, and, eventually, with the third affirmation that 'Guiglielmo Borsiere was a worthy man,' the two characters come face to face for the story's pungent exchange of words.

Benvenuto da Imola, glossing Guiglielmo Borsiere's appearance in Dante's *Inferno* (1375), describes him as 'quidam civis florentinus faciens bursas, vir secundum facultatem suam placibilis et liberalis, qui tractu temporis habens odio officium bursarum, quibus clauditur pecunia, factus est homo curialis et cepit visitare curias dominarum et domus nobilium' [a certain Florentine citizen who made purses, a man who was pleasant and liberal as his means permitted, who with the passage of time came to hate the job of making purses, in which money is contained, and he became a man of court and began to visit the courts of the lords and the homes of the nobles].[12] Boccaccio had said more about what it meant to be a 'man of court,' and how Guiglielmo fit that role in his *Esposizioni* on *Inferno* 16 (1373):

Questi fu cavalier di corte, uomo costumato molto e di laudevol maniera; ed era il suo essercizio, e degli altri suoi pari, il trattar paci tra grandi e gentili uomini, trattar matrimoni e parentadi e talora con piacevoli e

oneste novelle recreare gli animi de' faticati e confortargli alle cose
onorevoli; il che i moderni non fanno, anzi quanto più sono scellerate e
spiacevoli e con brutte operazioni e parole, più piacciono e meglio son
proveduti. (Boccaccio, *Esposizioni*, Canto XVI, §54)

[He was a knight of court, a very polite man of praiseworthy manner, and
it was his practice, and that of others like him, to negotiate peace between
great and noble men, to negotiate marriages and alliances, and sometimes
with pleasant and decorous tales to restore the spirits of the weary and
encourage them to do honourable things; things that the moderns do not
do, rather, the more wicked and displeasing they are with ugly actions
and words, the more they please and the better they fare.]

The passage condenses Lauretta's praise of Guiglielmo, words that had
burst into the bitter tirade on modern decadence at the heart of
Decameron I.8:

... arrivò a Genova un valente uomo di corte e costumato e ben parlante ...
non miga simile a quegli li quali sono oggi ... E là dove a que' tempi
soleva essere il lor mestiere e consumarsi la lor fatica in trattar paci,
dove guerre o sdegni tra gentili uomini fosser nati, o trattar matrimonii,
parentadi e amistà, e con belli motti e leggiadri ricreare gli animi degli
affaticati e sollazzar le corti e con agre riprensioni, sí come padri, mordere
i difetti de' cattivi, e questo con premii assai leggieri; oggi di rapportar
male dall'altro, in seminare zizzania, in dir cattività e tristizie ... e con
false lusinghe gli uomini gentili alle cose vili e scellerate ritrarre s'ingeg-
nano il lor tempo di consumare. E colui è più caro avuto e più da' miseri e
scostumati signori onorato e con premii grandissimi essaltato, che più
abominevoli parole dice o fa atti. (§§7–10)

[There arrived in Genova a worthy man of court, polite and well spoken
... not at all like those of the present day ... And whereas in those times it
used to be their job to negotiate peace, when wars or feuds had arisen
between noblemen, or negotiate marriages, alliances, and friendships,
and to restore the spirits of the weary and entertain the courts with witty,
graceful sallies, and to rebuke the misdeeds of the wicked with sharp
reproofs, father-like, and all this for precious few rewards; today they
manage to spend their time spreading evil report from one to another,
sowing discord, speaking wickedness and baseness ... and inciting gentlemen with false flattery to things vile and heinous. And he is held dearest

and most honoured by our miserable and ill-mannered lords, and exalted with grandest rewards, who says and does the most abominable words and deeds.]

Guiglielmo Borsiere, as Lauretta calls him back to life, was a model gentleman, the opposite of courtiers today, hypocrites who furnish evidence aplenty that the virtues have walked out of our world, leaving the living in dregs of vice. Her righteous indignation takes subtextual fuel from *Inferno* 16, as does the whole novella, which could exemplify what Pier Massimo Forni has called 'narrative realization' through elements of language rather than from a pre-existing plot motif, a process of *elocutio* as *inventio*, or 'logomimesis.'[13] The main elements of the story are all present in and about Dante's conversation with Iacopo Rusticucci: the desirability of courtesy ('si vuole esser cortese'); the coupling of courtesy with valour ('cortesia e valor'); Guiglielmo Borsiere, survivor from a Florence of better days, who can speak the truth, though its message hurt; a nouveau riche class, boasting of gains and spending conspicuously, 'beyond measure' ('la nuova gente e i sùbiti guadagni'; 'orgoglio e dismisura'); and, finally, as neighbors to the sodomites but not until early in Canto 17, the squatting misers, each with a pouch strung from his neck, the family-crested purse ('borsa'). Boccaccio connects into *Inferno* 16 and its appendix on avarice with a story that has shifted semantically from Dante's 'courtesy and worth' to the binomial pair 'court' and 'purse.' His tale multiplies and trades on possibilities clustered at those semantic poles, starting with 'borsa' and 'corte' narrowly, and pushing each term to wider senses.

'Borsa' is the metonymic equivalent of money, the stuff a purse contains, and as such, emblem par excellence of the miser. From Horace's Opimius, such a skinflint that he even hated to eat, to Disney's old Uncle Scrooge McDuck, the money hoarder is always close, one way or another, to his cache.[14] Moneybags, brightly escutcheoned, hang on Dante's misers, otherwise unrecognizable: 'dal collo a ciascun pendea una *tasca* / ch'avea certo colore e certo segno ... / in una *borsa* gialla vidi azzurro' [from the neck of each hung a *pouch*, which had a certain color and a certain device ... I saw, upon a yellow *purse*, azure (*Inf.* 17.55–9)]. Prudentius had cast Avaritia in the part of a scavenger hag cramming sacks with filthy lucre. In the medieval repertory, plentiful with examples, Midas endured as a favourite. His name provided the title of Boccaccio's eighth eclogue (perhaps about Niccola Acciaiuoli), and he led off the catalogue of figures depicted in the Triumph of

Wealth in *Amorosa visione* (cantos 13–14), which culminates with the poet's own banker father among a frantic mob violating the earth to grovel for buried treasure. Graphic among figurations in the canon is the repugnant creature looming with Love's enemies, as Guillaume de Lorris lined them up, outside his Garden of Diversion. When Amant pauses before the walled pleasance to study what he sees, Avarice makes a shocking sight. Ugly, dirty, thin, green, and miserable-looking, she wears a heavily patched dress and clutches in her hand a tightly drawn purse. These familiar images of self-scantlers converge in Ermino, 'contra il general costume de' genovesi che usi sono di nobile-mente vestire, sosteneva egli per non ispendere difetti grandissimi, e similmente nel mangiare e nel bere' [contrary to the general custom of the Genoese, who are wont to dress nobly, he endured the greatest privations in things necessary to his own person, and likewise in meat and in drink, rather than be at any expense (§5)].

Ironically, Boccaccio's tightwad meets his match in a man who is, *ad litteram*, 'of the purse.' A quondam purse-maker, if we can believe Benvenuto, Guiglielmo abandoned the trade as too materialistic. Now, critic of the coin sack that he carries in name only, he will correct Ermino, who kept a tight purse 'in hospitality' ('onorare altrui' §5). It seems significant that Guiglielmo's name reaches morphologically beyond 'borsa,' strictly speaking, to 'borsiere,' which need not be just 'purse-maker.' 'Borsiere' can mean 'bursar' or 'treasurer,' one who administers money, hence a person who knows how to collect and distribute it. The root 'borsa' in this novella has just such a positive capacity since it is a 'purser' who dispenses the virtue that teaches Ermino to open his purse strings and himself practise a model form of courtesy.

Considering the Dantean address of his detractor, in Ermino Grimaldi we can see the sort of person Boccaccio could have guessed Dante might mean when he lashes out against 'the new people and sudden gains.' Although Ermino is 'noble' – as merchants come – his behaviour is nouveau riche. He does not know the correct use of wealth. His money keeps piling up, until the hero Guiglielmo walks tall into town.

Going by Aristotle, the cupidity that Guiglielmo uproots from Ermino's soul could subsume tenacious avarice of two kinds. That vice, the Philosopher considers, is virtually incurable, for 'old age and every other disability make men miserly.' To complicate matters, there seem to exist many species of illiberality, which consists in essence of two elements, 'namely, deficient giving and needless grasping' (*Ethics* 1121b). Ermino's problem, a double defect defined as greed for gain and refusal to spend, even on himself for clothing necessities, finds outlet rhetorically in Boccaccio's insistence on its dual signifying terms, 'misero' and 'avaro,' 'miseria' and 'avarizia.' Even the name Ermino rings with an echo of the 'misero' that will compound his local interest as Ermino Avarizia.

But the adjective 'misero' does not just apply to Ermino in this tale. Lauretta's tirade on the decline of the courts attacks those 'miseri e scostumati signori' [miserable and ill-bred lords (§10)] just the opposite of Guiglielmo, who hold dearest the men of the most abominable words and deeds. Because of this corruption, the virtues have abandoned to dregs of vice 'i miseri viventi' [the miserable living (§10)]. Denoting 'miserly' in the strict sense, 'misero' opens a wider connotative space that comports the qualifiers miserable, mean-spirited, wretched, vile, and evil – the full panoply of suffering and wrong, in short, that Lauretta blames on 'men of court,' so-called, and their milieu in her day.

Like 'borsa,' 'corte' as a radical is also bivalent. In times past the fountainhead of old-fashioned virtue, the court now is a place of pure wickedness. The disparity is sharpened by Lauretta's back and forth between then and now. Her outburst first contrasts mannerly Guiglielmo with 'asses raised in filth' ('asini nella bruttura §7'). Its second half, built chiastically, mourns men like him, those peacemakers, marriage brokers, and courtly entertainers who have degenerated into poison tongues, strife makers, and goads to crime. Yet 'courtesy,' in the way we understand it, would hardly involve such a demanding range of social activity. How could that concept extend from civilized life at court, a simple virtue of good form, to the office of arranging marriages and negotiating peace treaties, a serious political responsibility? Compared with Avaritia, always a vice of the moneybagging miser, Cortesia was an unstable quality, susceptible during the Middle Ages of manifold meaning.

Clues to how some of Boccaccio's readers took Dame Courtesy in this story come from several illuminated manuscripts of the *Decameron* made at Paris in the first quarter of the fifteenth century. The miniaturist who illustrated each imagines that Guiglielmo conveniently happened to have in hand a picture of the woman who was on his mind. Scrolled in readiness at first, while Ermino asks Guiglielmo's advice on interior decoration, in a second scene the picture is unfurled, giving the miser his answer. One version has Guiglielmo, wearing a purse, display 'Cortesia' on what looks like a Veronica cloth. Standing, she is a regal lady whose skirts train over some long, lean person pinned under her feet. Her mashed prisoner, dark-robed with head upreared, is Avarice, telltale moneybag clutched in hand. In another miniature, Courtesy appears on a cloth as a queen with chalice and rosary, emblems of Charity, Faith, and Piety. In a third picture, while emptying a pail of coins, she carries a double cup. Made of two identical goblets fitted over each other at the lip, these were ceremonial cups, used as presentation gifts to honored persons.[15] To sum up, one artist shows Courtesy victorious over Avarice; the second suggests her affinity with Charity through the chalice and rosary; the third emphasizes Fair Welcoming with a double cup and Largesse with the stream of golden coins. What one painter implies in his quasi-Veronica cloth, the other two communicate with the role change they have taken the liberty of devising for Guiglielmo. We see not a courtier, but a cleric. In all three compositions, the point is the same. The power of the word ('la virtù della parola') in Guiglielmo's advice, 'Have Courtesy painted there,' has been transposed by the artists into the power of the picture. What Guiglielmo displays is a 'sign' capable of converting its beholder, a miracle-working image.[16]

One of this story's themes, Pier Massimo Forni has suggested, concerns the limits of representability. Sneezes cannot be visualized. Courtesy is something that can. The painter, whose mission was to depict things not seen, has the means to capture Courtesy in her essence by creating a personification.[17] But Ermino will not need to have the word painted; a verbalized idea alone is the sign by which Guiglielmo effects his conversion. Ermino promises to act on the word by acting it out. Like Guiglielmo, he will mirror Courtesy as a concept, rising to an ideal of the idea. With his crossover from a man of closed purse to 'courtesy,' the derisive nickname from his alienating vice, Avarizia, disappears. Ermino, whose miserliness had reached international proportions, can and will regain human dimension.[18] He does so through Cortesia, which restores him, with the tale's final words, to his native time and place. Once again, as at the beginning of the novella, Boccaccio appropriates fairy tale language with its 'forever after' happy endings: 'E da questo dì innanzi, di tanta virtù fu la parola da Guiglielmo detta, fu il più liberale e 'l più grazioso gentile uomo ... che in Genova fosse a' tempi suoi' [From that day forward, such was the power of the word spoken by Guiglielmo, that he was the most liberal and the most gracious gentleman ... in Genoa in those times (§18)].

How northern illuminators pictured *Decameron* I.8 still does not isolate the qualities of this vanished virtue as a Florentine in the mid-fourteenth century might have conceived it. From Italy there are no visual examples to help, at least not of the type recommended for Herman's new townhouse. Domestic interior wall decorations survive only beginning in the later fourteenth century, and Cortesia is not known among them. To recapture this elusive lady, then, we must sleuth in a territory of literary texts.

Twelfth-century France is where the words 'courtesy' and 'courteous' originate. They derive from the Old French noun base *'court'* (< Latin *cohors, cohortis,* i.e., farmyard, enclosure, cohort, retinue), which established itself as the Romance equivalent for the Latin *curia.* *'Courtois'* was a vernacular gloss for *'curialis'* ('pertaining to the court,' 'courtly'), *'urbanus,'* and *'facecus'* (= the Latin *'facetus,'* i.e., 'elegant in speech'). Associated with it was generosity, an idea preserved in the pun of a popular ditty: 'Fevrier de tous les mois / Le plus court et moins courtois.'[19] The *Romance of the Rose* brings Courtoisie into her own, assigning that feminine personification and her son, Bel Accueil, important roles as Love's allies in the Garden of Delight. The lady's enemy and opposite, locked in by rhymes, is Villanie. The contrasted pair, cortesia/villania return, rhyme-linked, in the thirteenth-century Tuscan adaptation of the *Rose, Il fiore,* which revives her offspring, Bellacoglienza, now a daughter to suit the Italian noun's gender. (It also attests the forms 'corteseggiare,' meaning 'to go about being courteous,' 'to carry on courteously,' and 'incortesito,' past participle of an implied verb 'incortesire,' meaning 'to cause to be courteous.') Dante will later mate the same antonyms when he refuses to wipe away Frate Alberigo's frozen tears: 'e cortesia fu lui esser villano' [and to be rude to him was courtesy (*Inf.* 33.150)].[20]

With Brunetto Latini's *Tesoretto,* Courtesy's ambiance shifts to embrace categories inherited from classical philosophy. Her identity, still 'courtly,' is here embedded in a taxonomy of the cardinal virtues and their facets that descends from Aristotle's *Nicomachean Ethics.* Widely read in Boccaccio's milieu,[21] the *Tesoretto* could figure *a fortiori* among sources for *Decameron* I.8, given the novella's lines of connection with *Inferno* 15, 16, and 17, a Brunettonian sphere of influence. Although Latini's fame today rests more on questions of his affectional preference than familiarity with what he wrote, this allegorical poem of ca. 1260 has a special distinction. It counts as one of the earliest examples in a genre for which Renaissance Italy would grow famous, the courtesy book.

Travelling horseback through a visionary landscape, the knight
Brunetto reaches a lovely plain, site of a grand court. Empress there is
Virtue. She has four daughters, the queens Prudence, Temperance, For-
titude, and Justice. Handmaidens accompany each, the most attractive
to Brunetto being those in the train of Justice: Cortesia, Larghezza,
Leanza, Prodezza [Courtesy, Largesse, Loyalty, Prowess]. Larghezza
delivers a speech that concludes with advice concerning 'court people.'
It is a passage that enriches our understanding of men in society like
Bergamino and Guiglielmo Borsiere:

> Hacci gente di corte
> che sono use ed acorte
> a sollazzar la gente,
> ma domandan sovente
> danari e vestimenti:
> certo, se tu ti senti
> lo poder di donare,
> ben déi corteseggiare,
> guardando d'ogne lato
> di ciascun lo suo stato. (ll. 1495–1504)

[There are people of court whose custom it is to entertain folk cleverly, but
they often ask for money and clothes; of course, if you feel you are in a
position to give, you certainly should carry on courteously, taking full
account of each one's status.]

Larghezza then sends the narrator errant to Cortesia, who imparts her
own long lesson on conduct, but not until she has said a bit about
herself:

> Sie certo che Larghezza
> è 'l capo e la grandezza
> di tutto mio mistero,
> sì ch'io non vaglio guero,
> e s'ella non m'aita
> poco sarei gradita. (ll. 1587–96)

[Be certain that Largesse is the head and greatness of all my mystery, so
that I am scarcely worth anything if she does not help me, and little favor
would I find.]

Obviously, Brunetto's Cortesia, so reliant on Larghezza, is similar to Boccaccio's, since the lady of whom Guiglielmo Borsiere speaks erases Ermino's 'Avarizia.'

As largesse opposed to avarice, courtesy finds another witness in Folgore da San Gimignano, a sonneteer active during the second decade of the fourteenth century. In his vignette, a reversal of the usual iconography, the virtue gets trampled by male figures. Perhaps the poet's hoped for patrons, they are at any rate men whose noblesse should oblige, yet they stand hooked on the vice that Courtesy can correct: 'Cortesia cortesia cortesia chiamo, / e da nessuna parte mi risponde; / ... / Avarizia le genti ha prese a l'amo, / ed ogne grazia distrugge e confonde: / però, se eo me doglio, eo so ben onde; / de voi, possenti, a Deo me ne richiamo. / Ché la mia madre cortesia avete / messa sì sotto 'l piè, che non si leva' [Courtesy, courtesy, courtesy, I call, and nowhere does she reply ... Avarice has caught the people with her hook, and she destroys and confounds all grace; therefore, if I lament, I have good reason; in my complaint about you, men of power, I call on God, for you are trampling Courtesy, my mother.].[22]

Information, near contemporary, from Dante's *Convivio* gives us more to go on. Glossing 'wise and courteous,' epithets of his lady in the first *canzone*, he affirms:

nulla cosa sta più bene in donna che cortesia. E non siano li miseri volgari anche di questo vocabulo ingannati, che credono che cortesia non sia altro che larghezza; e larghezza è una speziale, e non generale cortesia! Cortesia e onestade è tutt'uno: e però che ne le corti anticamente le vertudi e li belli costumi s'usavano, sì come oggi s'usa lo contrario, si tolse quello vocabulo da le corti, e fu tanto a dire cortesia quanto uso di corte. Lo qual vocabulo se oggi si togliesse de le corti, massimamente d'Italia, non sarebbe altro a dire che turpezza. (II, x, 7–8)

[Nothing more becomes a lady than courtesy. And let not miserable common folk, who think that courtesy is no different from largesse, be deceived by this word, because largesse is a special, not general, courtesy! Courtesy and honesty are one and the same, and since in the courts of olden days, virtues and fair manners were the custom, just as today the opposite is the custom, they took that word from the courts, and courtesy meant 'custom of the courts.' If that word were taken today from the courts, it would mean the same as turpitude.][23]

Largesse, then, is one particular aspect of courtesy, which stands more broadly for 'courtliness' in the most positive sense, being that virtue named for the place where people used to practise it, but no longer do. Here we are coming close, quite nicely so, to Lauretta's stance on its disappearance in *Decameron* I.8.

Luckily, we do not have to rest with Dante; we can hear Boccaccio himself on the subject of courtesy. He defines it in the *Esposizioni sopra la Comedìa* with glosses on 'cortesia e valor' of *Inferno* 16, line 67:

> 'cortesia' par che consista negli atti civili, cioè nel vivere insieme liberal-mente e lietamente, e fare onore a tutti secondo la possibilità; 'valore' par che riguardi più all'onore della republica, all'alteza delle 'mprese e ancora agli essercizi dell'arme, nelle quali costoro furono onorevoli e magnifichi cittadini. (*Espos.* 16.53)

> ['Courtesy' seems to involve civil acts, that is, living together generously and gladly, and honoring everyone according to one's means; 'valour' seems to concern more the honour of the republic, high undertakings, and again, the exercise of arms, in which things these men were honourable and magnificent citizens.]

On his source Boccaccio is silent. But intermediate aid from Brunetto Latini can help reconstruct it, since admonishments delivered by Lady Courtesy in the *Tesoretto* could be reduced to a kindred *sententia*. Corte-sia there, recall, was a handmaid to Justice, one of four sibling queens mothered by Virtue (Prodezza, Temperanza, Fortezza, Giustizia), each with her personal retinue of servants. What Brunetto's court holds is a moral pyramid: at the top, Virtue regnant; then her offspring, the four cardinal virtues; and, finally, grouped at the base with each, a retinue of satellite virtues, or facets. This system, which portrays the virtues with their character traits attendant, reflects Aristotle's basic defini-tions as they were expanded through many centuries. The most influ-ential accretions came from Cicero, who gave 'parts' to each virtue (*De inventione* 2, 53–4); the framework outlined by Macrobius (*Commentar-ium in somnium Scipionis* I.8); and a *Formula honestae vitae* ascribed in the Middle Ages to Seneca, but actually a treatise of the sixth century by Martin of Braga. Tuve has demonstrated how such elaborated cate-gories were 'completely habitual' from the late classical period, and that they continued in force through the end of the Renaissance, a powerful tradition compendiously attested by Spenser's *Faerie Queene*.[24] That Ser Brunetto's Cortesia should give advice on manners with the voice of Aristotle – the post-Hellenic, 'perfected' Aristotle – should not in the least surprise us.

Brunetto's philosophical allegory, putting Virtue in an Aristotelian context, finds space for Courtesy in the train of Justice. What suggests their relationship is the fact that both have a distributive function and strive to give every man his due. But if the *Tesoretto* is typical of medieval courtesy books for its scheme of virtues faceted, the author's particular collocation of Courtesy, peripheral to a core virtue, is unusual.[25] Why Brunetto slotted Cortesia where he did can be explained if we assume that he understood the term as equivalent to 'Friendship,' since from Macrobius on, 'Amicitia' was reckoned among the facets of Justice.

But Courtesy-as-Friendship could, and did, have another, more central place in the Philosopher's system. Hinted at by Brunetto's longer treatise on the virtues, which adapts into Old French Aristotle's *Ethics* (*Tresor* 2), it was clearly recognized by Boccaccio. The *Ethics* was a text Boccaccio must have poured over, wisdom so highly valued that he himself transcribed into his copy, which survives today, the commentary by Thomas Aquinas.[26] When glossing 'cortesia' in his *Esposizioni* on the *Comedy*, Boccaccio condenses what Aristotle had said about the one virtue among his twelve that goes 'without a name.' It is a quality, according to the Philosopher, that most closely resembles friendship.

Virtue, for Aristotle, is a mean. His nameless virtue 'like friendship' is the mean concerned with pleasantness and sadness arising from human intercourse. The man who has it 'seems to be concerned with the pleasure and pains of social life.' This virtue differs from friendship, however, because one does not apply it just to people for whom fondness is felt. Whoever possesses this virtue, which springs from right inner disposition, will use it both with strangers and intimates, doing the proper thing with each person in whatever measure appropriate. He will seek to give pleasure and decline to inflict pain, but if long-term benefits warrant, he will not hesitate to cause temporary grief. Common to the men who have this median virtue is the ability to live agreeably and gladly with others, always communicating becomingly (*Ethics* 1126b-1127a).

Boccaccio derives Guiglielmo Borsiere's courtesy initially from Dante's *Inferno*, where Guiglielmo was distressing Brunetto Latini's companions on the fiery desert with reports of that virtue's death. The substance of his virtue, though, a quiddity that he sought to promote in Genoa, has philosophical underpinnings as ancient as Aristotle. In its classical sense, 'cortesia' is Aristotle's 'near-friendship,' the ability to interact properly with other men as they merit and our means permit. From this ethical context comes Boccaccio's gloss on *Inferno* 16, line 67: '"cortesia" par che consista negli atti civili, cioè nel vivere insieme liberalmente e lietamente, e fare onore a tutti secondo la possibilità' (*Espos.* 16.53) ['courtesy' seems to consist in civil acts, that is, in living together generously and happily, and honoring everyone as one is able]. Aquinas, commenting on Aristotle's 'friendship,' explains that since the affable man observes the same behaviour with acquaintances as well as strangers, his virtue resembles liberality, the virtue that regards the correct use of riches and is the mean between avarice and prodigality. Like a man near-friendly (or, we could here say, like a courteous man), the liberal person gives, not because he is fond of someone but because his nature is to be a free spender.

With the benefit of definitions like these, we better appreciate aspects of *Decameron* I.8. Getting along with others, says Aristotle, may sometimes require reprimanding them. So Lauretta's ideal man of court can, 'father-like, rebuke the misdeeds of the wicked with sharp reproofs.' After Ermino has been cured of his incapacity to deal correctly with wealth, his avarice vanishes into its opposite, a form of generosity whose medieval names were liberality and largesse. Once converted, Ermino practises courtesy as much with compatriots as travellers: 'E da questo dì innanzi, di tanta virtù fu la parola da Guiglielmo detta, fu il più/ liberale e 'l più/ grazioso gentile uomo e quello che più/ e' forestieri e i cittadini onorò/ che altro che in Genova fosse a' tempi suoi' [And from that day forward, so great was the power of the word spoken by Guiglielmo, he was the most liberal and the most gracious gentleman, and the one most hospitable, both to outlanders and citizens, in the Genoa in those times (§18)]. Ermino's Genoese courtesy is none other than the nameless Greek virtue like friendship, amicable but sometimes stern, that makes for constancy in good behaviour, be it with intimates, be it with strangers. In Boccaccio's happy ending, pat phrasings of the fairy tale mingle with solid strands of Aristotle.

By the logic of medieval virtue systems, friendship and liberality shelter together under the umbrella of justice. There, for example, 'amicitia' and 'liberalitas' are assigned by Guillaume de Conches in his *Moralium dogma philosophorum*, a treatise of the mid-twelfth century with many European translations.[27] Ser Brunetto, writing a century later, attaches Larghezza and Cortesia (alias Amity) to Giustizia among the latter's following of virtue-facets. Thomas Aquinas, too, counts liberality and friendship as parts of justice, which concern 'those things that belong to our intercourse with other men, rendering to each one his right, or his own.' Again, Aquinas asserts, quoting Cicero's *De officiis*, justice has as its object to keep men together in society and mutual intercourse (*Summa theologica* II, II, Qu. 58, Art. 1–2).

If the female narrators in the *Decameron* are at a submerged level personifications of the Seven Virtues, Lauretta carries the banner of Justice. Narrator in eighth position on Day One, she is also given the eighty-eighth tale (IX.8), a pendant to I.8 that features other characters out of Dante's Hell: violent Filippo Argenti and the glutton Ciacco, who, unable to afford his appetite, decided to be 'non del tutto *uomo di corte* ma morditore e a usare con coloro che ricchi erano' [not quite a *man of court* but a satiric wit, and to frequent people who were rich]. Positioned to speak in eighth place on corresponding Days (the two Days without a set topic, One and Nine) in the chiastic structure around Day Five in the *Decameron*, the same young woman presides, not coincidentally, as her *brigata*'s ruler for the Eighth Day. This is so because justice, subject of the central tale on Day Eight and the virtue Lauretta represents, was equated in Pythagorean and Christian symbolism with the number 8.[28] Boccaccio assigns to the narrator most like Justice, whose aspects pertain to generosity and the friendship that lets men live together, his parable of greed cured by courtesy.

Grafted to the chivalric 'courtoisie' of Old French romance, Aristotle's virtue without a name, a kind of friendship related to liberality, made its way into the Middle Ages. On the one hand, what the ancient Greek authority called affability could authenticate a modern, vernacular concept. Conversely, Courtesy could be installed in an Aristotelian niche, just where the Master of Those who Know had left an opening for a quality ('like friendship') in need of a label.

Testimony to the hybrid's vitality is the courtesy book, a type already taking shape in Brunetto Latini's thirteenth-century *Tesoretto*. Another indicative treatise, one-part Aristotle and one-part chivalry, is the contemporary *Regiment of Princes* by Giles of Rome, Bishop of Bourges. His manual of conduct, designed to form an ideal prince, relies heavily for its precepts on the Philosopher's *Ethics* as well as the *Politics*. Of the twelve virtues reported from the former, that without a name is described under a rubric that in the Old Tuscan translation reads 'dibuonairetà' ('affability'). The introduction to discussion of all the virtues, though, gives the same term of near-friendship not as 'debonaireness,' but as 'cortesia.'[29]

In this mixed form as Aristotelian 'friendliness' and chivalry's highest virtue, courtesy flourished across Europe for at least four centuries. A prime example is the Renaissance epitome that still ranks today as Italy's Emily Post, *Galateo, ovvero de' costumi*. Giovanni della Casa named his dialogue on manners after its chief interlocutor, messer Galateo, a judge at the Council of Trent who in 1567 wrote the first vernacular commentary on Aristotle's *Ethics*. Historical credentials aside, this Galateo, whose name was to become synonymous with etiquette, fits a literary profile modelled on Boccaccio's gentlemen courtiers. He is 'piacevole e ben parlante, e di grazioso aspetto, e molto avea de' suoi dì usato alle corti de' gran signori' [pleasant and well spoken, graceful in appearance, and in his time he had much frequented the courts of the great lords]. Giving advice on how to tell an anecdote, Galateo actually refers to *Decameron* I.8, recollected in somewhat fuzzy fashion.[30]

Courtesy's most compendious Renaissance exponent was Edmund Spenser, who gave to that virtue the entire sixth book of the *Faerie Queene*. Figured by good Sir Calidore, Courtesie 'follows' Justice, the subject of Book 5. It is the virtue that 'of all goodly manners is the ground, / And roote of ciuill conuersation' (6.1.1). None is more fitting for knights and ladies, 'to bear themselues aright / To all of each degree' (6.2.1). In the heart of a pastoral land, far from the court where its name originated, the Graces teach 'all complements of curtesie': 'They teach vs, how to each degree and kynde we should our selues demeane, to low, to hie, to friends, to foes, which skill men call Ciuility' (6.10.23). Spenser is still transmitting the same heritage from Aristotle that had passed Boccaccio's way over two hundred years before.[31] In his acceptance as much as Boccaccio's, Courtesy is an ethical, civic virtue that forms the cement of society. Guiglielmo Borsiere, maker of peace treaties, marriages, pleasant recreation – and necessary reprimands – personifies the most civilized of human traits, a virtue that in action and eloquence brings and holds men together.

Lamenting Courtesy's demise, Lauretta sings in a time-honoured chorus of *laudatores temporis acti*. Like the old men Castiglione takes to task in his *Libro del Cortegiano*, they think the present much fallen off from the past, when they were young and things were right. (Ironically, to re-enter his golden circle at Urbino, Castiglione himself must retrogress twenty years.) Such nostalgia, which echoes through every era in myths of a Golden Age and Paradise Lost, finds expression in the poets' recurrent commonplace, Bygone was better. 'Le temps passé trop mieulx valoit,' wept Eustache Deschamps at the dark court of fifteenth-century France.[32] Kindred sadness creeps into the thoughts of

Don Fabrizio Salina, the fictional aristocrat modelled on Prince Tomasi di Lampedusa's forebearer, as he anticipates the sudden rise to power of a nouveau-riche class in nineteenth-century Sicily: 'Noi fummo i Gattopardi, i Leoni; quelli che ci sostituiranno saranno gli sciacalletti, le iene' [We were the Leopards, the Lions; those who take our place will be the jackals, the hyenas]. [33]

From the *Novellino*, microstories harking back to the reign of Emperor Frederick II, comes narrative tradition antecedent to Dante and Boccaccio. As the book's title-rubric announces, courtesy belongs more to the past than to the present: *Questo libro tratta d'alquanti fiori di parlare, di belle cortesie e di be' risposti e de belle valentie e doni, secondo che, per lo tempo passato, hanno fatto molti valenti uomini* [This book treats of a goodly number of flowers of speech, fair courtesies and fine replies and of fine worthy actions and gifts, according to what, in time past, many worthy men did]. A story about courtesy in a town called Brettinoro (near Forlì) makes explicit the theme of that virtue's passing:

> 'Intra gli altri bei costumi de' nobili di Brettinoro, era il convivare e che non voleano, che uomo vendereccio vi tenesse ostello. Ma una colonna di pietra era nel mezzo del castello, alla quale, come entrava dentro il forestiere, era menato; ed a una delle campanelle, che ivi erano, conveniali mettere le redine del cavallo, o arme, o cappello che avesse. E come la sorte gli dava, così era menato alla casa, per lo gentile uomo al quale era attribuita quella campanella, ed onorato secondo suo grado. La qual colonna e campanelle furon trovate, per tollere matera di scandalo intra li detti gentili; ché ciascuno prima correva a menarsi a casa li forestieri, sì come oggi quasi si fugge.'

> [Among the other fine customs of the Brettinoro nobles was their conviviality and refusal to have anyone keep an inn for money. Instead, in the middle of the castle there was a stone column, to which any stranger who entered was led; and he would have to hang the reigns of his horse, or his arms, or cape, or whatever, on one of the metal rings fastened there. And as luck decided, the gentleman who had claim to that ring would lead him to his house, and he would be entertained according to his rank. They devised that column with rings to prevent cause for discord among the said nobles, because each one used to rush first to bring home the outlanders, just as today they all but shun them.][34]

Dante takes the same stance when contending that 'courtesy and valour' are dead in Florence. He keeps to it fiercely throughout his *Commedia*. So his Guido del Duca recites regrets (*Purg.* 14.103–14) famous for their afterlife in the opening verses of Ariosto's epic:

> Non ti maravigliar s'io piango, Tosco,
> quando rimembro [...]
> le donne e' cavalier, li affanni e li agi
> che ne 'nvogliava amore e cortesia
> là dove i cuor son fatti sì malvagi.
> O Bretinoro, ché non fuggi via,
> poi che gita se n'è la tua famiglia
> e molta gente per non esser ria?

[Marvel not, Tuscan, if I weep when I remember ... the ladies and the knights, the toil and the sports to which love and courtesy moved us, there where hearts have become so wicked! O Bretinoro, why do you not flee away, now that your family has departed, with many another, in order to escape corruption?]

Marco Lombardo, too, speaks in the same vein, his denunciation echoing Iacopo Rusticucci's question from the corresponding canto of the first canticle (*Purg.* 16.115–16): 'In sul paese ch'Adice e Po riga, / solea *valore e cortesia* trovarsi' [On the land that is watered by the Adige and the Po *valor and courtesy* were once to be found]. Over and over again, Dante's application of courtesy in the *Commedia* reflects the animus of the etymology given in his *Convivio*. 'Cortesia' derives from 'corte,' and it is part of the Ghibelline society that no longer exists. Beings courteous in the Otherworld are, apart from God, consequently a select few, called forth from a past dim, remote. Virgil, at first a flickering, barely visible shade, takes on poetic presence as the 'courteous Mantuan spirit' (*Inf.* 2.58). Cacciaguida, the pilgrim's great-great-grandfather and a 'courteous' ancestor, takes us back to a Florence of better days, when that virtue must have been young in the city (*Par.* 15.48). Repeated references to the matter of courtesy in cantos analogous by position (*Inf.* 16, *Purg.* 16, *Par.* 15 and 17), chart a line of connected comments. Is courtesy dead, asks Iacopo Rusticucci? It is, answers Marco Lombardo. See, then, what it used to be, says Cacciaguida, who foretells the hospitality of another 'Lombardo' to Dante in his exile. For Boccaccio, no doubt, that Lombard was Can Grande, the Veronese lord whose 'courtesy' survives, momentarily marred, in the First Day of the *Decameron* beside the tale of Guglielmo Borsiere.

But if, in the *querelle des anciens et modernes*, Lauretta sides with Dante, Boccaccio as author seems to take a different view. No doubt there is, in the *Decameron*, a nostalgia for the days when knights were knights and ladies were ladies. Still, Boccaccio's anthology is quite sensibly anchored in its present. The *cortesia* disbursed by Guiglielmo Borsiere is a very Decameronian virtue, one quite alive and well in the comportment of the frame narrators. If the *Decameron* is the mercantile epic, written for a new social class who are knights not of the sword but the florin, Boccaccio shapes an ethical system suited to that historical reality – one that the new bourgeoisie could even read as 'an urban variant' of the medieval courtesy book.[35] Boccaccio must, perforce, make pronouncements on money, but he argues the preservation of older, stabilizing values in a society that was rapidly changing. There is a potential danger in the newly rich traders (the 'gente nuova') whose sudden wealth ('sùbiti guadagni') may give merchants wrong attitudes towards money. But 'cupidigia' [greed], a Dantesque gong word applied to Ermino, has shifted its meaning. No longer encompassing sin that suffocates Christian charity, avarice is now a secular problem, materialism that threatens social order. It matters not so much whether Ermino, as a result of his conversion, can get into heaven – although we assume his candidacy should be strong on the reformed ticket. What is more important is that he get into society, achieve the integration back into his community from which his vice had alienated him to anonymity. For Dante, the rising bourgeoisie were destroying Florence. For Boccaccio, their prosperity can be beneficent to the collective, provided gain not mean greed, provided money be wed to manners, provided the purse be carried by Courtesy.

NOTES

1 Thematics of *Dec.* I.7 suggest that Boccaccio took Dante's first host on the path of exile prophesied by Cacciaguida (*Par.* 17.70–2) to be Can Grande. The identity of Dante's 'great Lombard,' however, is problematic.

2 In ancient painting and statuary, as well as Renaissance medals, the purse was an attribute of Mercury. See Guy de Terverant, *Attributs et symboles dans*

l'art profane 1450–1600, 75–6. Boccaccio gives Mercury power over 'negociationes et emporia' [business dealings and market places] as well as 'eloquentia' when he catalogues that god's activities in *Genealogie* 2.7.5.

3 Dynamics connecting Days One and Six have attracted a growing circle of observers. See Barolini, 'Wheel of the Decameron'; Hollander, 'Boccaccio's Dante' and in *Boccaccio's Dante and the Shaping Force of Satire*, 21–52; Kirkham, *The Sign of Reason*, 173–97; Mazzotta, '*Decameron*: Marginality of Literature,' 64–81, and *World at Play*, 59 ff.; Stewart, *Rhetorica e mimica*, 19–38; van der Voort, 'Convergenze e divaricazioni.'

4 Boccaccio, *Decameron*, ed. Vittore Branca, in *Tutte le opere* (1976). This is the text cited throughout.

5 As Branca notes in his commentary, 1036, in 1365 Boccaccio would himself carry out a mission from the Florentine Signoria to the Doge of Genoa on behalf of certain Grimaldi family members. For that family's history, see the *Enciclopedia italiana* (1933), s.v. 'Grimaldi.'

6 Battaglia, *La coscienza*, 469: 'si vale di un fatto che è preformato e si condiziona su una intenzionalità aprioristica e tradizionale. Quel fatto o episodio, quel tema o frammento narrativo è un dato costante, di longeva discendenza, che si presenta anteriore alla stessa esperienza, nel momento stesso in cui intende esemplificarla e oggettivarla.' On the exemplum see also, e.g., Paolella, *Rettorica e racconto*; Delcorno, *Exemplum e letteratura*; and Kircher, 'The Modality of Moral Communication.'

7 Discussions of the *Psychomachia* can be found in Mâle, *The Gothic Image*, 99 ff., and Réau, *Iconographie*, 1: 177–8. Cf., with amusing deprecation, C.S. Lewis, *Allegory of Love*. For a classic introduction, see Katzenellenbogen, *Allegories*.

8 These examples, from Aulnay, France (12th c.), are cited by Mâle, *The Gothic Image*, 102, who refers to others at Notre Dame du Port at Clermont, the cathedral at Tournai, Notre Dame de la Coudre at Parthenay, St Hilaire at Melle, St Nicolas at Civray, Fenioux in Charente-Inférieure, and St Pompain in the Deux-Sèvres.

9 Mâle, *The Gothic Image*, 109.

10 Réau, *Iconographie*, 1: 176 ff., also mentions an English baptismal font at Stanton Fitzwarren, Wiltshire, where the virtues as warriors chase vices around the basin. Latin inscriptions identify them: Largitas-Avaritia, Modestia-Ebrietas, Humilitas-Superbia, Pietas-Discordia, Misericordia-Invidia, Temperantia-Luxuria, Patientia-Ira, Pudicitia-Libido. When, for requirements of structure or symmetry, the seven cardinal and theological figures need to be expanded to eight, the extra pair, as here, was usually Humility-Pride. See Kirkham, *The Sign of Reason*, 249–68.

11 Giorgio Petrocchi, ed., *La Commedia secondo l'antica vulgata*, Charles S. Singleton, trans., *The Divine Comedy, Inferno*; Franco Fido, 'Dante personaggio mancato.'

12 Cited from Biagi et al., *La Divina Commedia*, vol. 1, *Inf.* 16.

13 Boccaccio, *Comedia di Dante, Inf.* 16.54: 'Questi fu cavalier di corte, uomo costumato molto e di laudevol maniera, ed era il suo essercizio, e degli altri suoi pari, il trattar paci tra grandi e gentili uomini, trattar matrimoni e parentadi e talora con piacevoli e oneste novelle recreare gli animi de' faticati e confortargli alle cose onorevoli; il che i moderni non fanno, anzi quanto più sono scellerati e spiacevoli e con brutte operazioni e parole, più piacciono e meglio son proveduti'; *Decameron* I.8.7–10: 'arrivò a Genova un valente uomo di corte e costumato e ben parlante, il qual fu chiamato Guiglielmo Borsiere, non miga simile a quegli li quali sono oggi ... E là dove a que' tempi soleva essere il lor mestiere ... trattar paci, dove guerre o sdegni tra gentili uomini fosser nati, o trattar matrimonii, parentadi e amistà, e con belli motti e leggiadri ricreare gli animi degli affaticati e sollazzar le corti e con agre reprensioni, sì come padri, mordere i difetti de' cattivi, e questo con premii assai leggieri; oggi di rapportar male dall'uno all'altro, in seminare zizzania, in dir cattività e tristizie ... e con false lusinghe gli uomini gentili alle cose vili e scellerate ritrarre s'ingegno il lor tempo di consumare. E colui è più caro avuto e più da' miseri e scostumati signori onorato e con premii grandissimi essaltato, che più abominevoli parole dice o fa atti ... argomento assai evidente che le virtù, di qua giù dipartitesi, hanno nella feccia de' vizii i miseri viventi abbandonati.' Unless otherwise indicated, translations are mine. For a discussion of the concept of logomimesis, see Forni, *Adventures in Speech*, esp. ch. 4, 'The Poetics of Realization.'

14 Horace (*Satires* 2.2.142) lampoons Opimius, whose doctor hoped to save him from starvation by publically emptying the man's moneybags and warning him that if he did not spend to eat, he would die, and an heir would pounce into possession of all his wealth. See also, in the same context, the Roman poet's anecdote of Servius Oppidius and his sons, one a prodigal, the other a hoarder.

15 Paris, Bibliothèque de l'Arsenal, MS 5070, f. 32r; Vienna, Österreichische Nationalbibliothek, MS 2561, f. 38r; Paris, Bibliothèque Nationale, MS 12421, f. 36r. For reproductions see Branca, *Decameron* (1966), 1: 68–71. For descriptions of these princely copies of the *Decameron*, with accompanying reproductions of images from other tales, see Branca, *Boccaccio visualizzato*, 3: 218–30, nos. 85, 86. A photograph of a double cup appears in Hoving et al., *Secular Spirit*, 268. I thank Paul Watson for his thoughts concerning the manuscript illustrations of this story.

16 Thaumaturgical icons have a rich Western history, early witnessed by
   Emperor Constantine's conversion through the sign of the True Cross,
   which he saw in a dream, and likenesses of Saints Peter and Paul, shown
   him by Pope Sylvester. Famous cases later materialize in legends attached
   to St Francis of Assisi; St Catherine of Alexandria, recipient of a miraculous
   Madonna and Child; and her namesake, who was Boccaccio's contemporary, Santa Caterina of Siena. See Meiss, *Painting*, ch. 5, 'Texts and Images.'
   Christopher De Hamil, in *A History of Illuminated Manuscripts*, ch. 1, speaks
   of the power of the cross and pictures of saints carried by Augustinian mis-
   sionaries to Britain in the sixth century. So, too, in secular wise, Courtesy is
   the 'sign' that converts Ermino, whether we take her from the artists' imag-
   inings or the poet's.
17 Pier Massimo Forni, personal communication. Cennini's *Libro dell'arte*
   [1437], 4, asserts in the opening chapter that in the art of painting 'conviene
   avere fantasia e operazione di mano, di trovare cose non vedute, caccian-
   dosi sotto ombra di naturali [= facendole apparire come naturali], e fer-
   marle con la mano, dando a dimostrare quello che non è, sia' [one must
   have fantasy and a controlled hand to find things unseen, hidden under the
   shadow of natural things, and capture them with the hand, giving the
   impression that what is not, is].
18 Cottino-Jones, *Order from Chaos*, 42.
19 Carlo Battisti and Giovanni Alessio, *Dizionario etimologico italiano*, s.v.
   'corte,' 'cortese'; Tobler and Lommatzsch, *Altfranzösisches Wörterbuch*, s.v.
   'courtois,' 'courtoisie.'
20 Salvatore Battaglia, *Grande dizionario della lingua italiana*, cites numerous
   other examples, s.v. 'cortesia': 'Amor che in sé virtode: / del vile uom face
   prode, / s'egli è villano in cortesia lo muta, / di scarso largo a divenir lo
   aiuta' (Bonagiunta) [Love that in itself is virtue makes the coward brave; if
   he is coarse, it makes him courteous; it helps him change from stingy to
   generous]; and s.v. 'cortese': 'Mostrava il candido petto, del quale, mercé
   del vestimento cortese nella sua scollatura, gran parte se n'apriva a' riguar-
   danti' (Boccaccio) [she showed her white breast, a good part of which was
   open to the beholders, thanks to her dress, courteous in its plunging neck-
   line]. For Courtesy in the *Roman de la Rose*, ed. C. Langlois, see vv. 777 ff.
   (she dances in garden of Deduit); vv. 1229 ff. (she is characterized as wise,
   reasonable); vv. 10449 (she is among the barony of the God of Love); vv.
   10719 ff. (Courtesy coupled with generosity); vv. 21277 ff. (Courtesy prays
   that her son grant the rose to the lover). Cf. *Il fiore*, ed. Gianfranco Contini,
   in Dante Alighieri, *Opere minori*, vol. 1, pt. 1.

21 Although only ten manuscripts of the *Tesoretto* survive, they represent a wide range of families, indicating that it enjoyed great popularity throughout the Trecento but fell rapidly out of favor in the next century. The text can be found in Gianfranco Contini, ed., *Poeti del Duecento*, 2: 172 and 869 ff.

22 Connection noted by Branca in his commentary on the *Decameron*, 1036; text cited from Muscetta and Rivalta, *Poesia del Duecento*, 1: 402.

23 *Convivio*, ed. Giuseppe Busnelli and Giuseppe Vandelli, rev. Antonio Enzo Quaglio.

24 Tuve, *Allegorical Imagery*, 61–77.

25 I have found it only in the *Tesoretto*. To discover exactly which perfecting tradition(s) Brunetto relied on for his virtue families would require some research. In the *Tesoretto* he gives only the facets of Justice; for aspects of the other three virtues the reader is invited to look 'nel gran Tesoro' (v. 1351). His discussion in *Li livres dou Tresor*, ed. F.J. Carmody, 2: 55 ff., makes reference to Tully, Seneca, and Alain. Not always clearly drawn, the alignments seem to be as follows: I. Prudence with (1) Memoire, (2) Porveance, (3) Garde (cf. Lat. *cautio*), (4) Cognoissance (*circumspectio* ?); II. Tempérance with, (1) Honesté, (2) Chasteté, (3) Sobrieté, (4) Retenance, (5) Continence; III. Force with (1) Magnanimité, (2) Fiance, (3) Seurté, (4) Constance, (5) Patience; IV. Justice with (1) Reddeur (*vindicatio*), (2) Liberalité, (3) Religion, (4) Pitié, (5) Innocense, (6) Charité, (7) Amitié, (8) Reverance, (9) Concorde, (10) Misericorde.

26 Auzzas, 'I codici autografi,' 1–20. I cite Aristotle and the commentary by Thomas Aquinas from *Commentary on the Nicomachean Ethics*.

27 Tuve, *Allegorical Imagery*, 60–1.

28 The Pythagoreans called 8 Justice because that number could be divided into two equal halves. In patristic commentary on the Bible, 8 became associated with the justice awaiting at the Last Judgement. See Kirkham, *The Sign of Reason*, 233, 247, 278. On the 'psychomachia' between vice and virtue in the *Decameron*, see also Kirkham's entry, 'Morale,' 262–3, in *Lessico critico decameroniano*, ed. Renzo Bragantini and Pier Massimo Forni.

29 Giles of Rome, *Del reggimento de' principi*, 27, 73.

30 Della Casa, *Galateo ovvero de' costumi*, 21: 411.

31 Greenlaw, *Fairie Queene*, 325–7, cites William Fenn DeMoss, *Spenser's Twelve Moral Virtues 'According to Aristotle,'* who relates the Spenserian concept of courtesy to Aristotle's Near-Friendliness. In *F.Q.* 6, Courtesy's enemies, Maleffort, Crudor, Sir Turpine, and Mirabella, maltreat all who cross their paths.

32 Huizinga, *Waning*, 36.

33 Tomasi di Lampedusa, *Il gattopardo*, 127.
34 Manganelli, ed., *Il Novellino*, 137.
35 Branca, 'L'epopea dei mercatanti,' in *Boccaccio medievale*, 134–65. David Wallace, *Boccaccio: Decameron*, 33, suggests that the *Decameron* could itself serve as a manual of courtesy for the new merchant class.

The Tale of the King of Cyprus and the Lady of Gascony (I.9)

PIER MASSIMO FORNI

Upon re-reading the story of the king of Cyprus and the lady of Gascony, I found it impossible to dismiss the fact that there are two kinds of novellas in the *Decameron*: those to which we want 'to do service,' and those which we want to serve us. That is to say, we encounter stories that demand a privileged critical treatment, and others from which we want merely to lift an idea. Although this may not be an exceedingly insightful notion, it helped me to envision my approach to a reading of *Decameron* I.9.

We have been seduced by the novellas of the first kind. We want to lose and find ourselves again and again in them. We overindulge them, we are ready to respond to them with our most elaborate intellectual and critical strategies. These are stories about which 'there is a lot to say,' even though they possess a hypnotic quality which at times compels us to just 'watch them work.' We may feel that they have in some fashion explained us even before we have begun to explain them. We do not perceive their significance on the basis of what they can tell us about other stories or even about the book. Endowed with a strong centripetal force, they appear as objects powerfully affirming their autonomy.[1] As professional readers, we want to put ourselves at their service rather than consider them to be service-texts. The first stories that come to mind as belonging to this category are those of Rinaldo d'Asti, Andreuccio da Perugia, Zima, Tancredi and Ghismonda, Lisabetta da Messina, Girolamo and Salvestra, Federigo degli Alberighi, and Messer Torello.

There are then the novellas of the second kind. We may find them satisfactory, even endowed with a perfection of their own, but we hardly perceive them as engaging absolutes. Although they make us think without engrossing us, they seem to demand a different kind of critical attention. A novella of this kind is not the first we might choose to study. There is something centrifugal in it and we think that we could be satisfied by simply putting to use that centrifugal force. To put it in rather coarse terms: we do not really want to speak about the text; rather, we want the text to speak about other things, we want its allegorical potential exploited. Boccaccio himself, with the *novelletta* of the goslings ('non una novella intera ... ma parte d'una' [not a complete novella ... but part of one (IV Intro. §11)] created a text with a declared functional value: a centrifugal text that serves to justify and interpret other texts. Although Guido Almansi's reading of the story of Madonna Oretta (VI.1) may not be totally convincing, I am ready to acknowledge that a good part of the interest of that story lies in what it tells us about other things.[2] I would be reluctant to try to build a complex critical apparatus around VI.1 for its own sake, but I certainly consider that novella an excellent tool for illustrating important aspects of the *Decameron*.

I recognize the simplistic nature of this argument, to which one can easily respond that a text does not attract critical work merely for its own sake. Moreover, the centripetal force of certain texts can be a function of their allegorical nature. I am ready to admit that it is often difficult to determine what makes us devote an inordinate amount of time and energy to a story. However, the fact remains that there are novellas that have the power to impose an elaborate scheme of centripetal critical action upon us, and there are those that do not. When interpreting one of the first kind, we want to construct an ample critical edifice around it – a structure that somehow matches the impact that the text has made upon us. From other novellas we want only to steal a few bricks.

To me, the novella of the king of Cyprus is allegorical. In many ways it is a very simple story – it is, for one thing, the shortest in the book. When I started working on it, I found its simplicity not merely disarming, but almost painful: the text did not seem to yield itself easily to a translation into an essay. As I undertook the task of having to work on a painful text, I decided to respond to it with an 'effortless' reading. I resolved not to overindulge the text artificially. I chose, that is, to look for a single idea which I could snatch, swiftly and painlessly, from the text. Eventually, a viable idea took shape. It is an idea that could have been suggested by readings of other stories: that of Ghino di Tacco (X.2), for example, or that of Cisti (VI.2). However, these are more complex and colourful stories, crowded with signification. In the case at hand, simplicity of form may have helped identify a rewarding interpretation.

The very short story of the King of Cyprus and the lady of Gascony is a most convenient pedagogical tool. Through it, the teacher can demonstrate that in the *Decameron* 'together with the ample and complex novella form, which represents the great innovation of the Boccaccian genius, the exemplum is preserved.'[3] Of course, it is an exemplary tale with a Boccaccian flair, which when viewed in contrast to the version found in the *Novellino* allows one to observe the cardinal directions of Boccaccio's artistic innovation. As a matter of fact, this contrast is an ideal complement to Auerbach's essay on Frate Alberto, wherein a primary goal is the measuring of the distance between Boccaccio and his predecessors.[4]

I will begin by reproducing the version of the story that appears in the *Novellino*, followed by a brief contrastive reading, with the help of current critical texts, of that version and Boccaccio's text.

Novellino LI[5]

Qui conta d'una guasca, come si richiamò a lo re di Cipri:
Era una guasca in Cipri, alla quale fu fatta un dì molta villania e onta tale, che non la poteo sofferire. Mossesi e andonne al re di Cipri, e disse:
– Messere, a voi sono già fatti diecimila disinori, e a me n'è fatto pur uno; priegovi che voi, che tanti n'avete sofferti, m'insegniate sofferire il mio uno. – Lo re si vergognò e cominciò a vendicare l[i] su[oi], e a non voler[n]e più sofferire.

[*This is about a Gascon woman, how she lay a complaint before the king of Cyprus:*
There was a Gascon woman in Cyprus who one day received such an indignity that she could not bear it. She went to the King of Cyprus and said: – Sire, you suffered ten thousand affronts and I but one; you who have sustained so many, please teach me how to sustain mine. – The king was ashamed and began to avenge his affronts and ceased to tolerate them.]

It may be useful to adopt Renato Barilli's terminology, where he speaks of the transition from a *fabula nuda* to a *fabula ornata*. The *Novellino* relies on 'bare plot and the values of essence, of synthesis, and of ellipsis rather than on those of explication and profusion.'[6] We can also use Marga Cottino-Jones's concise and precise definition of pre-Decameronian narrative: 'The earlier form of tale can be described as a reduced and compact structure developing only in one direction out of a close-knit narrative nucleus, created by brief and condensed syntactical constructions and limited lexical choice and centered around a minimal set of main characters.'[7] A *fabula ornata* entails a more generous amount of information about 'circumstances and details of place, time, mores, and psychological make-up.'[8] Boccaccio, indeed, provides his readers with a real, if sketchy, historical background.

The story takes place 'ne' tempi del primo re di Cipri' [during the reign of the first King of Cyprus, cf. the unqualified, more fabulous 're di Cipri,' King of Cyprus, in the *Novellino*], dopo il conquisto fatto della Terra Santa da Gottifré di Buglione' [after the conquest of the Holy Land by King Godfrey of Bouillon]. Boccaccio also accounts for the circumstances of the affront to the woman (who is a 'gentil donna di Guascogna' [gentlewoman of Gascony] rather than simply 'una guasca' [Gascon woman], as in the earlier collection). He then articulates the lady's intention and tells us how she learned of the king's character and behaviour. These elements are absent from the *Novellino*. Mario Baratto finds the essence of Boccaccio's version in this sentence: 'La qual cosa udendo la donna, disperata della vendetta, ad alcuna consolazione della sua noia propose di voler mordere la miseria del detto re' ['On hearing this, the woman lost all hope of obtaining justice, but she decided, to alleviate her woes, to taunt this king with his vileness' (§6)]. He explains:

> that resolve creates a character – one barely sketched, but real. She is an 'intellectual,' in the Boccaccian sense of the word, and the reader will be able to understand the subtlety of her speech, even within the feeble layout of the novella. The rhetorical construction of that speech with its mordancy will be the consolation of the gentlewoman, the only compensation allowed to her. She believes in the values of intelligence and decides to uphold them even when they offer only a gratuitous consolation, one devoid of practical consequences. Hence, the polemic finesse of her brief speech (in the *Novellino* it is extremely brief and crude, because its effect is already a given). In the *Decameron*, the speech is elaborate – built with great polemic sagacity, of a series of subordinate clauses, crafty parenthetical segments, and implied pauses. The well-crafted speech exhausts the woman's action, and it is prepared by tears that are not those of an offended woman who is out to seek justice, but rather those of an actress who cries because she knows that she will not obtain justice and only

wants to create a dramatic effect in front of the coward she intends to sting [...].[9]

Luigi Russo called the lady of Gascony 'an artist of revenge,' and, indeed, Baratto acknowledges his indebtedness to Russo.[10]

The *Novellino* tale ends with the king's shame and change in behavior. We know that the pride that came to him through the woman's words will no longer allow him to tolerate offences committed against him. On the other hand, we are not told if he avenged the offence borne by the courageous woman. In Boccaccio's version there is no mention of shame, rather the sense of the breaking of a spell: Il re, infino allora stato tardo e pigro, quasi dal sonno si risvegliasse [It was as though the king, who until that moment had been laggard and submissive, had been roused from sleep (§7)]. And the lady is the first to benefit from the modification of his behaviour: cominciando dalla ingiuria fatta a questa donna, la quale agramente vendicò, rigidissimo persecutore divenne di ciascuno che contro allo onore della sua corona alcuna cosa commettesse da indi innanzi [He harshly avenged the injury done to this lady, and, from that time on, became the inflexible persecutor of anyone who did anything to discredit the honor of his crown (§7).

Elissa's introductory words seem to leave no trace in the readings of Russo, Battaglia, and Barilli. Alfonso Paolella reproduces the two versions of the story in his monograph on the *Novellino*, but apparently, for his purposes, sees no need to include Elissa's introduction.[11] Yet the introduction, as Baratto observes, gives psychological likelihood to the king's conversion:

> 'Giovani donne, spesse volte già addivenne che quello che varie riprensioni e molte pene date a alcuno non hanno potuto in lui adoperare, una parola molte volte, per accidente non che ex proposito detta, l'ha operato.' (§3)

> [Young ladies, it has happened over and over that a single word, uttered by chance rather than *ex proposito*, has managed to bring about a positive change in a person previously unaffected by reproaches and punishments.]

From this, it seems, Boccaccio is not only interested in the psychology of the lady (that which motivates her to address the king), but in 'this instant that reveals the story of a soul, this fleeting moment in the psychology of individuals in which an action, against all rational expectations, suddenly elicits a positive reaction.'[12]

Similar positive reactions can be found in most stories of the First Day. In I.3, the Saladin's cunning plan to extort money from rich Melchizedech is countered by the latter's ingenuity. In the end, the moneylender's apologue of the three rings inspires a new and positive course of action in the Sultan. Cangrande della Scala (I.7) is a prince who acts in a way not befitting his well-known munificence. With the story of Primas and the Abbot of Cluny, his antagonist, Bergamino manages to modify that behavior. In I.5, a more elaborate counter-plan, one which entails 'e con opere e con parole' [words and actions (§4)] is laid out by the marchioness, who finds herself in a vulnerable position. As the rubric reads: 'La marchesana di Monferrato con un convito di galline e con alquante leggiadre parolette reprime il folle amore del re di Francia' [The Marchioness of Monferrato, by dint of a chicken banquet and a few nimble-witted words, restrains the ill-conceived passion of the king of France]. And again, with a clever remark the 'buon uomo' of I.6 saves himself from persecution by the Inquisitor. Master Alberto (I.10) defends himself from the benevolent mocking of ladies through a clever, self-effacing analogy with leeks, compelling his interlocutors to make amends. The threat of an awkward situation is defused to everybody's satisfaction by Guiglielmo Borsiere's smart repartee (I.8), which has such an impact on the tight-fisted Ermino de' Grimaldi that Ermino becomes the most liberal and civil gentleman in Genoa. Even the story of the sinful monk and of his no less sinful abbot (I.4) culminates with a witty retort – one which is the verbal crystallization of the monk's resourcefulness. The two former antagonists restore harmony to the monastery by reaching a secret pact of connivance: 'E perdonatogli e impostogli di ciò che veduto aveva silenzio, onestamente misero la giovanetta di fuori e poi più volte si dee credere ve la facesser tornare' [(the abbot) pardoned the monk and ordered him not to reveal what he had seen; then they slipped the girl out of the monastery, and we can assume that they afterwards brought her back time and again (§22)].

It is precisely this verbal art, in which the *arte di vivere* manifests itself, that will reappear at the core of the stories of Day Six. It is an art that the reader is invited to appreciate not only on aesthetic, but also on ethical grounds – ethics as the healing power of the word, the need for restoring harmony, and lessons in the *arte di vivere*. Boccaccio's heroes wage a war against the inept, the pompous, the coarse, the hypocritical, the ignorant, the impudent, and the imprudent. Their weapon is often a muffled form of impertinence, a witty impertinence, a pertinent *insolentia*. There is indeed a 'meno che onesto motteggiare' [less than honest witticism] (VI.3.1) and a 'dire onestamente villania' [an honest calling of names/ an elegant way to offend] ('ci ha detta onestamente ... villania' VI.9.14). This *insolentia* is usually met by the benevolent disposition of the victim. In the words of Thomas M. Greene, 'it frequently happens in the *Decameron* that the success of an invention depends not only on its own brilliance but the capacity of those affected to accede, to fall into line, to compromise.'[13] From this nimble combination a supreme Boccaccian moment is born. The reader feels that he or she has witnessed what it means to be alive in a heightened, somewhat exalted way. In this moment the needs of the individual and those of the community coincide, and humankind is able to find an intelligent and genial solution within the complexity of existence. Fredi Chiappelli defines this Boccaccian moment with his usual intellectual elegance:

> The archetypal situation entails a momentary annulment, thanks to a spark of intelligence, of an otherwise unbreakable convention; usually we are presented with an inferior who, being spirited and quick, manages to elicit a smile from a superior. This is accomplished on a level of intellectual fellowship, of charming and breezy complicity in taste, which is a common denominator of humanity. The inferior is thus forgiven, rewarded, or praised. It is the situation of Chichibio, of Cisti, and of a multitude of other minor characters.[14]

The story of the king of Cyprus presents a serious reproof of the character of higher social standing: though shame is not mentioned, the lady has indeed put the king to shame. From this point of view, I.9 relates more closely to the story of Monna Nonna de' Pulci (VI.3) than to that of Chichibio (VI.5). Merriment and zaniness are excluded. Nevertheless, the story belongs entirely to the same tradition of the 'dire onestamente villania.'

One should not lose sight of the social inequality of the protagonists, a fundamental element which continues to appear in these stories. The resourceful heroes and heroines (the lady of Gascony, Melchizedech, the Marchioness of Monferrato, Bergamino, Cisti, Chichibio, Nonna de' Pulci) are all engaged in conflict with a superior. Their victory is the modest but exhilarating triumph allowed to socially weaker individuals. Boccaccio is evidently fascinated by the configuration of a conflict which entails a felicitous tampering with the social codes on the part of the inferior. He seems to relish the lull and leniency that are unexpectedly produced. With an approving smile, he contemplates the bracketing of social tension and the light-footed step into the realm of the ideal. These stories recount the elegance of this moment, and its social auspiciousness: the king of Cyprus 'rigidissimo persecutore divenne di ciascuno che contro allo onore della sua corona alcuna cosa commettesse da indi innanzi' [from that time on, became the inflexible persecutor of anyone who did anything to discredit the honor of his crown (§7)]. What happens is both charming and good.

I would like to suggest that these stories continue to represent another step: that of the author himself from one social sphere (the one allotted to him by virtue of his birth) into a more privileged one. They are stories about access, about the holes in the fabric of destiny that allowed the illegitimate offspring of a Florentine merchant to breathe the rarefied and gentle air of the aristocratic Neapolitan circles.

It is not necessary here to review in detail the seminal years that Boccaccio spent in Naples during his youth. The pages of Branca, Sabatini, Padoan, and many others, are more than adequate to illustrate how much Boccaccio owed to his coming of age in an extremely varied cultural universe comprising the Neapolitan mercantile establishment, the Neapolitan Studium, and the Neapolitan aristocratic society.[15] The *Caccia di Diana, Filocolo, Fiammetta*, and the *Decameron* as well, are vivid testimonials to his Neapolitan experience. The Florentine mercantile and financial colony controlled Angevin finances, making it possible for its more prominent and enterprising members not only to gain access to the court, but even to reach positions of political leadership at the highest levels. Exemplary in this respect was the brilliant career of Niccola Acciaiuoli, a childhood friend of Boccaccio's who became 'Gran Siniscalco,' and, in the words of Branca, the 'real arbiter of the kingdom' in the 1350s and 1360s.[16]

Boccaccio was not destined to become an actor in Neapolitan politics, but he did benefit from the position that his father Boccaccino had reached at the court. A representative of the Bardi bank in Naples, Boccaccino is called 'familiaris et fidelis noster' and 'consiliarius, cambellanus, mercator, familiaris, et fidelis,' in royal documents of 1328 and 1329.[17] Beginning a narrative of the *De casibus*, Boccaccio recalls the time when he 'was still a young man and frequented the court of Robert, king of Jerusalem and Sicily' (IX xxvi, 1). Although we can envision his stay in Naples between 1327 and 1340–1 as a joyous blurring of social lines, we should not be so ingenuous as to disregard the implications of his protracted visit in the Neapolitan gilded open house. We may underscore the essential happiness of that interaction (for there seems to be enough evidence), but we may also postulate a lingering sense of inadequacy. Indeed, it seems unlikely that the young foreigner of bourgeois origins would blissfully feel and act as a peer within that society.

Idalogos, speaking in the *Filocolo* (V.8) as an alter ego of Boccaccio, reveals that he was born of a daughter of the king of France. And this is not the only instance in Boccaccio's works of an allusion to the author's royal blood. Under the veil of the beloved Fiammetta, the reader is supposed to see Maria d'Aquino, illegitimate daughter of King Robert of Anjou. All this may well be 'genealogical snobbism' and literary fantasizing, but perhaps the literary game derives from deeply felt needs.[18] The creation of fictional credentials may be a way of coping with inadequacy, legend coming to the rescue of reality.

In Book IV of the *Filocolo*, the protagonist and his companions are thrown by a storm onto the shores of 'ancient Parthenope,' and after a few days come in contact with the local youth. Exquisite music emanates from a garden in which a festive gathering is taking place.

... i quali canti a Filocolo piacque di stare alquanto a udire, acciò che la preterita malinconia, mitigandosi per la dolcezza del canto, andasse via. Ristette adunque ad ascoltare: e mentre che la fortuna così lui e i campagni fuori del giardino tenea ad ascoltare sospesi, un giovane uscì di quello, e videli, e nell'aspetto nobilissimi e uomini da riverire gli conobbe. Per che egli sanza indugio tornato a' compagni, disse: 'Venite, ono-riamo alquanti giovani, ne' sembianti gentili e di grande essere, i quali, forse vergognandosi di passare qua entro sanza essere chiamati, dimorano di fuori ascoltando i nostri canti.' (IV.14. 3–4)

[It pleased Filocolo to stand and listen for a while to these songs, in the hope that his melancholy, perhaps mitigated by the sweetness of the song, might go away. So he stood and listened; and while fortune kept him and his companions listening outside the garden in this way, a young man came out and saw them, and realized from their appearance that they were most noble gentlemen deserving of being honoured. Therefore, he immediately returned to his companions and said: 'Come, let us pay our respects to these young men, who appear to be courteous and of high station, and who are perhaps hesitant to come in without being invited and stand outside listening to our songs.']

As a meditation on the condition of the outsider ('i quali, forse vergognandosi di passare qua entro senza essere chiamati ...'), this passage is particularly meaningful for our purposes. In the guise of Filocolo, Boccaccio returns to the scene of his acceptance into the circles of young Neapolitan aristocrats. Through fiction, he experiences again the difficulty of belonging, this time not as the son of Boccaccino, but as the son of King Felice and heir to the throne of Marmorina.[19]

Several years later, in 1363, Boccaccio will recall those encounters of his youth in his famous letter to Francesco Nelli. The letter, written in the safe haven of Petrarch's home in Venice, recounts the indignities suffered by Boccaccio during his stay in Naples the preceding fall and winter. He had returned in the hope of securing an honourable position for himself at the court, but he had been ill-treated by Nelli and Acciaiuoli, the very friends who had invited him. It is therefore with a heart brimming with resentment and indignation that he addresses Fran-cesco Nelli. How can Nelli marvel if he, Boccaccio, finally could not bear to remain in the dreadful and disgraceful lodgings allotted to him by the 'generosity' of Niccola Acciaiuoli?

Se tu nol sai, amico, io sono vivuto, dalla mia puerizia infino in intera età nutricato, a Napoli ed intra nobili giovani meco in età convenienti, i quali, quantunque nobili, d'entrare in casa mia né di me visitare si vergognavano. Vedevano me con consuetudine d'uomo e non di bestia, ed assai dilicatamente vivere, sì come noi fiorentini viviamo; vedevamo ancora la mia casa e la masserizia mia, secondo la misura della possibilità mia, splendida assai. Vivono molti di questi, ed insieme meco nella vecchiezza cresciuti, in degnità sono venuti. Non voleva, se io avessi potuto, che, volendo essi continuare l'amicizia, che eglino m'avessono veduto disorrevolmente vivere a modo di bestia e che cio avvenire per mia viltà pensassono.

[If you don't know it, my friend, I lived, from my childhood until I came of age, in Naples, and amongst noble youth of my same age, and even though they were noble, they were not ashamed to enter my home and visit me. They could see that I was living like a man and not like an animal – very comfortably, the way we Florentines live; they also saw that my home and my household goods were, according to my means, very handsome. Several of these people are still alive. We grew in age together, and they have become, in the meanwhile, dignified people of consequence. I did not want those people who still prized my friendship to see me living disgracefully like an animal and think that this was due to my baseness. (XII, 153–4)][20]

Of particular interest is the notion that his Neapolitan companions 'quantunque nobili' [even though they were noble] were not ashamed to enter his home. The writer mentions his social inferiority while asserting his worth. This scene of entrance into the author's Neapolitan house somehow complements the one of the entrance into the Neapolitan garden we found in the *Filocolo*. From a different point of view, with a different twist, it is a retelling of the outsider's story. Of course this is a painful moment for Boccaccio. The treatment inflicted upon him by his friends, Nelli and Acciaiuoli, makes him feel more than an outsider, a veritable outcast. However, our concern is less with the reaction to present circumstances than with the feeling transcending the episodes. An implicit, central concern of the letter is that of a man who finds himself in the position of having to rely on the acknowledgment of a group superior to his own in order to define his own worth. Is not this also a central theme in the story of Cisti?

Fortune made Cisti a baker, but he is a man of high worth ('d'altissimo animo fornito'; VI.2.3). His behaviour is charmingly perfect, from the moment he sets about honouring men of much higher status with his precious wine, to the moment he sends the rest of the wine to messer Geri. As Getto stated, he is indeed an 'artist of life,' a 'lover of form, of form translated into words and things.'[21] The appropriateness of his witty reply to the servant who has gone to fetch wine with a big flask, is promptly acknowledged by messer Geri: 'Cisti dice vero' [Cisti is right (VI.2.26)]. What matters in the story is not only that a man of humble trade can be provided with an 'altissimo animo' [great soul (VI.2.3)] and that he can teach a lesson in the art of living to a superior, but also that his worth receives sanction from a higher social level. The distinction of Cisti's soul is now adequately measured, because it has proven itself in an exchange with a gentleman. The gentleman is in a way the loser, but he is also victorious in that he crowns the winner and has the power to make the victory prestigious. The higher class, in other words, cannot lose. From a metatextual perspective, 'Cisti is right' means that Cisti is given the ultimate legitimation for his existence in the realm of literature. It is as if messer Geri had said: 'Cisti, you rightly belong in this book.'

As in Cisti's case, both the marchioness of Monferrato and Monna Nonna de' Pulci have opponents who are socially superior to them. The marchioness acts as 'savia e avveduta' [wise and judicious (I.5.9)], outwitting the king of France who had planned to seduce her. With a sharp retort, Nonna de' Pulci rebukes the bishop of Florence who had addressed her less than respectfully. The value of the two women is known at the beginning of the two novellas. Their successful interactions with king and bishop are the best possible proof of that value because of the exceptionally high social standing of their opponents. Again, the greatness of the victory is in proportion to the prestige of the interlocutor. We can, of course, apply these considerations to the story of the lady of Gascony.

To obtain access to a superior circle (and this does not mean necessarily to abandon one's original social class), to prove one's worth in that circle, to search for one's identity there: these are central concerns in Boccaccio's world. The lady of Gascony, Cisti, and messer Torello are characters in search of legitimation, characters who are evidently dear to an author in search of legitimation both for himself and for his work.[22]

Within this interpretive framework, it is almost impossible to ignore the novella of Ghino di Tacco (X.2). The author delights in the events that transform this rebel and brigand into an honourable member of society. The turning point in Ghino's criminal career is the kidnapping of the abbot of Cluny. The abbot, during his forced stay, has the opportunity to appreciate his host's *saviezza* and *liberalità* [wisdom and generosity]. Ghino explains to him the good reasons that have compelled him to become a highway robber and an enemy of the pope. Eventually, the abbot goes to Rome and pleads the case of Ghino with the pope, arguing that the outlaw's wicked ways are 'molto maggiore peccato della fortuna che suo' [more the fault of Fortune than his own (X.2.28)]. Eventually, Ghino is invited to the papal court:

né guari appresso del Papa fu che egli il reputò valoroso, e riconciliatoselo gli donò una gran prioria di quelle dello Spedale, di quello avendol fatto far cavaliere; la quale egli, amico e servidore di santa Chiesa e dello abate di Clignì, tenne mentre visse. (X.2.31)

[nor had he been with the Pope long before the latter acknowledged his worth, and, having made peace with him, granted him a large priory of those of the Hospitallers, having first made him a knight of that order. This priory he held for the rest of his days, remaining a friend and servant of the holy Church and the abbot of Cluny.]

From outcast and outlaw to prior in the order of the Hospitallers, Ghino is yet another character in search of legitimation. Boccaccio's heartfelt approval goes not only to this master in the *arte di vivere*, but also to those (the abbot and the pope) who are magnanimous enough to acknowledge and reward his merits. One is reminded, of course, of Boccaccio's complaint in the letter to Nelli (written several years after the completion of this story), that his own worth had been left unrewarded at the Angevin Court. And Niccola Acciaiuoli comes to mind, too, portrayed in that letter as unable to protect the *minori*, and to discharge his princely duties in a dignified and just way.

> When he comes out [of his chambers, after making the postulants wait for a long time] the poor wretches address him, pleading justice with entreaties fraught with tears and sorrow; but he, as if absorbed in grave thoughts, pretends, if he is not well disposed, not to hear what they are telling him, and when he answers, he mocks them, uttering vain promises and inconsequent words, letting the matter stand. (XII, 161–2)

This is almost a portrait of the king of Cyprus before the conversion.

Boccaccio opened his *Decameron* with a series of stories contemplating the positive results of a perfect verbal exchange between inferior and superior. He insisted on these configurations in Day Six, and ended the book with stories in which the perfect interaction between heroes belonging to different social spheres can be relished again (X .1, 2, 6, 7, 9, and 10). Indeed, it seems rewarding to underscore the rich production of social harmonies in the *Decameron*, to read the book as a showcase of 'artifices of reconciliation,' or as an anthology of 'forms of accommodation' (these are the words of Thomas M. Greene).[23] Within this strategy of reading, it is relevant to bring to the fore the notion of legitimation (or certification) – legitimation as an archetypal producer of meaning. It also seems advisable to mention Boccaccio's role as a dispenser of literary certification in the cultural arena of the fourteenth century.

In the realm of literature he was a Saladin or an abbot of Cluny, rather than an Acciaiuoli, never remiss in acknowledging value wherever he could find it, rescuing value from lowly status. He was a dispenser of legitimation from that day when a real or fictional Fiammetta first asked him to give literary decorum to the lovely story of Florio and Biancifiore, which had been left languishing in the 'fabulosi parlari degli ignoranti' [fantastic yarns of the ignorant (*Filocolo* I.i, 25)], and from the day he decided to follow Dante's example and use the vulgar tongue as a tool that would vie with Latin in the service of true poetry.

I have shaped my reading of the story of the king of Cyprus around data pertaining to the author's life. It is certainly possible, while maintaining the focus on the issue of certification, to reorganize the critical strategy in such a way as to steer clear of individual biography. Strictly from a metatextual perspective, every utterance and every narrative tells the story of its own being, of its own status as artifact and as information. Every speech-act tells the story of a voyage from a 'no' (the no of non-existence and of intention) towards the 'yes' of actualization, from the 'outside' where the self resides, to the 'inside' – the locus where the self and the 'other' meet under the auspices of the verbal exchange.

As with any journey, this one is laden with anxiety, with presumptions of inadequacy as well as expectations of successful accomplishment. Not only is every speech-act the stipulation of a contract between interlocutors (more or less identifiable), but also a plea for legitimation. Every speech-act carries encoded in itself a yearning for acknowledgment and validation. In this sense, Filocolo's entrance into the Neapolitan garden is the metaphorical equivalent of the verbal event. In this same sense are we all characters in search of legitimation, together with Filocolo, Cisti, messer Torello and messer Giovanni Boccaccio.

NOTES

1 By this of course I do not mean that the microtexts (the individual novellas) should be studied with little or no regard for their belonging to the macrotext (the novella collection). In fact, in my *Forme complesse nel* Decameron I have tried to show, among other things, the critical advantages of the opposite strategy.
2 Almansi, *Writer as Liar*, 20–4.
3 Battaglia, *La coscienza*, 564.
4 Auerbach, *Mimesis*, 177–203.
5 From *Il Novellino*, ed. Cesare Segre, 839.

6 Barilli, 'Retorica e narrativa,' 44.

7 Cottino-Jones, 'Observations,' 379.

8 Barilli, 'Retorica e narrativa,' 44.

9 Baratto, *Realtà*, 39.

10 Russo, *Letture critiche del* Decameron (1956), 149. Baratto, *Realtà*, 37.

11 Paolella, *Retorica e racconto*, 110.

12 Baratto, *Realtà*, 38.

13 Greene, 'Forms of Accommodation,' 302.

14 Chiappelli, *Il legame musaico*, 23.

15 Cf. Branca, *Boccaccio: Man and His Works*; Sabatini, *Napoli angioina*; and Padoan, *Il Boccaccio, le muse*.

16 Branca, *Boccaccio: Man and His Works*, 133.

17 Ibid., 11, 15.

18 Ibid., I, 28.

19 Another figure representing the author in this part of the *Filocolo* is Caleon, one of the Neapolitan youngsters who welcome the strangers. As Carducci has observed: 'Caleone is Boccaccio, the plebeian already made noble by virtue of love and art' (Carducci, *Discorsi letterari e storici*, 273).

20 The references are to the edition of this letter published in Boccaccio, *Opere latine minori*.

21 Getto, *Vita di forme*, 145–6.

22 Todd Boli ('Dante's "Fathers" and Boccaccio's Search for Legitimacy,' unpub. essay, 1992) has a different, but I believe fruitful, approach to these issues. Further investigations should include a careful review of Boccaccio's pronouncements on the issue of nobility. I have in mind in particular his endorsement of the traditional stance (Seneca, Juvenal, Boethius, Andreas Capellanus, Dante) which upholds the primacy of nobility of heart over nobility of blood. For the ideology of social classes in the *Decameron*, see the fifth chapter of Surdich, *La cornice di amore*.

23 Greene, 'Forms of Accommodation.'

The Tale of Maestro Alberto (I. 10)

MILLICENT MARCUS

As figure 1 reveals, this study rests on an interest in *Decameron* I.10 that is vegetal, and will argue that when we peel away the textual layers of this complex little narration, what we come to is neither a celebration of stilnovist love, as Luigi Russo and Mario Baratto have suggested, nor a simple example of the *rovesciamento* technique which seems to govern all the tales of Day One, as Georgio Padoan and Antonio D'Andrea argue, nor a lesson on witty repartee, as Pampinea herself proposes in her prefatory remarks to the tale.[1] What we come to instead when we penetrate to the core of this story is a vegetable, a leek, whose metaphoric significance has much to teach us about sexuality and textuality in the *Decameron*.

The protagonist of I.10 is maestro Alberto, a world famous member of the Bolognese medical establishment, who, at the age of 70, becomes infatuated with the beautiful young widow Malgherida dei Ghisolieri. Nor is the maestro subtle in his attentions to the lady as he parades up and down the street in front of her house to the amusement of all Bologna. One feast day, while Alberto is making his usual rounds, he is confronted by Malgherida and her *brigata* who invite him into a courtyard for refreshments and ridicule. When asked how he dares compete with the lady's many young admirers, Alberto answers with a witticism about senior male sexuality. He points out the ladies' erroneous preference for the green leaves of the leek, whose flavour is decidedly inferior to that of the savoury white head. Chastened by Alberto's witty defence of sex with a septuagenarian, Malgherida accedes to his suit. And though Boccaccio chooses to omit the happiest element of the happy ending (for reasons I'll consider later on), history tells us that indeed Alberto de' Zancari, physician and professor of medicine at the

CVII

PORRVM

❦ Porrū aliud domeſticū aliud ſilueſtre:caliduȝ in
tertio ſiccū in ſecūdo gradu. Et ſilueſtre eſt calidius
& ſiccius ꝓpter illud ē deterius. Porrum nocet ſto-
macho cauſans inflationem ac uentoſitatē. Et cuȝ
ſui acumine neruos mordet faciet enim fumos me-
lancolicos ex alate caput obfuſcādo uiſum. Et eius
uſus cauſat ſomnia terribilia. unde caueant acco-
lerici & melancolici ſeu inaniati & opilationem in
                                                            o iii

Source: *De virtutibus herbarum* (Venice: Giunta, 1502), p. 109. Courtesy of the
Harry Ransom Humanities Research Center, University of Texas at Austin.

University of Bologna, married the widow Malgherida dei Ghisolieri in the early 1300s.[2]

Though the critical neglect suffered by this tale makes my task here somewhat easier, it comes as a distinct surprise, given what we know about literary structure in general, and about Boccaccio's architectonic interests in particular. Since beginnings, middles, and ends are privileged positions in any work with a temporal component, *Decameron* I.10, enjoys a triple privilege of place. It participates in the important central portion of the *Decameron* by foreshadowing the opening and closing stories of Day Six – Filomena's didactic introduction to the tale of Madonna Oretta (VI.1) is a close paraphrase of Pampinea's opening remarks in I.10, while the leek offers an imagistic anticipation of Boccaccio's notorious talking onion, Frate Cipolla himself (VI.10).[3] But even before reading our tale, without the benefit of allusions to the *Decameron*'s structural core, its textual position makes strong claims on our attention. As the end of the beginning, *Decameron* I.10 gives closure to the inaugural day of storytelling, fulfilling all the thematic and formal requirements that such a location would entail. Frank Kermode argues that literary form satisfies the deep and abiding human need for finality by offering 'concord fictions,' where beginnings and middles make sense in terms of their endings, and conclusions retrospectively order the plot into a coherent totality.[4] In collections of short stories, the juxtaposition of a number of completed plots brings our awareness of form to the forefront and multiplies our satisfaction by enabling us to experience a series of concord fictions in close succession. When tales are in turn organized in larger units (such as storytelling days), each of which affords us the pleasure of closure on a higher level, the possibilities for formal satisfaction increase exponentially. Thus, as the ending of the first full day of storytelling, *Decameron* I.10 must fulfil the cumulative expectations for closure generated by the preceding tales of the day. But it must also serve as a beginning – the first in the series of ten day-ending tales, and the only one to escape the authorship of Dioneo, with his privilege of exemption from the daily themes. Through the image of the leek, Boccaccio is able to give closure to the tales of Day One while maintaining the interpretive open-endedness which will be Dioneo's trademark throughout the text.

The world of Day One, like its counterparts in the plague-ridden city, is rife with corruption, wrong-headedness, and greed. Its protagonists choose to address their delinquent authorities through verbal wit, and in so doing they prove the reformatory power of the word. Thus

recalcitrant rulers are brought into line by the witty expedients of
Melchisedech (I.3), the marchioness of Monferrato (I.5), and the
woman of Gascony (I.9), the Church is chastised by Abraham the Jew
(Abraam giudeo I.2), and the would-be victim of the Inquisition (I.6),
while delinquent aristocrats are called to task by Bergamino (I.7) and
Guiglielmo Borsiere (I.8). Though all these stories exhibit the dynamic
of *rovesciamento*, or reversal, it is significant that what transforms the
initial situation into its opposite is not dramatic action, but language,
specifically figurative language. In Roland Barthes's terms, these plots
pivot on linguistic transgression, where the paradigmatic spills over
onto the syntagmatic axis, making language the determinate of the
narrative outcome.[5] Thus in Day One, words not only assume the status of events, they become superior events in their ability to shape
plots. And in *Decameron* I.10, we have an example of how metaphors
in general, and erotic metaphors in particular, function in the text
'come momento propulsore dell'azione strutturale' [as the propell-
ing moment of the structural action] to use Mirko Bevilacqua's apt
formulation.[6]

Indeed, Boccaccio's Day One may be read as an *amplificatio* of
Cicero's rather cursory remarks in *De oratore* on the rhetorical efficacy
of those jests 'which spring from some allegorical phraseology, or from
a metaphorical use of some one word.'[7] Such *motti* are admirably
suited to the critic who seeks to reproach someone in a position of
superior authority without giving offence.[8] By casting his criticism in
figurative language, the speaker avoids directly attacking his listener
and staves off that immediate defensive posture which would preclude
receptivity to reform. Such indirect censure encourages the listener to
become his own critic through the very act of interpretation. In the cognitive journey from the vehicle to the tenor of the metaphoric discourse, the listener actively participates in the making of meaning and
becomes a kind of co-author of the reproach.[9] By the same token, the
critic flatters his listener by giving him credit for superior understanding and enough potential self-awareness for the witticism to register at
all. Even messer Ermino de' Grimaldi, alias Ermino Avarizia, had that
'faviluzza di gentilezza' [spark of civility, I.8.12] which could be fanned
into a flame of generosity by Guiglielmo's incendiary wit.

Boccaccio's insistence on the power of witty reproach to reform the
listener by involving him in the interpretive process becomes clear
when comparing Days One and Six in the *Decameron* to their sources
in classical jest literature. Though Cicero and Quintilian consider

humour an important oratorical aid, their catalogues of jests invariably end at the punchline without dramatizing their reformatory effects on a listening public. Macrobius, whose second book of the *Saturnalia* is commonly cited as a source for Boccaccio's First and Sixth Days, does tell us, for example, that Augustus was shamed by a witticism into appearing in court on an old soldier's behalf or recompensing an impoverished Greek poet for his epigrams, but such listener responses conclude a distinct minority of Macrobius's many examples.[10] For Boccaccio, on the other hand, the witty rejoinder is never an end in itself. We are always privy to its transforming effect on the listener, be he the French monarch who gets tired of eating chicken à la king in Monferrato, or the abbot who cheerfully joins his young colleague in sin.

There is, of course, a meta-literary message in these tales of conversion by witty retort. The invitation to a figurative understanding of language, the plea to abandon literal-mindedness and consider hidden truths, seems to correct for the obsessive attachment to things, to appearances, or to the flesh, which makes gentlemen and friars avaricious, abbots hypocritical, monarchs lustful, extortionary, or lethargic. The journey of understanding from the literal to the figurative occasions a moral journey from self-interest to magnanimity, from malevolence to goodwill. It would be no exaggeration to say that the movement within each tale of Day One recapitulates the overall comic design of the *Decameron* itself, which begins with the decrepitude of the plague-ridden city and ends with the triumphant humanity of Day Ten.

In its marriage of textuality and sexuality, *Decameron* I.10 synthesizes the metanarrative preoccupations of the preceding nine tales. Literal-mindedness, the inability to speak and understand in anything but the most obvious terms, is equated with excessive body interest on the part of the women in Pampinea's long diatribe against female dull-wittedness. 'Quella virtú,' Pampinea complains, 'che già fu nell'anime delle passate hanno le moderne rivolta in ornamenti del corpo' [That virtue which once resided in the souls of women, has been redirected, by modern women, into the adornment of the body (§5)].[11] By invoking the *laudatio temporis acti* topos and hypothesizing a mythical past of female virtue, Boccaccio is able to see contemporary womanhood as falling away from an imagined earlier ideal. And, by giving the dyads of *virtú/ornamenti* and *anime/corpo* the temporal dimension of *passate/moderne*, he suggests that a rejection of corporeality would amount to a Golden Age return, a recuperation of lost innocence, a Paradise regained. This fictive past could be as recent as the *Novellino*, or as distant as the past examples of *bel parlare* to which the *Novellino* itself so vividly points. But today's woman, in her mania for fashion, for bangles, baubles, and stripes, is either unable to speak in polite company at all (a reticence she would pass off as modesty), or confines her conversation to servants, laundresses, and bakers. Obsession with physical adornment or with household matters (another form of corpo-reality) excludes the higher understanding prerequisite to polite social intercourse – the art of 'sapere tralle donne e co' valenti uomini favellare' [knowing how to speak among worthy men and women (§6)] – is lost on a woman consumed by the complexities of high fashion or home economics.[12]

The relationhship between textuality and sexuality constitutes the very theme of maestro Alberto's climactic encounter with madonna Malgherida. When chided by the lady and her *brigata* for loving a woman so much his junior, Alberto must teach them, through figurative language, that sexuality, like textuality, demands a superior understanding – one that goes beyond the letter to the hidden meaning of words, and one that goes beyond the obvious physical appeal of youth to the subtler attractions of older lovers. To put it simply – sex, like texts, requires interpretation.

But here is where Boccaccio complicates his lesson and makes maestro Alberto's tale both an ending and a beginning. In its insistence on the reformatory power of figurative language, the tale reaffirms the rhetorical theme of Day One.[13] But it looks ahead to Dioneo's subsequent stories (terminal stories by his own request), which will parody and subvert each Day's preceding tales. Figurative language may edify listeners, Pampinea argues, but does it point to any one, univocal truth? In other words, can a polysemous text ever free itself from ambiguity?

And this is where the leek comes in. Though fruits and vegetables are commonplace figures for allegorical works where the fictive surface gives way to a hidden kernel of truth, when we peel the leek we find a series of inner layers which enclose a seedless core. And, indeed, when we seek the underlying significance of *Decameron* I.10, we find in it no unitary truth, no allegorical *sovrasenso*. Instead we encounter a plurality of readings which contradict and subvert one another in defiance of interpretive closure. Though maestro Alberto takes us on none of the semantic wanderings of Frate Cipolla, his leek nonetheless serves as a kind of antipasto for the rhetorically equivocal banquet to be served up by Boccaccio's talking onion at the end of Day Six.[14]

But what about the didactic framing of *Decameron* I.10? Surely Pampinea's prefatory remarks point to the unitary lesson we are to glean from her tale: that ladies must cultivate the art of witty repartee and must learn to be careful in choosing their targets. Accordingly, Pampinea ends her preface with an intertextual note of considerable importance to an interpretation of her didactic intent. She concludes:

> Questa ultima novella di quelle di oggi, la quale a me tocca di dover dire, voglio ve ne renda ammaestrate, acciò che, come per nobiltà d'animo dall'altre divise siete, così ancora per eccellenzia di costumi separate dall'altre vi dimostriate. (§8)

> [I wish that this last story of those for today, which it is my turn to tell, should instruct you so that just as you stand apart from other women by virtue of your noble character, so will you show yourselves to be separate from the others in your excellent manners.]

The recall here is to the proem of the *Novellino*, which warrants lengthy citation for its relevance to Pampinea's instructional purpose.

> Facciamo qui memoria d'alquanti fiori di parlare, di belle cortesie e di belli risposi e di belle valentie, di belli donari e di belli amori, secondo che per lo tempo passato hanno fatto già molti. E chi avrà cuore nobile e intelligenzia sottile sì li potrà simigliare per lo tempo che verrà e per innanzi, e argomentare e dire e raccontare in quelle parti dove averanno luogo, a prode e a piacere di coloro che non sanno e disiderano di sapere.[15]

> [Let us call to mind here a good many flowers of speech, of beautiful courtesies and responses and worthy deeds and gifts and loves, according to what many have already done in the past. And he who will have a noble heart and intelligence thus will be able to imitate them in the future and persuade and speak and recount wherever he may be, to the benefit and pleasure of those who do not know and who want to.]

Boccacccio thus seems to share the *Novellino* author's elevated storytelling objective: to activate the inner nobility of his public through edifying examples. Both writers share the conviction that their publics require external agents – peer instruction, behavioral models, exemplary texts – before *nobiltà d'animo* can produce *eccellenzia di costumi*, and both accord *bel parlare* pride of place in a list of courtly virtues, including 'belle cortesie,' 'belle valentie,' 'belli donari' and 'belli amori.' Such privileging of speech acts reveals the survival of Aristotelian *eutrapelia*, as Victoria Kirkham points out, and its importance as an index of moral worth in medieval ethical thought.[16]

Boccaccio further reinforces the didactic import of this tale by building into the story an internal public of gentlewomen reminiscent of the *cornice* ladies themselves, whose edification by wit will follow on the model of Malgherida and her entourage.[17] This lady is strategically situated among 'molte altre donne' [many other women] (§12) – the phrase occurs twice in the tale – and at the climactic moment of enlightenment, Boccaccio insists on the plurality of Alberto's listeners. 'La gentil donna,' Pampinea tells us, *'insieme con l'altre* alquanto vergognandosi, disse: "Maestro, assai bene e cortesemente gastigate n'avete della *nostra* presuntuosa impresa"'* [The gentlewoman, together with the others somewhat ashamed, said: 'Master, well and courteously you have chastised us for our presumptuous enterprise' (§19, emphases mine)], where the 'nostra' is not so much the editorial *we* as a declaration of the collective impact of Alberto's teaching.

Like the *cornice* [framing tale], *Decameron* I.10 is set in a genteel world of leisure, wherein 'una fresca corte' [a cool courtyard] stocked with 'finissimi vini e confetti' [delicate wines and sweets (§14)] provides the stage for the sparring of wits. Such marked affinities between internal narrative public and *cornice* suggest that Alberto's teachings are not to be lost on the female-dominated ranks of the frame story *brigata*, and by implication on the 'donne oziose' [idle ladies] of Boccaccio's fictive reading public.

But when we peel away the didactic outer covering of this tale, we find far more than a bland lesson in courtly conversation worthy of etiquette books for ladies. The obscene euphemisms at the heart of the story suggest that what Alberto is arguing for here is the acceptability of a certain kind of love – a love whose meaning is implied not in the leek image alone, but in its juxtaposition with the other vegetal protagonist of the tale, the lupin. 'Io sono stato piú volte già là,' boasts Alberto,

là dove io ho vedute merendarsi le donne e mangiare lupini e porri; e come che nel porro niuna cosa sia buona, pur men reo e piú piacevole alla bocca è il capo di quello, il quale voi generalmente, da torto appetito tirate, il capo vi tenete in mano e manicate le frondi, le quali non solamente non sono da cosa alcuna, ma son di malvagio sapore. Che so io, madonna, se nello eleggere degli amanti, voi vi faceste il simigliante? (§17)

[I have already been there many times where I have seen women snacking and eating lupins and leeks, and although in the leek nothing is good, yet less offensive and more agreeable to the taste is the head, which you, generally led by a mistaken appetite, hold in your hands and eat the leaves which not only are no good, but have a bad flavour. How do I know, madam, if you do the same in choosing your lovers?]

It is significant that Alberto invokes the lupin early in his simile, but fails to develop its implications for lovemaking. If the leek, with its tasty white head and insipid green leaves, offers him a favourable comparison between senior and junior male sexual performance, then the lupin stands by in silent disagreement. As Pliny tells us, not only does the lupin look like a penis, it also acts like one: 'To such a degree is it attached to the earth, that even though left upon a soil thickly covered with brambles, it will throw out a root amid the leaves and brakes and so contrive to reach the ground.'[18] What the lupin and leek reveal about junior male sexuality is that it might be insipid, but it is also fecundating, while the senior male passion, like the head of the leek, might be tasty but can serve little procreative purpose. Maestro Alberto's suit, therefore, goes beyond the question of age-appropriate behavior to the very acceptability of a courtly love code as a non-procreative, adulterous passion whose end is the self-justifying pursuit of pleasure. And it is to preserve the courtly love referent of the tale that Boccaccio omits the marital happy ending of the couple's historical counterparts.

In Alberto's very use of figurative language to further his adulterous desires, he distances himself from the kind of sexuality celebrated by Reason in Jean de Meun's *Romance of the Rose*. When the Lover scolds her for speaking directly of Saturn's testicles, Reason replies:

Fair friend, without disgrace I will name
Quite openly and by the proper term
A thing that's nothing if it be not good
[. . .]

In open text without resort to gloss,
As God the Father made in Paradise

With his own hands, and other instruments
Intended to perpetuate the race
Which without them had fallen in decay. (6933–35, 6941–46)[19]

Of course, Reason is talking here about reproductive biology and its divinely ordained part in the providential plan, according to the naturalist philosophy of the School of Chartres. If it is this procreative sexuality that requires no linguistic masking, then by implication the kind of eros which must be disguised by figurative language is the non-fecundating, adulterous passion of courtly love. Thus such passion sets itself apart from socially sanctioned sexuality in the very doubleness of its linguistic expression.

By giving this frank celebration of courtly love the bland packaging of a ladies' how-to book of conversational pointers, Boccaccio opens an interpretive gap between framing and tale, between overt didacticism and hidden textual significance. In its plurality of readings which contradict and call each other into question, *Decameron* I.10 becomes a companion piece to the terminal tales of the collection: that of Panfilo in *Decameron* I.1, whose theological-frame remarks about divine benevolence are undermined by Ser Ciappelletto's hagiographic spoof and that of Dioneo in *Decameron* X.10, whose pornographic gloss sabotages Griselda's exemplum of superhuman steadfastness and suffering. Thus Alberto's story, as it strays from its didactic justification, offers one more argument for the interpretive open-endedness of the text.

Throughout this tale, various and mutually exclusive theories of love vie with each other in variant literary registers to confound the critic in search of exegetical consistency. Many astute readers of *Decameron* I.10, from Russo to Baratto, have argued for a 'stilnovist' approach to the story. The Bolognese setting and time frame suggest the world of Guido Guinizelli, as do the descriptives 'vago e dilicato viso' [lovely and delicate face (§11)], the chorus of women who seem to hover about the streets ready to harass young poets in love (cf. *Vita nuova*, 18), or old doctors in lust. Most suggestive of stilnovist thought is the linkage of love and the gentle heart so reminiscent of Guinizelli's celebrated 'al cor gentil rempaira sempre amore' and Dante's reworking of the twin theme in 'amor e 'l cor gentil sono una cosa.'[20] But how can we reconcile such a stilnovist reading with leeks and lupins? Natural imagery may abound in the *dolce stil novo* lexicon, but sex organs masquerading as vegetables come from an entirely different literary universe. Salacious double entendres are not the stuff of ethereal poets whose *donne angelicate* exist in the material world only to dispense greetings and to inspire metaphysical awe. Obscene euphemisms are far more the province of Tindaro and Licisca, the brawling servants of the Introduction to Day Six, than aspirants to stilnovist dignity.

By building the two halves of *Decameron* I.10 on mutually exclusive theories of love, one dedicated to disembodied ideals of the Gunizel-lian school, the other to a frankly carnal passion, Boccaccio deliberately thwarts the critic's quest for interpretive consistency. Malgherida's response to Alberto's witticism only reinforces the ambiguity of the tale. Her answer makes it unclear whether she is in agreement to be the *donna angelicata* or the flesh-and-blood mistress of her elderly beau. 'Tuttavia il vostro amor m'è caro, sí come di savio e valente uomo esser dee, e per ciò, salva la mia onestà, come a vostra cosa ogni vostro piacere imponete sicuramente' [Nonetheless your love is dear to me, just as the love of a wise and worthy man should be, and therefore, preserving my honour, impose your every desire on me with confidence, as if I were your possession (§19)]. On the surface, this sounds like a stilnovist response. Malgherida acknowledges her suitor's wisdom and moral worth and she insists on maintaining a virtue-preserving distance from him. But the phrase 'salva la mia onestà' raises some serious questions. For *onestà* is such a fluid and slippery term in the *Decameron*, denoting sometimes honour and sometimes the mere appearance of it, that Malgherida's qualification reveals little about the real limits she would place on their intimacy.

Nor are the stilnovist and pornographic approaches to love the only ones present in the tale. Maestro Alberto is, after all, a physician, and we would expect him to be treated in appropriate medical fashion. Thus in the very passage which articulates the stilnovist linkage of love and the gentle heart, medical terminology intrudes to debunk the high-minded poetic teaching. Of Alberto we are told, 'essendo già vecchio di presso a settanta anni, tanta fu la nobiltà del suo spirito, che, essendo già del corpo quasi ogni natural caldo partito, in sé non schifò di ricevere amorose fiamme' [although already old, approaching seventy years, such was the nobility of his spirit that, although almost all natural warmth had already left his body, he was not averse to receiving amorous flames (§10)]. If the two clauses beginning with *essendo* were struck from this period, then we would have the standard stilno-vist equation of noble spiritedness and love. But the medical commentary entirely reverses the metaphysical movement of stilnovist thought. For Maestro Alberto, 'spirito' is no disembodied poetic ideal, it is the *spirito vitale* which motors the body's physical plant. Likewise, the 'amorose fiamme,' in their association with natural *caldo*, cease to function as the refining fire of spiritualizing ardour, and suggest instead the thermal accompaniment of sexual excitation. Thus the mind-over-body motif, which for the stilnovist meant metaphysical transcendence, for Alberto comes to signify the mind's power to renew the flagging body. Alberto's passion is clearly confined neither to the heart nor to the brain alone. Not surprisingly, the maestro mixes stilnovist, medical, and pornographic strategies in his climactic retort to Malgherida. 'Madonna,' he begins, 'che io ami, questo non dee esser meraviglia a alcun savio, e spezialmente voi, per ciò voi il valete' [Madam, that I love, this should not amaze any wise person, and especially you, because you are worthy of it (§15)]. This *captatio benevolentiae* is appropriately couched in the idealizing terms of the Guinizellian school, with its allusions to the lady's *valore* and her consequent intellectual appeal. But medical lore intervenes again to temper any unwarranted idealism:

> E come che agli antichi uomini sieno naturalmente tolte le forze le quali agli amorosi esercizii si richeggiono, non è per ciò lor tolto la buona volontà né lo intendere quello che sia da essere amato, ma tanto più dalla natura conosciuto, quanto essi hanno più di conoscimento che i giovani.' (§16)

> [And though the forces required for amorous exercises are lacking in elderly men, not for that reason is goodwill lacking, nor the understanding of what should be loved, which is so much better known to them by nature as they have more empirical knowledge than young men.]

Here the metaphysical *conoscenza* so tauted by the stilnovists, is reduced to the worldly wisdom of the sexually experienced, while love itself is relegated to 'esercizii,' calisthenics.

Boccaccio's interest in maestro Alberto is not without a pseudo-autobiographical element, as Baratto suggests.[21] Indeed, when Boccaccio uses the leek to refer to his own mature sexuality in the Introduction to Day Four, he gives a retrospective pseudo-autobiographical gloss to the tale of maestro Alberto. Boccaccio's authorial investment in stories of older lovers who use verbal wit, or their actual writings, to spar with their youthful heartthrobs (especially of the widowed variety) surfaces later in *Decameron* VIII.7, in the tale of the scholar Rinieri who takes ago-

nizing and interminable revenge on the young widow Elena who made
a mockery of his love. When Rinieri accompanies his physical punishment of Elena with torrents of verbal abuse, he begins to sound very
much like the *Corbaccio*'s Boccaccio. 'Le forze della penna,' gloats the
scholar, 'son troppo maggiori che coloro non estimano che quelle con
conoscimento provate non hanno' [The power of the pen is far greater
than those who have not experienced it suppose (§99)]. And in a successive passage of the same tale, the writer reveals such a close identification with his protagonist that he temporarily replaces Rinieri's fictional
character with his own narrative persona.[22] Though we have been told
on several occasions that the scholar is 'un giovane,' Boccaccio has him
defend older lovers in a language we've come to know only too well:

> E oltre a ciò gli stimate miglior cavalieri e far più miglia le lor giornate che
> gli uomini più maturi. Certo io confesso che essi con maggior forza scuo-
> tano i pillicioni, ma gli attempati, sì come esperti, sanno meglio i luoghi
> dove stanno le pulci, e di gran lunga è da elegger più tosto il poco e saporito
> che il molto e insipido; e il trottar forte rompe e stanca altrui, quantunque
> sia giovane, dove il soavemente andare, ancora che alquanto più tardi
> altrui meni all'albergo, egli il vi conduce almen riposato. (§§102–3)

> [And furthermore you consider them better horsemen and able to ride
> more miles a day than older men. Certainly I confess that they shake the
> fleece with more vigour, but older men, since they're experts, know better
> the places where the fleas hide, and it's far better to choose something
> small and tasty than something copious and tasteless, and hard trotting
> breaks and wearies another, no matter how young, where gentle progress
> brings one to the inn at least rested, if somewhat later.]

In this piling up of obscene euphemisms, whose density and intensity
reflect Rinieri's own vindictive hysteria, Boccaccio reveals how much
his literary imagination is stimulated by the question of senescent love
for young widows – a stimulus which will result in the book-length
anti-feminist diatribe of the *Corbaccio*. Careful readers will see in
Rinieri's catalogue a summa of Boccaccian euphemisms – horseback
riding occurs as a frequent erotic metaphor throughout the *Decameron*,
while fur-shaking appears in the pornographic framing of the Griselda
tale (X.10.69). The gastronomic reference to *saporito* and *insipido* is what
interests us here, for it recalls the image of the leek and its age-specific
commentary on male sexual appeal. What we realize, retrospectively,

is that *Decameron* I.10 and VIII.7 present two alternative outcomes for
the same scenario – the comic and near-tragic results of January's love
for May.

Why does Rinieri fare so poorly when Alberto meets with such
resounding success? Perhaps because his tale occurs in a day when
things turn out well, when wit can effectuate positive change. Rinieri's
tale, instead, takes place in the squalid days of the latter *Decameron*
when human nature is reduced to so much mutual exploitation. The
two stories also reveal Boccaccio's ambivalent literary approach to
women – an ambivalence which can give rise to the philogyny of the
frame story or the misogyny of VIII, 7.[23] When we see how easy it
would be for Malgherida to become Elena through a simple failure of
figurative understanding (if leeks remained literal leeks in Malgherida's story the outcome would have been far different), we can see
how much is at stake in Boccaccio's invocation of a female readership
for his *Decameron*. I.10 is especially important in this regard, for it is the
first to consolidate Boccaccio's address to a female readership through
concrete behavioral directives. In the Proem, Boccaccio tells us that the
Decameron is written to alleviate the tedium of idle women in love, and
his first nine stories, as well as his introduction, invariably invoke a
female listenership with such flattering descriptives as *graziosissime,
carissime, amorose, valorose,* etc. Apart from these perfunctory invoca-
tions, only two of the tales are cast as gender-specific *exempla*: that of
the marquess of Monferrato, which warns women against loving
above their station, and our tenth, which shares the distinction of having the longest prefatory remarks in the entire *Decameron* (the other
being Emilia's disquisition on the taming of the shrew in IX. 9).[24] If rhetorical length is an index of meta-literary importance, then the introduction to our tale must be seen as a crucial statement about the fictive
readership which Boccaccio conjures up for his text.

First, let me insist on the label 'fictive.' Boccaccio's work was clearly
intended for a general public, as the early circulation of his manuscript
reveals. Victoria Kirkham shows that Boccaccio's most enthusiastic
contemporary readers were *il popolo grasso*, and that he discouraged
friends from allowing their women access to such morally equivocal
writings.[25] The address to a female audience, then, is a literary ploy
which Boccaccio uses both to appropriate a tradition of secular writing
on love, and then to re-distance himself from it, as I shall argue later
on. Surely he was not the first to privilege a female readership,
Kirkham notes, when she recalls the troubadour poets' appeals to their

lady loves, Andreas's address to Eleanor of Aquitaine and Marie de Champagne, or the intended female audience of Guido Cavalcanti's 'Donna mi prega' and of Dante's 'Donne ch'avete.'[26] Janet Smarr observes that women offered an excuse for writing in the vernacular, according to Dante's arguments in his *De vulgari eloquentia*, *Vita nuova*, and *Epistle* XIII, 10.[27] And since women were the prime consumers of medieval romance, as Francesca da Rimini and the *Corbaccio* widow imply, then an intended female readership would require not only writing in the vernacular, but writing on a certain prescribed subject (love), in a predetermined style (intermediate).[28] But Boccaccio's *donne oziose* serve as far more than a mere device to align his text with a medieval tradition of erotic literature in the vulgar tongue. Even a cursory reading of his Introduction to the Fourth Day will reveal the centrality of women to Boccaccio's defence of his *Decameron* against its detractors. The writer's decision to interrupt his stories at the end of Day Three and to make explicit his poetic principles reflects the failure of his first defensive strategy: to present the text as a gentlewoman's Galateo whose entire justification is to provide *utile consiglio* [useful counsel] for refined ladies lacking the distractions of spindle and loom. Obviously such pseudo-didacticism could not stave off those critics who saw in his text a far more bold and subversive literary experiment. And here we must call our attention to the leek, which recurs in the Introduction to Day Four and rears his white head in defense of senior sexuality once again.[29] Like maestro Alberto, Boccaccio is also taken to task for loving women in his dotage. His detractors claim that at his age 'non sta bene l'andare omai dietro a queste cose, cioè a ragionar di donne o a compiacer loro' [it is not appropriate to pursue these matters, that is, to speak of women or to seek to please them (IV Intro. §6)]. But if the tale of Filippo Balducci is the parable of the storyteller who obeys the dictates of Boccaccio's critics, that is, gives up writing about the things of this world in his old age and retires to a mountaintop to sojourn with the Muses, then Filippo's failure to shield his son from temptation is the failure of the writer who seeks either to escape the reality of sexual desire or to mask it through verbal camouflage. Indeed, the young Balducci's attraction to women is hardly thwarted by his father's metaphoric recourse to poultry.

In arguing that literature should be brought down to earth, or at least down the mountain, Boccaccio uses the leek image to perform the same demystifying function that it did for Maestro Alberto. Just as the stilnovist idealism and the high literary register of the first half of the tale met its opposite in the frank carnality and the obscene double entendre of its conclusion, so Boccaccio's impassioned plea for the inspirational value of love, a plea couched in such stilnovist terms as 'la vertú della luce degli occhi vostri, la soavità delle parole melliflue e la fiamma accesa da' pietosi sospiri' [the power of the light of your eyes, the gentleness of your mellifluous words and the flame ignited by your piteous sighs (IV Intro. §32)], ends in the equivocal figure of the leek. 'E quegli che contro alla mia età parlando vanno, mostra mal cha conoscano che, perché il porro abbia il capo bianco, che la coda sia verde' [and those who go speaking against my age reveal how they do not know that although the leek has a white head, its tail is green (§33)]. Though this leek, in its exclusive reference to older men, serves a slightly different metaphoric purpose than that of maestro Alberto, which figured a comparison between junior and senior male sexual appeal, both nonetheless perform the same meta-literary function: to demystify the stilnovist teaching about poetic language and love. And what better way to debunk the *dolce stil novo* than to invoke its favourite sons as justifications, not for Boccaccio's own early literary career, but for his persistent senile philandering?

> Io mai a me vergogna non reputerò infino nello stremo della mia vita di dover compiacere a quelle cose alle quali Guido Cavalcanti e Dante Alighieri già vecchi e messer Cino da Pistoia vecchissimo, onor si tennero, e fu lor caro il piacere loro. (IV Intro. §33)

> [I will never consider it shameful to bring pleasure as long as I live to those whom Guido Cavalcanti and Dante Alighieri already old, and Cino da Pistoia very old, honoured, and endeavoured to please.]

Thus when Boccaccio joins the company of Guido, Dante, and Cino, it is not as another poet in the stilnovist pantheon, but as one more dirty old man unable to renounce a lifetime propensity for womanizing.

But women's role in Boccaccio's defensive strategy goes beyond the inspiration of literary 'realism.' For Boccaccio's best textual defence is self-deprecation, and women are crucial to the success of this pose. Throughout his authorial interventions, Boccaccio invokes the modesty topos to argue that his text is indeed below reproach. Why would a work written in vernacular prose, without a title and in a humble and subdued style, excite critical attention of any sort? Thus the address to women serves as yet another critical dodge – as one more device for undermining the literary seriousness of the text and minimizing its vulnerability to attack. When Boccaccio says in his author's conclusion that his stories were told neither in church nor in school but 'ne' giardini, in luogo di sollazzo, tra persone giovani' [in gardens, in a place of recreation, among young persons (Concl. §7)], the writer specifies the kind of critical immunity he seeks in his text. The garden that Boccaccio cultivates here is a new literary space free from the didactic expectations of the schoolmen or the clergy. Far from a self-deprecating plea to ignore his trifling stories 'scritte per cacciar la maliconia delle femine' [written to rid women of melancholy (Concl. §23)], the address to a fictive female public constitutes a powerful argument for authorial freedom – freedom from the educational imperatives of the academy and the Church.

In the absence of didactic certainty, in the refusal of a *sovrasenso* to which the literal level unconditionally points, interpretation becomes a relative process whose morality inheres in the mind of the reader. 'Niuna corrotta mente intese mai sanamente parola,' Boccaccio argues in his conclusion, 'e cosí come le oneste a quella non giovano, cosí quelle che tanto oneste non sono la ben disposta non posson contaminare' [No corrupt mind ever interpreted a word in a healthy manner, and just as honourable words do not help it, so those less honourable ones cannot contaminate a mind well disposed (§11)].[30] It is here that Boccaccio defends himself against those detractors who take aim at his word when he subtitles the *Decameron* 'Principe Galeotto' – an allusion to the archetypal panderer of medieval romance. But Dante tells us where readers end up who allow books to become pimps and act out in their own lives the grand passions of literary lovers. Boccaccio's ironic subtitle is not only a warning about the seductions of the text, but it is also a rejection of a certain kind of writing – the kind of writing which inspired a literal-minded imitation of its fictive surface. The word can have a powerful, persuasive effect on its public, bringing about total transformations in the misguided or malevolent authorities of Day One, for example, but such conversions depend on figurative language which implicates the listener in the very act of interpretation.[31] It is the discriminating reader, one able to transcend literal-mindedness, who actualizes the transformatory power of the work. The *Decameron* will thus play neither Galeotto nor Galateo to readers seeking blueprints for their lives. If it exemplifies anything, it is the need to think figuratively, to go beyond the letter of experience, be it the literal level of a text, the sexual appeal of young male bodies, or even the fixed allegories of the clerics and the schoolmen. Literature must be free from absolute systems of meaning and their consequent imperatives to teach univocal truths. Like the leek, which figures the joys of non-reproductive sexuality, Boccaccio's writing is self-justifying, needing no external recourse to legitimize the multiple and ambiguous pleasures of the text.

NOTES

1 *Il Decameron*, ed. Luigi Russo, 87–9n.; Baratto, *Realtà*, 333-4; Padoan, 'Mondo aristocratico,' 164–5; D'Andrea, 'Le rubriche del *Decameron*,' 48.
2 See Muscetta, *Giovanni Boccaccio*, 185.
3 On the links between I.10, VI.1, and VI.10 see Stewart, 'La novella di Madonna Oretta,' 34–5.
4 See, in particular, the chapter 'Fictions' in Kermode, *The Sense of an Ending*, 35–64.
5 See Barthes, *Writing Degree Zero*, 186.
6 Bevilacqua, 'L'amore,' 417.
7 *Cicero on Oratory and Orators*, trans. J.S. Watson, 298–9.
8 Stories of underlings who chide their superiors through wit were already popular in pre-Boccaccian Tuscan narrative, according to Chiappelli, 'L'episodio di Travale,' 141–2.
9 Cok van der Voort analyses the persuasive power of wit in Day One, which he describes as *ars puniendi* as opposed to its defensive use (*ars defendendi*) in Day Six. See 'Convergenze e divaricazioni,' 241.
10 See Macrobius, *The Saturnalia*, 174–5.
11 Giovanni Boccaccio, *Decameron*, ed. Vittore Branca (Florence: Accademia della Crusca, 1976), 65. All quotes will be from this edition.
12 Angelo Marchese sees in this lament for the disappearance of conversationally gifted ladies a parallel to the elegy for the lost breed of male courtiers which opens *Decameron* I.8. See Marchese, *Metodi e prove strutturali*, 277.
13 In fact, the tale invests language with such power that it can bring inanimate objects to life, according to Giuseppe Mazzotta, who notes that tongue-tied women, 'come statue di marmo mutole e insensibili,' are brought to life by Alberto's conversational example. See Mazzotta, *World at Play*, 37.
14 For a discussion of Cipolla's dubious rhetorical strategy in VI.10, see the chapter 'Boccaccio's Singular Cicero,' in Marcus, *Allegory of Form*, 64–78.
15 *Novellino e conti del Duecento*, ed. Sebastiano Lo Nigro, 62–3.

16 See Kirkham, 'The Word, the Flesh,' 181–2.
17 Cottino-Jones remarks on the important link between the internal public of the tale and the cornice ladies, in *Order from Chaos*, 46.
18 The *Natural History* of Pliny, IV, trans. John Bostock and H.T. Riley (London: Bohn, 1856), 49–50. That Boccaccio had access to the *Historia Naturalis* is proved by his copious citations from the text in his *Genealogia Deorum Gentilium* and in *Commento a Dante*. See Hortis, *Studi sulle opere latine*, 433–4.
19 Guillaume de Lorris and Jean de Meun, *Romance of the Rose*, trans. Harry Robbins, 143.
20 See *Il Decameron*, ed. Luigi Russo, 87–9n.; and Baratto, *Realtà*, 333–4.
21 Baratto makes fleeting mention of an authorial identification with the protagonist in *Realtà*, 333.
22 Boccaccio's apparent identification with his scholar protagonist has led many critics to read the tale as thinly disguised autobiography. For a bibliography of such readings, see my article 'Misogyny as Misreading,' *Stanford Italian Review* 4 (Spring 1984): 25n.
23 On Boccaccio's problematic approach to women in the *Decameron*, see Shirley S. Allen, who reads the text as a complex, multi-faceted plea for women's rights in 'The Griselda Tale,' 1–13; and Joy H. Potter, who emphasizes the misogynous bias in many of Boccaccio's narrative and authorial pronouncements in 'Woman in the *Decameron*.' For a comprehensive overview of the problem, see Cazalé Bérard, 'Filoginia/Misoginia.'
24 See R. Hollander, 'Utilità,' 224n.
25 Kirkham, 'Boccaccio's Dedication,' 118. I would also like to thank Professor Kirkham for the many bibliographical leads as well as critical insights she offered me in informal conversations during the course of this writing.
26 Kirkham, 'Boccaccio's Dedication,' 121.
27 Smarr, *Boccaccio and Fiammetta*, 170.
28 Kirkham, 'Boccaccio's Dedication,' 125; and Smarr, *Boccaccio and Fiammetta*, 170.
29 See Potter, *Five Frames*, 129.
30 For a similar statement of the reader's responsibility for textual morality see the *Genealogie deorum gentilium*, where Boccaccio argues that 'poets are not corruptors of morals. Rather, if the reader is prompted by a healthy mind, not a diseased one, they will prove actual stimulators to virtue.' See Boccaccio, *Boccaccio on Poetry*, 74.
31 Boccaccio's insistence on going beyond the letter of the text in search of hidden, allegorical significance constitutes the very basis of his fervent defence of poetry in the final two books of the *Genealogie deorum gentilium*.

Bibliography

Primary Sources

Ambrose, Saint. *Hexameron, Paradise,* and *Cain and Abel.* Trans. John J. Savage. New York: Fathers of the Church, 1961.

Andreas Capellanus (André le Chapelain). *Andreae capellani regii Francorum de amore libri tres.* Ed. Amadeu Pagès Castelló de la Plana : Sociedad castellonense de cultura, 1930.

Aristotle. *Ethics: Introduction to Aristotle.* Ed. Richard McKeon. New York: Modern Library, 1947.

Augustine, Saint. *Confessions.* Trans. William Watts. London: Heinemann, 1912.

L'Avventuroso ciciliano. Ed. G.F. Nott. Milan: Giovanni Silvestri, 1836.

Benedict, Saint. *Regula.* Ed. Gregorio Penco, O.S.B. Florence: La Nuova Italia, 1958.

– *Opera Omnia.* Ed. J.P. Migne. *Patrologia Latina* 66. Paris, 1859.

Benvenuto da Imola. *Comentum super Dantis Aldigherii Comoediam.* Cited in Vol. 1. *La Divina Commedia nella figurazione artistica e nel secolare commento,* by Guido Biagi et al. Turin: UTET, 1924.

Boccaccio, Giovanni. *Boccaccio on Poetry, Being the Preface and the Fourteenth and Fifteenth Books of Boccaccio's* Genealogia Deorum. Trans. Charles G. Osgood. New York: Liberal Arts Press, 1956.

– *Comedia delle ninfe fiorentine.* Ed. Antonio Enzo Quaglio. *Tutte le opere di Giovanni Boccaccio.* Vol. 2. Milan: Mondadori, 1964. 665–835.

– *The Corbaccio.* Ed. and Trans. Anthony K. Cassell. Urbana and Chicago: University of Illinois Press, 1975.

– *Decameron.* Ed. Luigi Russo. Florence: Sansoni, 1939.

– *Decameron.* Ed. Giuseppe Petronio. 2 vols. Turin: Einaudi, 1950.

– *Decameron.* Ed. Vittore Branca. 3 vols. Florence: Sadea/Sansoni, 1966.

- *Decameron*. 3 vols. illustrated. Florence: Sadea, 1966.
- *Decameron*: 49 *novelle commentate da Attilio Momigliano* [1924]. Ed. E. Sanguineti. Turin: G.B. Petrini, 1968.
- *Decameron*. Trans. G.H. McWilliam. Middlesex: Penguin, 1972.
- *Decameron*. Ed. Vittore Branca. *Tutte le opere di Giovanni Boccaccio.* Vol. 4. Milan: Mondadori, 1976.
- *Decameron*: *15th Century Manuscript*. Ed. Edmond Pognon. Trans. J. Peter Tallon. New York: Miller Graphics, 1978.
- *Decameron*. Trans. John Payne. Revised with commentary by Charles S. Singleton. Berkeley and Los Angeles: University of California Press, 1982 [1886].
- *Decameron*. Trans. Mark Musa and Peter Bondanella. New York: Norton, 1982.
- *Decameron*. Ed. Vittore Branca. Turin: Giulio Einaudi editore, 1984 [1980].
- *Decameron: Con le illustrazioni dell'autore e di grandi artisti fra Tre e Quattrocento.* Ed. Vittore Branca. Florence: Le Lettere, 1999.
- *Eclogues*. Trans. with Introduction by Janet L. Smarr. New York: Garland Publishing, 1987.
- *Esposizioni sopra la Comedia di Dante*. Ed. Giorgio Padoan. *Tutte le opere di Giovanni Boccaccio.* Vol. 6. Milan: Mondadori, 1965.
- *Filocolo*. Ed. Antonio Enzo Quaglio. *Tutte le opere di Giovanni Boccaccio.* Vol. 1. Milan: Mondadori, 1967.
- *Filostrato*. Ed. Vittorio Branca. *Tutte le opere di Giovanni Boccaccio.* Vol 2. Milan: Mondadori, 1964. 15–228.
- *Genealogie deorum gentilium*. Ed. Vittorio Zaccaria. *Tutte le opere di Giovanni Boccaccio.* Vols. 7–8. Milan: Mondadori, 1998.
- *Genealogie deorum gentilium libri*. Ed. Vincenzo Romano. 2 vols. Bari: Laterza, 1951.
- *Opere latine minori*. Ed. Aldo Francesco Massèra. Bari: G. Laterza e figli, 1928.
- *Rime: Caccia di Diana*. Ed. Vittorio Branca. Padua: Liviana, 1958.
- *Teseida delle nozze di Emilia*. Ed. Alberto Limentani. *Tutte le opere di Giovanni Boccaccio.* Vol. 2. Milan: Mondadori, 1964. 245–664.
- *Trattatello in laude di Dante*. Ed. Pier Giorgio Ricci. *Tutte le opere di Giovanni Boccaccio.*Vol. 3. Milan: Mondadori, 1965.
Brito, Guillelmus. *Summa Britonis sive Guillelmi Britonis Expositiones Vocabulorum Biblie.* Ed. Lloyd W. Daly and Bernadine A. Daly. Padua: Antenore, 1975.
Carmina burana. Ed. P. Rossi. Milan: Bompiani, 1989.
Cennini, Cennino. *Il libro dell'arte*. 2d ed. Franco Brunello. Vicenza: Neri Pozza, 1982.

Cicero, Marcus Tullius. *Cicero on Oratory and Orators.* Trans. J.S. Watson. London: George Bell and Sons, 1903.

Dante, Alighieri. *La Commedia secondo l'antica vulgata.* Ed. Giorgio Petrocchi. Milan: Mondadori, 1966–7.

– *The Divine Comedy.* Edited with translation and commentary by Charles S. Singleton. 6 vols. Bollingen Series 80. Princeton: Princeton University Press, 1970–5.

– *Il Convivio.* Ed. Maria Simonelli. Bologna: Pàtron, 1966.

– *Il Convivio.* Ed. Giuseppe Busnelli and Giuseppe Vandelli. Rev. by Antonio Enzo Quaglio. Florence: Le Monnier, 1968.

– *La vita nuova.* Ed. Domenico De Robertis. Milan: Riccardo Ricciardi, 1980.

– *The New Life of Dante Alighieri.* Trans. Dante Gabriel Rossetti. New York: R.H. Russell Publisher, 1901.

– *Opere minori.* Ed. Domenico De Robertis and Gianfranco Contini. Milan and Naples: Ricciardi, 1984.

Della Casa, Giovanni. *Galateo ovvero dei costumi.* Ed. Carlo Cordié. *Baldassare Castiglione: Giovanni Della Casa, Benvenuto Cellini, Opere.* Milan: Ricciardi, 1960.

Etienne de Bourbon. *Tractatus de diversis materiis praedicabilibus. Anecdotes historiques, légendes et apologues, tirés du recueil inédit d'Etienne de Bourbon Dominicain du XIIIe siècle, publiés pour la Société de l'Histoire de France par A. LeCoy de la Marche.* Paris: Renouard, 1877.

Gelli, Giovan Battista. *Commento edito e inedito sopra la Divina Commedia.* Ed. Carlo Negroni. Florence, 1887 [1553].

Gesta romanorum. Ed. H. Oesterley. Berlin: Weidman, 1872.

Giles of Rome. *Del Reggimento de' principi.* Ed. Francesco Corazzini. Florence: Le Monnier, 1858.

Gregory, Saint. *Opera omnia.* Ed. J.P. Migne. *Patrologia Latina* 75–8. Paris, 1896.

Groto, Luigi [il Cieco d'Adria]. *Le lettere familiari di Luigi Grotto: Cieco d'Adria.* Venice: Gioacchino Brugnolo, 1606.

Guido da Pisa. *Expositiones et glose super Comediam Dantis or Commentary on Dante's Inferno.* Ed. Vincenzo Cioffari. Albany: State University of New York Press, 1974.

Guillaume de Lorris and Jean de Meun. *The Romance of the Rose.* Trans. Harry Robbins. New York: Dutton, 1962.

– *The Romance of the Rose.* Trans. Charles Dahlberg. Princeton: Princeton University Press, 1971.

Henri d'Andeli. *Le Lai d'Aristote.* Ed. M. Delbrouille. Paris: Société d'edition 'Les Belles Lettres,' 1951.

Horace. *Satires, Epistles, and Ars Poetica.* 1926. Trans. H. Rushton Fairclough. Loeb Classical Library. Cambridge: Harvard University Press, 1966.

Isidore of Seville. *Etymologiarum sive originum libri XX.* Ed. W.M. Lindsay. Oxford: Clarendon, 1911.

Johannes de Alta Silva, *Dolopathos, or, The King and the Seven Wise Men.* Trans. Brady B. Gilleland. Binghamton, NY: Center for Medieval and Early Renaissance Studies, 1981.

John of Bromyard. *Summa praedicantium.* Nürenberg, 1518.

Latini, Brunetto. *Li livres dou Tresor.* Ed. F.J. Carmody. Berkeley: University of California Press, 1948.

– *Il tesoretto: Poeti del Duecento.* Ed. Gianfranco Contini. Vol. 2. Milan and Naples: Riccardo Ricciardi, 1960.

Lessing, Gotthold Ephraim, *Werke.* 8 vols. Ed. H. Göpfert. Munich: Carl Hanser Verlag, 1970–9.

Li dis dou vrai aniel. Ed. A. Tobler. Leipzig: Hirzel, 1884.

Macrobius, Ambrosius Theodosius. *The Saturnalia.* Trans. Percival Vaughn Davies. New York: Columbia University Press, 1969.

Manuzio, Aldo, the Younger. *Lettere.* Rome, 1572.

Minnis, Alastair J., and A. Brian Scott, eds. *Medieval Literary Theory and Criticism, c. 1100–c. 1375: The Commentary-Tradition.* Oxford: Clarendon Press, 1991.

Montale, Eugenio. 'I limoni.' *Ossi di seppia.* Turin: Fratelli Ribet, 1928.

Muratori, Lodovico Antonio. *Antiquitates Italicae Medii Aevi.* In *Opere.* Ed. G. Falco and F. Forti. Vol 1. Milan and Naples: Ricciardi, 1964.

Il Novellino. La prosa del Duecento. Ed. C. Segre and Mario Marti. Milan and Naples: Riccardo Ricciardi Editore, 1959.

Il Novellino. Ed. Giorgio Manganelli. Milan: Rizzoli, 1975.

Il Novellino. Ed. Cesare Segre. *Prosatori del Duecento: Trattati morali e allegorici, novelle.* Turin: Einaudi, 1976.

Il Novellino e conti del Duecento. Ed. Sebastiano Lo Nigro. Turin: UTET, 1968.

Ovid [Publius Ovidius Naso]. *Heroides and Amores.* Trans. Grant Showerman. Loeb Classical Library [1914]. Rev. ed. G.P. Goold, 1977.

– *The Art of Love and Other Poems.* Trans. J. H. Mozley. Loeb Classical Library [1929]. Rev. ed. G.P. Goold, 1979.

Peter Lombard. *Opera Omnia.* Ed. J.P. Migne. *Patrologia Latina* 192. Paris, 1880.

Plato. *Plato's Cosmology: The Timaeus of Plato.* Trans. with commentary by F.M. Cornford. Indianapolis: Bobbs-Merril (Library of Liberal Arts), 1975.

Pliny the Elder [Gaius Plinius Secundus]. *The Natural History of Pliny.* Trans. John Bostock and H.T. Riley. Vol 4. London, 1856.

Rudel, Jaufré. *The Songs of Jaufré Rudel.* Ed. Rupert T. Pickens. Toronto: Pontifical Institute of Mediaeval Studies, 1978.

Spenser, Edmund. *The Faerie Queene*. In *The Works of Edmund Spencer: A Variorum Edition*. Ed. Edwin Greenlaw, et al. Vol. 6. Baltimore: Johns Hopkins University Press, 1938.

Stendhal. *Vie de Henry Brulard. Oeuvres intimes*. Ed. H. Martineau. Paris: Pléiade, 1955.

Thomas Aquinas, Saint. *In X libros Ethicorum ed Nichomachum expositio: Opera omnia*. Vol. 21. Parma, 1867.

– *Summa theologica*. Bernardo Maria de Rubeis, Charles René Billuart et al. 4 vols. Turin: Marietti, 1948–50.

– *In Aristotelis librum De anima commentarium*. Ed. Angelo M. Pirotta, O.P. 4th ed. Turin: Marietti, 1959.

– *Commentary on the Nichomachean Ethics*. Trans. C.I. Litzinger, O.P. Chicago: Henry Regnery, 1964.

Tomasi di Lampedusa, Giuseppe. *Il Gattopardo*. Milan: Feltrinelli, 1957.

Secondary Sources

Agamben, Giorgio. *Stanze: La Parola e il fantasma nella cultura occidentale*. Turin: Einaudi, 1977.

Allen, Shirley S. 'The Griselda Tale and the Portrayal of Women in the *Decameron*.' *Philological Quarterly* 56 (1977): 1–13.

Almansi, Guido. *L'estetica dell'osceno*. Turin: Einaudi, 1974.

– *The Writer as Liar: Narrative Technique in the* Decameron. London: Routledge and Kegan Paul, 1975.

Ascoli, Albert Russell. 'The Vowels of Authority (Dante's *Convivio* IV.vi. 3–4).' In Brownlee, Kevin, and Walter Stephens, eds. *Discourses of Authority in Medieval and Renaissance Literature*, 23–46. Hanover, N.H.: University Press of New England, 1989.

– 'Pyrrhus' Rules: Playing with Power from Boccaccio to Machiavelli.' *Modern Language Notes* 114 (1999): 14–57.

Asor Rosa, Alberto. *Letteratura italiana I: Il letterato e le istituzioni*. Turin: Einaudi, 1982.

Auerbach, Erich. *Mimesis: The Representation of Reality in Western Literature*. Princeton: Princeton University Press, 1957.

Auzzas, Ginetta. 'I Codici autografi: Elenco e bibliografia.' *Studi sul Boccaccio* 7 (1975): 1–20.

Bailet, Michel Henri. *L'homme de verre: Essai d'interprétation thématique de l'échec et de la maîtrise dans le* Décaméron. Nice [L'imprimerie universelle: Pour diffusion exclusive par le Studio bibliografico Antenore, Padua], 1972.

Bakhtin, Mikhail. *Rabelais and His World.* Trans. Helene Iswolsky. Bloomington: Indiana University Press, 1984.

Baldissone, Giusi. 'Il piacere di narrare a piacere.' In *Prospettive sul* Decameron. Ed. Giorgio Barberi Squarotti. Turin: Tirrenia Stampatori, 1989. 9–23.

– *Le voci della novella: Storia di una scrittura da ascolto.* Florence: Olschki, 1992.

Baratto, Mario. *Realtà e stile nel* Decameron. Vicenza: Neri Pozza, 1970.

Barberi Squarotti, Giorgio. 'La cornice del *Decameron* o il mito di Robinson.' *Il potere della parola: Studi sul Decameron.* Naples: Federico & Ardia, 1983. 5–63.

– ed. *Prospettive sul* Decameron. Turin: Tirrenia Stampatori, 1989.

Barilli, Renato. 'Retorica e narrativa.' *Attualità della retorica.* Atti del primo convegno italo-tedesco, Bressanone, 1973. Padua: Liviana, 1975. 37–54.

Barolini, Teodolinda. 'The Wheel of the *Decameron*.' *Romance Philology* 36 (1983): 521–39.

Barthes, Roland. *Writing Degree Zero and Elements of Semiology.* Trans. Annette Lavers and Colin Smith. Boston: Beacon Press, 1970.

– 'The Death of the Author.' 'From Work to Text.' In *The Rustle of Language.* Trans. Richard Howard. New York: Hill & Wang, 1986. 49–64.

Battaglia, Salvatore. 'Premesse per una valutazione del *Novellino*.' *Filologia romanza* 2 (1955): 259–86.

– Review of 'Présence du Saladin dans les littératures romanes,' by Américo Castro, *Filologia romanza* 2 (1955): 329–36.

– *La coscienza letteraria del Medioevo.* Naples: Liguori, 1965.

– *Giovanni Boccaccio e la riforma della narrativa.* Naples: Liguori, 1969.

Battaglia Ricci, Lucia. *Boccaccio.* Rome: Salerno Editrice, 2000.

Bernardo, Aldo S. 'The Plague as Key to Meaning in Boccaccio's *Decameron*.' In *The Black Death: The Impact of the Fourteenth-Century Plague,* ed. D. Williman. Binghamton, N.Y.: Medieval and Renaissance Texts and Studies, 1982. 39–64.

Bettinzoli, Attilio. 'Per una definizione delle presenze dantesche nel *Decameron*: 1. I registri "ideologici," lirici, drammatici.' *Studi sul Boccaccio* 13 (1981–82): 267–326; 2. 'Ironizzazione e espressivismo antifrastico-deformatorio.' *Studi sul Boccaccio* 14 (1983–84): 209–40.

Bevilacqua, Mirko. 'L'amore come "sublimazione" e "degradazione": Il denudamento della donna angelicata nel *Decameron*.' *Rassegna della letteratura italiana* 79 (1975): 415–32.

Biagi, Guido, et al. *La Divina Commedia nella figurazione artistica e nel secolare commento.* 3 vols. Turin: UTET, 1924–9.

Birus, H. 'Das Rätsel der Namen' in Gotthold Lessing. *Nathan der Weise.* Ed. K. Bohnen. Darmstadt: Wissenschaftliche Buchgesellschaft, 1984.

Biscaro, Girolamo. 'Inquisitori ed eretici a Firenze (1319–1334).' *Studi medievali* ns 2 (1929): 347–75; 3 (1930): 266–87; 6 (1933): 161–207.

Bloch, R. Howard. *Etymologies and Genealogies: A Literary Anthropology of the French Middle Ages.* Chicago: University of Chicago Press, 1983.

Boyle, Leonard. 'The date of the *Summa praedicantium* of John of Bromyard.' *Speculum* 48 (1973): 533–47.

Bragantini, Renzo, and Pier Massimo Forni, eds. *Lessico critico decameroniano.* Turin: Bollati Boringhieri, 1995.

Branca, Vittore. *Boccaccio: The Man and His Works.* New York: NYU Press, 1976.

– *Boccaccio medievale e nuovi studi sul* Decameron. 6th ed. Florence: Sansoni, 1986.

– *Boccaccio medievale.* [1956.] Florence: Sansoni, 1987.

– 'Boccaccio visualizzato: Amore sublimante, amore tragico, amore festoso dalla novella alla figuratività narrativa.' *La novella italiana.* Atti del Convegno di Caprarola, 19–24 septembre 1988. Rome: Salerno Editrice, 1989. 283–302.

– 'Le due redazioni del *Decameron* e la presenza di Genova nel capolavoro del Boccaccio.' *Atti dell'Accademica ligure di Scienze e Lettere.* Serie 6. Vol. 3 (2000): 21–38.

– ed. *Boccaccio visualizzato: Narrare per parole e immagini dal Medioevo al Rinascimento.* 3 vols. Turin: Einaudi, 1999.

Branca, Vittore, and Chiara Degani. 'Studi sugli *exempla* e il *Decameron*.' *Studi sul Boccaccio* 14 (1983–4): 178–208.

Brownlee, Kevin, and Walter Stephens, eds. *Discourses of Authority in Medieval and Renaissance Literature.* Hanover, N.H.: University Press of New England, 1989.

Campbell, Anna Montgomery. *The Black Death and Men of Learning.* New York: Columbia University Press, 1931.

Capozzi, Frank. 'Food and Food Images in the *Decameron*.' *Canadian Journal of Italian Studies* 10 (1987): 1–13.

Cappelletti, Licurgo. *Studi sul Decamerone.* Parma: Luigi Battei, 1880.

Carducci, Giosuè. *Discorsi letterari e storici.* 3d ed. Bologna: Zanichelli, 1905.

Castro, Américo. 'Présence du Saladin dans les littératures romanes.' *Diogène* 8 (1954): 18–47.

Cavallini, Giorgio. *Brevi studi stilistici e letterari.* Genoa: Di Stefano, 1968.

Cazalé Bérard, Claude. 'La strategia della parola nel *Decameron*.' *Modern Language Notes* 109.1 (1994): 12–26.

– 'Filoginia/Misoginia.' In *Lessico critico decameroniano*, ed. Renzo Bragantini and Pier Massimo Forni. Turin: Bollati Boringhieri, 1995.

Cerisola, Pier Luigi. 'La questione della cornice del *Decameron*.' *Aevum* 49 (1975): 137–56.

Chiappelli, Fredi. 'L'episodio di Travale e il "dire onestamente villania" nella narrativa toscana dei primi secoli.' *Studi di filologia italiana* 9 (1951): 141–53.

– *Il legame musaico.* Ed. Pier Massimo Forni. Rome: Edizioni di Storia e Letteratura, 1984.

Chiecchi, Giuseppe. 'Narrativa, *Amor de lonh,* epistolografia nelle opere minori del Boccaccio.' *Studi sul Boccaccio* 12 (1980): 175–95.

– *'Dolcemente Dissimulando': Cartelle Laurenziane e* Decameron *Censurato. 1573.* Padua: Editrice Antenore, 1992.

Chiecchi, Giuseppe, and Luciano Troisio. *Il* Decameron *sequestrato: Le tre edizioni censurate nel Cinquecento.* Milan: Unicopli, 1984.

Cian, Vittorio. 'L'organismo del *Decameron.' Scritti minori.* Turin: G. Gambino, 1936.

Ciavolella, Massimo. 'La tradizione dell'*aegritudo amoris* nel *Decameron.' Giornale Storico della letteratura italiana* 147 (1970): 496–517.

– *La 'malattia d'amore' dall'antichità al medioevo.* Rome: Bulzoni, 1976.

Comparetti, Domenico. *Intorno al libro dei sette savi di Roma.* Pisa: Tipografia Nistri, 1865.

Cottino-Jones, Marga. 'Ser Ciappelletto or "Le Saint Noir": A Comic Paradox.' *An Anatomy of Boccaccio's Style.* Naples: Cymba, 1968. 23–51.

– 'Saggio di lettura della prima giornata del *Decameron.' Teoria e critica* 1 (1972): 111–38.

– 'Observations on the Structure of the *Decameron* Novella.' *Romance Notes* 15 (1973): 378–87.

– *Order from Chaos: Social and Aesthetic Harmonies in Boccaccio's* Decameron. Washington, D.C.: University Press of America, 1982.

Croce, Benedetto. 'Il Boccaccio e Franco Sacchetti.' *Poesia popolare e poesia d'arte.* 2d ed. Bari: Laterza, 1946. 81–105.

Culler, Jonathan. 'The Turns of Metaphor.' *The Pursuit of Signs: Semiotics, Literature, Deconstruction.* Ithaca: Cornell University Press, 1981.

Dällenbach, Lucien. *Le récit spéculaire: Essai sur la mise en abîme.* Paris: Seuil, 1977.

– *Mirrors and After: Five Essays on Literary Theory and Criticism.* Ed. Tamara S. Evans. New York: Graduate School, City University of New York, 1986.

D'Ancona, Alessandro. 'Del *Novellino* e delle sue fonti.' Pt. 1 of *Studi di critica e storia letteraria.* 2d ed. Bologna: Zanichelli, 1912.

D'Andrea, Antonio. *Il Nome della Storia: Studi e Ricerche di Storia e Letteratura.* Naples: Liguori, 1982.

– 'Le rubriche del *Decameron.' Yearbook of Italian Studies* (1973–75): 41–67. Rpt. in *Il Nome della Storia* (1982). 98–119.

- 'Esemplarità, ironia, retorica nella novella interrotta del *Decameron*.' In *La Nouvelle: Genèse, Codification et rayonnement d'une genre médiéval*, ed. Michelangelo Picone, G. Di Stefano, and P.D. Stewart. Montréal: Plato Academic Press, 1983. 123–30.

Davis, Walter R. 'Boccaccio's *Decameron*: The Implications of Binary Form.' *Modern Language Quarterly* 42 (1981): 3–20.

Degani, Chiara, with Vittore Branca. 'Studi sugli *exempla* e il *Decameron*, I. Riflessi quasi sconosciuti di *exempla* nel *Decameron*,' *Studi sul Boccaccio* 14 (1983–84): 189–207.

De Hamil, Christopher. *A History of Illuminated Manuscripts*. Boston: David R. Godine, 1986.

Delcorno, Carlo. 'Ironia/parodia.' In *Lessico critico decameroniano*, ed. R. Bragantini and P.M. Forni. Turin: Bollati Boringhieri, 1955. 162–91.

- 'Note sui dantismi nell'*Elegia di madonna Fiammetta*.' *Studi sul Boccaccio* 11 (1979): 251–94.

- 'Studi sugli *exempla* e il *Decameron*. II. Modelli esemplari in tre novelle (I 1, III 8, II 2).' *Studi sul Boccaccio* 15 (1985–6): 189–214.

- *Exemplum e letteratura: Tra Medioevo e Rinascimento*. Bologna: Il Mulino, 1989.

De Man, Paul. *Allegories of Reading: Figural Language in Rousseau, Nietzsche, Rilke, and Proust*. New Haven: Yale University Press, 1979.

- 'Autobiography as De-Facement.' *The Rhetoric of Romanticism*. New York: Columbia University Press, 1984. 67–81.

Dembowski, Peter F. 'Quelques considérations sur les titres littéraires en France au Moyen Age.' In *Miscellanea di studi romanzi offerta a Giuliano Gasca Queirazza*, ed. Anna Cornagliotti et al. Vol. 1. Turin: Edizioni dell'Orso, 1988, 251–69.

De Michelis, Cesare. *Contraddizioni nel* Decameron. Milan: Guanda, 1983.

De' Negri, Enrico. 'The Legendary Style of the *Decameron*.' *The Romanic Review* 43 (1952): 166–89.

Derrida, Jacques. 'Title (to be specified).' *Sub-Stance* 31 (1981): 5–22.

- 'White Mythology: Metaphor in the Text of Philosophy.' In *Margins of Philosophy*, trans. Alan Bass. Chicago: University of Chicago Press, 1982. 207–71.

Di Francia, Letterio. 'Alcune novelle del *Decameron* illustrate nelle fonti.' *Giornale storico della letteratura italiana* 44 (1904): 94–103.

- 'La IV novella del *Decameron* e le sue fonti.' *Miscellanea a Vittorio Cian*. Pisa: C.F. Mariotti, 1909. 63–9.

- *Novellistica*. 2 vols. Milan: Vallardi, 1924–5.

Di Pino, Guido. 'Il proemio e l'introduzione alla quarta giornata.' *La polemica del Boccaccio*. Florence: Vallecchi, 1953. 209–20.

Dizionario etimologico italiano. Ed. Carlo Battisti and Giovanni Alessio. Florence: Università degli Studi, 1951.

Enciclopedia italiana. Rome: Istituto dell'Enciclopedia, 1933.

Fido, Franco. 'Dante personaggio mancato del *Decameron.*' In *Boccaccio: Secoli di vita.* Atti del congresso internazionale: Boccaccio 1975. University of California, Los Angeles, 17–19 October 1975. Ed. Marga Cottino-Jones and Edward F. Tuttle. Ravenna: Longo, 1977. 177–89.

Forni, Pier Massimo. *Forme complesse nel* Decameron. Turin: Petrini, 1986.

– *Adventures in Speech: Rhetoric and Narration in Boccaccio's* Decameron. Philadelphia: University of Pennsylvania Press, 1996.

Foucault, Michel. 'What Is an Author?' In *Language, Counter-Memory, Practice,* ed. Donald F. Bouchard, trans. Donald F. Bouchard and Sherry Simon. Ithaca, N.Y.: Cornell University Press, 1977. 113–38.

Gaeta, Franco. 'Dal comune alla corte feudale.' In *Letteratura italiana* I: *Il letterato e le istituzioni,* ed. Alberto Asor Rosa. Turin: Einaudi, 1982. 215–28.

Garbaty, Thomas Jay. '*Pamphilus, De Amore*: An Introduction and Translation.' *Chaucer Review* 2 (1967): 108–34.

Genette, Gérard. 'Structure and Functions of the Title in Literature.' *Critical Inquiry* 14 (1988): 692–720.

Getto, Giovanni. *Vita di forme e forme di vita nel* Decameron. Turin: G.B. Petrini, 1958.

Gibaldi, Joseph. 'The *Decameron* Cornice and the Responses to the Disintegration of Civilization.' *Kentucky Romance Quarterly* 24 (1977): 349–57.

Girard, René. 'The Plague in Literature and Myth.' *'To Double Business Bound':* *Essays on Literature, Mimesis, and Anthropology.* Baltimore: Johns Hopkins University Press, 1978. 136–54.

Gottfried, Robert S. *The Black Death: Natural and Human Disaster in Western Europe.* New York: Macmillan, 1983.

Grande dizionario della lingua italiana. Ed. Salvatore Battaglia. Turin: UTET, 1964.

Greene, Thomas L. 'Forms of Accommodation in the *Decameron.*' *Italica* 45 (1968): 297–313.

Grimaldi, Emma. *Il privilegio di Dioneo: L'eccezione e la regola nel sistema* 'Decameron.' Naples and Rome: Edizioni scientifiche italiane, 1987.

Gröber, Gustav. *Über die Quellen von Boccaccio's* Dekameron. Strasburg: J.H.E. Heitz, 1913.

Hexter, Ralph J. *Ovid and Medieval Schooling: Studies in Medieval School Commentaries.* Munich: Arbeo-Gesellschaft, 1986.

Hirdt, W. 'Boccaccio in Germania.' In *Il Boccaccio nelle culture e letterature nazionali,* ed. F. Mazzoni. Florence: Olschki, 1978. 27–51.

Hollander, John. '"Haddocks' Eyes": A Note on the Theory of Titles.' *Vision and*

Resonance: Two Senses of Poetic Form. 2d ed. New Haven: Yale University
    Press, 1985. 212–26.

Hollander, Robert. *Allegory in Dante's* Commedia. Princeton: Princeton University Press, 1969.

– *Boccaccio's Two Venuses.* New York: Columbia University Press, 1977.

– 'Boccaccio's Dante: Imitative Distance *(Decameron* I.1 and VI.10).' *Studi sul
    Boccaccio* 13 (1981–2): 169–98.

– *Il Virgilio dantesco.* Florence: Olschki, 1983.

– *'Decameron:* The Sun Rises in Dante.' *Studi sul Boccaccio* 14 (1983–4): 241–53.
    Rpt. in *Boccaccio's Dante and the Shaping Force of Satire.*

– *'Utilità* in Boccaccio's *Decameron.' Studi sul Boccaccio* 15 (1985–6): 215–23.

– *Boccaccio's Last Fiction:* Il Corbaccio. Philadelphia: University of Pennsylvania Press, 1988.

– *Boccaccio's Dante and the Shaping Force of Satire.* Ann Arbor: University of
    Michigan Press, 1997.

Holloway, John. 'Supposition and Supersession: A Model of Analysis for Narrative Structure.' *Critical Inquiry* 3 (1976): 39–55.

Hortis, Attilio. *Studi sulle opere latine del Boccaccio.* Trieste: Julius Dase, 1879.

Hoving, Thomas, Timothy B. Husband, and Jane Hayward. *The Secular Spirit:
    Life and Art at the End of the Middle Ages.* New York: The Metropolitan
    Museum of Art, 1975.

Huizinga, Johan. *The Waning of the Middle Ages.* New York: Doubleday,
    1924.

Huygens, R.B.C. *Accessus ad Auctores: Bernard d'Utrecht, Conrad d'Hirsau, Dialogus Super Auctores.* Leiden: E.J. Brill, 1970.

Katzenellenbogen, Adolf. *Allegories of the Virtues in Medieval Art.* London: The
    Warburg Institute, 1939.

Kermode, Frank. *The Senses of an Ending: Studies in the Theory of Fiction.* New
    York: Oxford University Press, 1975.

Kircher, Timothy. 'The Modality of Moral Communication in the *Decameron's*
    First Day, in Contrast to the Mirror of the Exemplum.' *Renaissance Quarterly*
    54 (2001): 1035–73.

Kirkham, Victoria. 'Painters at Play on the Judgement Day *(Decameron* VIII 9).'
    Studi sul Boccaccio 14 (1983–84): 256–77. Rpt. in *The Sign of Reason in Boccaccio's Fiction.* 215–35.

– 'An Allegorically Tempered *Decameron.' Italica* 62 (1985): 1–23. Rpt. in *The
    Sign of Reason in Boccaccio's Fiction.* 131–71.

– 'Boccaccio's Dedication to Women in Love.' *Renaissance Studies in Honor of
    Craig Hugh Smyth,* ed. Andrew Morrogh et al. Florence: Giunti Barbàra,
    1985. 333–43. Rpt. in *The Sign of Reason in Boccaccio's Fiction.* 117–29.

- 'The Word, the Flesh, and the *Decameron.*' *Romance Philology* 41 (1988): 127–49. Rpt. in *The Sign of Reason in Boccaccio's Fiction.* 173–97.
- 'The Last Tale in the *Decameron.*' *Mediaevalia: A Journal of Medieval Studies* 12 (1989): 205–23. Rpt. in *The Sign of Reason in Boccaccio's Fiction.* 249–68.
- *The Sign of Reason in Boccaccio's Fiction.* Florence: Olschki, 1993.
Klapisch-Zuber, Christiane. 'The Name "Remade": The Transmission of Given Names in Florence in the Fourteenth and Fifteenth Centuries.' In *Women, Family, and Ritual in Renaissance Italy,* trans. Lydia Cochrane. Chicago: University of Chicago Press, 1985. 283–309.
Kleinhenz, Christopher. 'Stylistic Gravity: Language and Prose Rhythms in *Decameron* I, 4.' *Humanities Association Review/ La Révue de l'Association des Humanités* 26 (1975): 289–99.
Knox, Dilwyn. *Ironia: Medieval and Renaissance Ideas on Irony.* Leiden: E.J. Brill, 1989.
Landau, Marcus. *Die Quellen des Dekameron.* Stuttgart: J. Sheible, 1884.
Lee, A.C. *The* Decameron *and Its Sources and Analogues.* London: David Nutt, 1909.
Levenstein, Jessica. 'Out of Bounds: Passion and Plague in Boccaccio's *Decameron.*' *Italica* 73 (1996): 313–35.
Levin, Harry. 'The Title As a Literary Genre.' *Modern Language Review* 72 (1977): xxiii–xxxvi.
Lewis, C.S. *The Allegory of Love* [1936]. Rpt. New York: Galaxy Books, 1958.
Littré, E. 'Opuscule relatif à la peste de 1348, composé par un contemporain.' *Bibliothèque de l'Ecole des Chartes* 2 (1840–41): 201–43.
Lomperis, Linda. 'From God's Book to the Play of the Text in the *Cosmographia.*' *Medievalia et Humanistica* 16 (1988): 51–71.
Mâle, Emile. *The Gothic Image: Religious Art in France in the Thirteenth Century.* Trans. Dora Nussey. 1913. New York: Harper Torchbooks, 1958.
Marchese, Angelo. 'Strutture narrative della prima giornata del *Decameron.*' *Metodi e prove strutturali.* 2d Ed. Milan: Principato, 1974.
Marcus, Millicent Joy. 'Faith's Fiction: A Gloss on the Tale of Melchisedech.' *Canadian Journal of Italian Studies* 2 (1978–9): 40–55.
- *An Allegory of Form: Literary Self-Consciousness in the* Decameron. Saratoga, Calif.: Anma Libri, 1979.
- 'Mysogyny as Misreading: A Gloss on *Decameron* VIII 7.' *Stanford Italian Review* 4 (1984): 23–40.
Marino, Lucia. *The* Decameron *'Cornice': Allusion, Allegory, and Iconology.* Ravenna: Longo Editore, 1979.
Markulin, Joseph. 'Emilia and the Case for Openness in the *Decameron.*' *Stanford Italian Review* 3 (1983): 183–99.

Mazzacurati, Giancarlo. 'Alatiel, ovvero gli alibi del desiderio.' *Forma e ideologia.* Naples: Liguori, 1974. 25–65.

Mazzotta, Giuseppe. 'The *Decameron*: The Marginality of Literature.' *University of Toronto Quarterly* 42 (1972): 64–81.

– 'The *Decameron*: The Literal and the Allegorical.' *Italian Quarterly* 18 (1975): 53–73.

– *The World at Play in Boccaccio's* Decameron. Princeton: Princeton University Press, 1986.

McCann, Dom Justin. *Saint Benedict.* London: Sheed & Ward, 1938.

Meiss, Millard. *Painting in Florence and Siena after the Black Death.* 1951. New York: Harper Torchbooks, 1964.

Moleta, Vincent. 'The Illuminated *Canzoniere*, Banco Rari 217.' *La Bibliofilia* 78 (1976): 1–36.

Mordenti, R. 'Le due censure: La collazione dei testi del *Decameron* "rassettati" da Vincenzo Borghini e Lionardo Salviati.' *La pouvoir et la plume.* Paris: Université de la Sorbonne Nouvelle, 1982. 253–73.

Muscetta, Carlo. *Giovanni Boccaccio.* Bari: Laterza, 1972, 1974.

Muscetta, Carlo, and Paolo Rivalta, eds. *Poesia del Duecento e del Trecento.* Parnaso Italiano 1. Turin: Einaudi, 1956.

Musso, Olimpio. 'Una leggenda monferrina nel Boccaccio (*Decameron* I.5).' *Studi sul Boccaccio* 11 (1979): 243–9.

Neri, Ferdinando. 'Il disegno ideale del *Decameron*.' *Storia e poesia.* Turin: Chiantore, 1936.

Neuschäfer, Hans-Jörg. *Boccaccio und der Beginn der Novelle: Strukturen der Kurzerzählung auf der Schwelle zwischen Mittelalter und Neuzeit.* Munich: Wilhelm Fink Verlag, 1969.

Noakes, Susan. 'The Double Misreading of Paolo and Francesca.' *Philological Quarterly* 62 (1983): 221–39.

O Cuilleanáin, Cormac. *Religion and the Clergy in Boccaccio's* Decameron. Rome: Edizioni di Storia e Letteratura, 1984.

Olson, Glending. *Literature as Recreation in the Later Middle Ages.* Ithaca: Cornell University Press, 1982.

Padoan, Giorgio. 'Mondo aristocratico e mondo communale nell'ideologia e nell'arte di Giovanni Boccaccio.' *Studi sul Boccaccio* 2 (1964): 81–216. Rpt. in *Il Boccaccio, le muse, il Parnaso e l'Arno.* 1–91.

– *Il Boccaccio, le muse, il Parnaso e l'Arno.* Florence: Olschki, 1978.

– *L'avventura della commedia rinascimentale.* Padua: Vallardi, 1996.

Paolella, Alfonso. *Rettorica e racconto: Argomentazione e finzione nel Novellino.* Naples: Liguori, 1987.

Paris, Gaston. *La légende de Saladin.* Paris: Imprimeur National. 1893.

– 'La parabole des trois anneaux.' *La poésie du Moyen Age*. 2d Series. Vol. 2. Paris: Hachette, 1895. 131–63.

Penna, Mario. *La parabola dei tre anelli e la tolleranza nel Medio Evo*. Turin: Rosenberg and Sellier, 1953.

Perella, Nicholas J. *Midday in Italian Literature: Variations on an Archetypal Theme*. Princeton: Princeton University Press, 1979.

Pézard, André. 'Figures françaises dans les contes de Boccaccio.' *Revue de littérature comparée* 12 (1948): 5–34.

Picone, Michelangelo. 'Dal fabliau alla novella: il caso di Chichibío (*Decameron* VI.4).' In *La Nouvelle: Genèse, codification et rayonnement d'un genre médiéval*, ed. M. Picone, G. Di Stefano, and P.D. Stewart. Montréal: Plato Academie Press, 1983. 111–22.

– 'Giulleria e poesia nella *Commedia:* Una lettura intertestuale di *Inferno* XXI–XXII.' *Letture Classensi* 18 (1989): 11–30.

– 'Lettura macrotestuale della prima giornata del *Decameron*.' In *Feconde venner le carte: Studi in onore di Ottavio Besomi*, ed. Tatiana Crivelli. Vol. 1. Bellinzona: Casagrande, 1997. 107–22.

Picone, Michelangelo, G. Di Stefano, P.D. Stewart, eds. *La Nouvelle: Genèse, codification et rayonnement d'un genre médiéval*. Montréal: Plato Academic Press, 1983.

Polzer, Joseph. 'Aspects of the Fourteenth-Century Iconography of Death and the Plague.' In *The Black Death: The Impact of the Fourteenth-Century Plague*, ed. Daniel Williman. Binghamton, N.Y.: Medieval and Renaissance Texts and Studies, 1982. 107–30.

Potter, Joy H. *Five Frames for the* Decameron: *Communication and Social Systems in the Cornice*. Princeton: Princeton University Press, 1982.

– 'Woman in the *Decameron*.' In *Studies in the Italian Renaissance: Essays in Memory of Arnolfo B. Ferruolo*, ed. Gian Paolo Biasin, Albert Mancini, and Nicolas Perella. Naples: Società Editrice Napolitana, 1985. 87–103.

Prato, Stanislao. 'L'orma del leone.' *Romania* 12 (1883): 535–65; 14 (1885): 132–5.

Prete, Antonio. 'Ritmo esterno e tempi spirituali nella cornice del *Decameron*.' *Aevum* 28 (1964): 33–61.

Réau, Louis. *Iconographie de l'arte chrétien*. 3 vols. Paris: Presses Universitaires de la France, 1955.

Ritter Santini, L. *Da Vienna a Napoli in carrozza: Il viaggio di Lessing in Italia*. Naples: Diffusione Electra, 1991.

Rochon, André. *Formes et significations de la 'beffa' dans la littérature italienne de la Renaissance*. 2 vols. Paris: Université de la Sorbonne Nouvelle, 1972–5.

Rossi, Luciano. 'Ironia e parodia nel *Decameron*: Da Ciappelletto a Griselda.'

La novella italiana. Atti del Convegno di Caprarola. 19–24 settembre 1988. Rome: Salerno Editrice, 1989. 365–405.

– 'Presenze ovidiane nel *Decameron*.' *Studi sul Boccaccio* 21 (1993): 125–37.

Rovida, C. 'La novella V della giornata I.' In *Il Decameron, dipinto di Giovanni Servi*. Milan [?], 1842.

– 'La marchesana di Monferrato: Novella volta in lingua spagnola con note e saggio bibliografico.' Vicenza, 1851.

Russo, Luigi. *Letture critiche del* Decameron. [1944] Bari: Laterza, 1956, 1973.

– ed. *Novelle scelte del 'Decameron' con un'appendice delle opere minori. Commento storico-linguistico di L. Russo*. Florence: G.C. Sansoni, 1943.

Sabatini, Francesco. *Napoli angioina: Cultura e società*. Naples: Edizioni Scientifiche Italiane, 1975.

Sanguineti, Edoardo. 'Gli "schemata" del *Decameron*,' *Studi di filologia e letteratura dedicati a Vincenzo Pernicone*. Genoa: Istituto di Letteratura Italiana, 1975. 141–53.

Scaglione, Aldo D. *Nature and Love in the Late Middle Ages*. Berkeley and Los Angeles: University of California Press, 1963.

Schilling, Bernard. 'The Fat Abbot.' *The Comic Spirit: Boccaccio to Thomas Mann*. Detroit: Wayne State University, 1965. 21–42.

Seung, T.K. 'The Sovereign Individual in the *Decameron*.' *Cultural Thematics: The Formation of the Faustian Ethos*. New Haven: Yale University Press, 1976. 207–16.

Shoaf, R. Alan. *Dante, Chaucer, and the Currency of the Word*. Norman, Okla.: Pilgrim Books, 1983.

Singleton, Charles S. 'On Meaning in the *Decameron*.' *Italica* 21 (1944): 117–24.

Šklovskij, Victor. *Lettura del* Decameron: *Dal romanzo d'avventura al romanzo di carattere*. Trans. Alessandro Ivanov. Bologna: Il Mulino, 1969.

Smarr, Janet L. 'Symmetry and Balance in the *Decameron*.' *Mediaevalia* 2 (1976): 159–87.

– *Boccaccio and Fiammetta: The Narrator as Lover*. Urbana and Chicago: University of Illinois Press, 1986.

– 'Ovid and Boccaccio: A Note on Self-Defense.' *Mediaevalia* 13 (1987): 247–55.

Spettacoli conviviali dall'antichità classica alle corti italiane del '400. Atti del VII convegno di studi, Viterbo, 27–30 May 1982. Viterbo: Agnesotti, 1983.

Stewart, Pamela D. 'La novella di Madonna Oretta e le due parti del *Decameron*.' *Yearbook of Italian Studies* (1977): 27–40. Rpt. in *Retorica e mimica nel* Decameron *e nella commedia del Cinquecento*. 19–38.

– *Retorica e mimica nel* Decameron *e nella commedia del Cinquecento*. Florence: Olschki, 1986.

Stillinger, Thomas C. 'The Language of Gardens: Boccaccio's *Valle delle Donne.'* *Traditio* 39 (1983): 301–21.
– 'The Form of *Filostrato.'* *Stanford Italian Review* 9 (1990): 191–210.
– *The Song of Troilus: Lyric Authority in the Medieval Book.* Philadelphia: University of Pennsylvania Press, 1992.
Surdich, Luigi. *La cornice di amore. Studi sul Boccaccio.* Pisa: ETS Editrice, 1987.
Taylor, Karla. 'A Text and Its Afterlife: *Inferno* V and *Troilus and Criseyde.'* *Chaucer Reads the Divine Comedy.* Stanford: Stanford University Press, 1989. 50–77.
Terverant, Guy de. *Attributs et symboles dans l'art profane 1450–1600: dictionnaire d'un langue perdu.* Geneva: Droz, 1958.
Tobler, Adolf, and Ernst Lommatzsch. *Altfranzosisches Worterbuch.* Berlin: Weidmann, 1936.
Todorov, Tzvetan. *Grammaire du Décaméron.* The Hague: Mouton, 1969.
Toldo, Pietro. 'La conversione di Abram.' *Giornale storico della letteratura italiana* 42 (1903): 355–9.
Tuve, Rosemund. *Allegorical Imagery: Some Mediaeval Books and Their Posterity.* Princeton: Princeton University Press, 1966.
Valesio, Paolo. 'Federigo degli Alberighi e i fabliaux.' New England Inter-University Seminar in Italian Studies. Cambridge, Mass., 1985.
Van der Voort, Cok. 'Convergenze e divaricazioni tra la Prima e la Sesta Giornata del *Decameron.'* *Studi sul Boccaccio* 11 (1979): 207–41.
Wallace, David. *Giovanni Boccaccio, Decameron.* Landmarks of World Literature. Cambridge: Cambridge University Press, 1991.
Wenzel, Siegfried. *The Sin of Sloth: Acedia in Medieval Thought and Literature.* Chapel Hill: University of North Carolina Press, 1967.
Williman, Daniel, ed. *The Black Death: The Impact of the Fourteenth-Century Plague.* Binghamton, N.Y.: Medieval and Renaissance Texts and Studies, 1982.
Zatti, Sergio. 'Federigo o la metamorfosi del desiderio.' *Strumenti critici* 36–7 (1978): 236–52.

Contributors

Marga Cottino-Jones is professor emerita of Italian at the University of California, Los Angeles. She is the author of *An Anatomy of Boccaccio's Style* (1968), *Metodi di critica letteraria americana* (1972), *Order From Chaos: Social and Aesthetic Harmonies in Boccaccio's* Decameron (1982), *Introduzione a Pietro Aretino* (1993); and *Il dir novellando: modello e deviazioni* (1994). She co-edited, with Edward Tuttle, *Boccaccio: secoli di vita* (1977), and has edited two volumes on Italian cinema and language. She was one of the founding members of the American Boccaccio Association and served as president, 1977–8.

Dante Della Terza is professor emeritus of Italian and comparative literature at Harvard University. His major publications include *Forma e memoria: Saggi e ricerche sulla tradizione letteraria da Dante a Vico* (1979), *Da Venezia a Baltimora: La diaspora degli intellettuali europei negli Stati Uniti d'America* (1987), *Tradizione ed esegesi: Semantica dell'innovazione da Agostino a DeSanctis* (1988), *Letteratura e critica tra Otto e Novecento: itinerari di ricezione* (1989), *Strutture poetiche, esperienze letterarie: percorsi culturali da Dante ai contemporanei* (1995). He edited Eric Auerbach, *Studi su Dante* (1963), Scipione Gonzaga, *Commentarii* (1987), *Pasolini in periferia* (1992); *Da una riva e dall'altra: studi in onore di Antonio D'Andrea* (1995); and *Per Vittorio Russo* (2000).

Franco Fido is professor of Italian at Harvard University. His work on Boccaccio includes *Le metamorfosi del centauro: Studi e letture da Boccaccio a Pirandello* (1977) and *Il regime delle simmetrie imperfette. Studi sul* Decameron (1988). He has written extensively on the Renaissance, especially on Machiavelli, Renaissance comedy, and eighteenth- and nineteenth-century literature, especially the literature of Venice. He published *Machiavelli*, a reception history in 1965. Among his many studies of Carlo Goldoni are *Guida a Goldoni: Teatro e società nel Settecento* (1977), *Da Venezia all'Europa: Prospettive sull'ultimo Goldoni* (1984), *Le inquietudini di Goldoni* (1995), and *Nuova guida a Goldoni: Teatro e società nel Settecento* (2000). He has also published *Il paradiso dei buoni compagni: Capitoli di storia letteraria veneta* (1987), *Le muse perdute e ritrovate: Il divenire dei generi letterari fra Sette e Ottocento (1989)*, *La serietà del gioco: Svaghi letterari e teatrali nel Settecento* (1998); and he has edited works by Goldoni and Giuseppe Baretti, and co-edited *Studies for Dante: Essays in Honor of Dante Della Terza* (1998).

Pier Massimo Forni is professor of Italian at Johns Hopkins University. He is author of *Forme complesse nel* Decameron (1992) and *Adventures in Speech: Rhetoric and Narration in Boccaccio's* Decameron (1996). He has edited *Il legame musaico*, a collection of essays by Fredi Chiappelli (1984), and Boccaccio's *Ninfale fiesolano* (1991); and has co-edited, with Renzo Bragantini, *Lessico critico decameroniano* (1995).

Robert Hollander is professor emeritus in European literature at Princeton University. He has written extensively on Boccaccio and Dante. His major publications include *Allegory in Dante's* Commedia (1969), *Boccaccio's Two Venuses* (1977), *Il Virgilio dantesco* (1983), *Boccaccio's Last Fiction:* Il Corbaccio (1988), *Dante and Paul's Five Words with Understanding* (1992), *Dante's Epistle to Cangrande* (1993), *Boccaccio's Dante and the Shaping Force of Satire* (1997), *Dante: A Life in Works* (2001). Together with Jean Hollander, he has also translated Dante's *Inferno* (2000) and *Purgatorio* (2003). In 1997 he was made *cittadino onorario* of Certaldo.

Victoria Kirkham is professor of Romance languages at the University of Pennsylvania. She is the author of *The Sign of Reason in Boccaccio's Fiction* (1993) and of *Fabulous Vernacular: Boccaccio's* Filocolo *and the Art of Medieval Fiction* (2001); and of a catalogue of the portraits of Boccaccio with a monographic essay in *Boccaccio visualizzato*, ed. Vittore Branca (1999). She co-authored, with Anthony K. Cassell, *Diana's Hunt: Caccia di Diana, Boccaccio's First Fiction* (1991), and co-edited with Kevin Brownlee, *Boccaccio 1990: The Poet and his Renaissance Reception, Studi sul Boccaccio*, vol. 20 (1992). She has published articles on Boccaccio, Dante, and the Counter-Reformation poet Laura Battiferra degli

Ammannati, and is currently preparing an anthology of Battiferra's poetry. She was president of the American Boccaccio Association, 1988–92.

Millicent Marcus is Mariano DiVito professor of Italian studies at the University of Pennsylvania. Her areas of specialization include Italian cinema and medieval literature. She is the author of *An Allegory of Form: Literary Self-Consciousness in the* Decameron (1979), *Italian Film in the Light of Neorealism* (1986), *Filmmaking by the Book: Italian Cinema and Literary Adaptation* (1993), and *After Fellini: National Cinema in the Post-modern Age* (2002). She has also published numerous articles on Boccaccio and on film, and is currently working on an interdisciplinary collaborative project entitled *Italy 1919*.

Ronald Martinez is professor of Italian Studies at Brown University. He has co-authored, with Robert Durling, *Time and the Crystal: Studies in Dante's 'Rime petrose'* (1990), and has co-authored the introduction and notes to Durling's translation of Dante's *Inferno* (1996) and *Purgatorio* (2003). He has published numerous articles on Italian medieval and Renaissance authors, especially Boccaccio, Dante, Petrarch, Machiavelli, and Ariosto.

Michelangelo Picone is professor of Italian literature at the 'Romanisches Seminar' of the University of Zürich. He is the author of *Il mito della Francia in Alessandro Manzoni* (1974), *Vita nuova e tradizione romanza* (1979), and *Percorsi della lirica duecentesca: dai Siciliani alla* Vita nova (2003), as well as numerous articles on medieval Romance literature. He has edited several volumes, including *Il racconto* (1985), *Dante e le forme dell'allegoresi* (1987), *Il giuoco della vita bella: Folgóre da San Gimignano* (1988), *L'Enciclopedismo medievale* (1994), *Guittone d'Arezzo: nel settimo centenario della morte* (1995), *Dante, da Firenze all'aldilà* (2001) *Autori e lettori di Boccaccio* (2002); he also co-edited *La Nouvelle: Formation, codification et rayonnement d'un genre médiéval* (1983), *I cantari: struttura e tradizione* (1984), *Studi di italianistica in onore di Giovanni Cecchetti* (1988), *L'illusione della realtà: Studi su Luigi Capuana* (1990), *Sciascia, scrittore europeo* (1994), *Ovidius redivivus: Von Ovid zu Dante* (1994), *Der Antike Roman und Seine Mittelalterliche Rezeption* (1997), *Scritti danteschi: Giovanni Andrea Scartazzini* (1997), *Gli Zibaldoni di Boccaccio: Memoria, scrittura, riscrittura* (1998), *Dante, mito e poesia* (1999), and Lectura Dantis turicensis (3 vols., 2000–02).

Janet Levarie Smarr is professor of theatre and Italian studies at the University of California, San Diego. Her publications include *Boccaccio and Fiammetta: The Narrator As Lover* (1986), translations of Boccaccio's *Eclogues* (1987) and of *Italian Renaissance Tales* (1983), along with articles on Boccaccio, Dante, Petrarch, Chaucer, and Renaissance authors, including Italian and French women writers. She has also edited *Historical Criticism and the Challenge of Theory* (1993), and is currently president of the American Boccaccio Association.

Pamela D. Stewart is professor emerita of McGill University. She is author of *Innocent Gentillet e la sua polemica antimachiavellica* (1969), *Retorica e mimica nel* Decameron *e nella commedia del Cinquecento* (1986), and *Goldoni fra letteratura e teatro* (1989). She has co-edited *La Nouvelle: Formation, codification et rayonnement d'un genre médiéval* (1983) and *Studies for Dante: Essays in Honor of Dante Della Terza* (1998).

Thomas C. Stillinger is associate professor of English at the University of Utah. He is the author of *The Song of Troilus: Lyric Authority in the Medieval Book* (1992), on the dynamics of literary form in Dante, Boccaccio, and Chaucer. He has also edited *Critical Essays on Geoffrey Chaucer* (1998).

Elissa B. Weaver is professor of Italian at the University of Chicago. She is author of *Convent Theatre in Early Modern Italy: Spiritual Fun and Learning for Women* (2002), and has edited Francesco Buoninsegni and Suor Arcangela Tarabotti, *Satira Antisatira* (1998), and Beatrice del Sera, *Amor di virtú*, a dramatization of Boccaccio's *Filocolo* (1990). She has co-edited, with Elizabeth Rodini, the catalogue of *A Well-Fashioned Image: Costume and Clothing in European Art, 1500–1850*, a Smart Museum show (2002). She has also published articles on Boccaccio, on the Renaissance epic-chivalric tradition, and on convent literature. She was president of the American Boccaccio Association, 1981–5.

Index